Institutions, Transaction Costs and Environmental Policy

NEW HORIZONS IN ENVIRONMENTAL ECONOMICS

General Editors: Wallace E. Oates, *Professor of Economics, University of Maryland, USA* and Henk Folmer, *Professor of Economics, Wageningen Agricultural University, The Netherlands and Professor of Environmental Economics, Tilburg University, The Netherlands*

This important series is designed to make a significant contribution to the development of the principles and practices of environmental economics. It includes both theoretical and empirical work. International in scope, it addresses issues of current and future concern in both East and West and in developed and developing countries.

The main purpose of the series is to create a forum for the publication of high quality work and to show how economic analysis can make a contribution to understanding and resolving the environmental problems confronting the world in the twenty-first century.

Recent titles in the series include:

The Political Economy of Environmental Taxes
Nicolas Wallart

Trade and the Environment
Selected Essays of Alistair M. Ulph
Alistair M. Ulph

Water Management in the 21st Century
The Allocation Imperative
Terence Richard Lee

Institutions, Transaction Costs and Environmental Policy
Institutional Reform for Water Resources
Ray Challen

Valuing Nature with Travel Cost Models
A Manual
Frank A. Ward and Diana Beal

The Political Economy of Environmental Protectionism
Achim Körber

Trade Liberalisation, Economic Growth and the Environment
Matthew A. Cole

The International Yearbook of Environmental and Resource Economics
2000/2001
A Survey of Current Issues
Edited by Tom Tietenberg and Henk Folmer

Economic Growth and Environmental Policy
A Theoretical Approach
Frank Hettich

Principles of Environmental and Resource Economics
A Guide for Students and Decision-Makers
Second Edition
Edited by Henk Folmer and H. Landis Gabel

Institutions, Transaction Costs and Environmental Policy

Institutional Reform for Water Resources

Ray Challen

University of Western Australia

NEW HORIZONS IN ENVIRONMENTAL ECONOMICS

Edward Elgar
Cheltenham, UK • Northampton, MA, USA

Published by
Edward Elgar Publishing Limited
Glensanda House
Montpellier Parade
Cheltenham
Glos GL50 1UA
UK

Edward Elgar Publishing, Inc.
136 West Street
Suite 202
Northampton
Massachusetts 01060
USA

A catalogue record for this book
is available from the British Library

Library of Congress Cataloguing in Publication Data

Challen, Ray.
    Institutions, transaction costs and environmental policy: institutional reform for water resources / Ray Challen.
    (New horizons in environmental economics)
    Includes bibliographical references and index.
    1. Transaction costs. 2. Institutional economics—Case studies.
3. Water resources development—Australia—Case studies. 4. Water resources development—Environmental aspects—Australia—Case studies. I. Title. II. Series.

HB846.3.C46 2000
333.91'00994—dc21

99–049033

ISBN 1 84064 250 5

Printed and bound in Great Britain by Bookcraft (Bath) Ltd.

To Anne

Contents

List of Figures

List of Tables

Preface and Acknowledgements

This work grew out of a disenchantment with the fragmentation of economics research in areas of property rights and institutional structures. This fragmentation has a long history, being based in pro-market and pro-intervention ideologies. Modern institutional economics that has grown from the seminal works of Ronald Coase has, by and large, maintained this ideological divide. On the one hand, there is the school of thought that suggests the answer to any allocation problem is the establishment of unattenuated property rights in the resource or asset, or, when taken to extremes, the absence of markets is itself the allocation problem. On the other hand, there are those expressing doubt and disillusionment in respect of markets as a panacea for all allocative ills. Scepticism of markets arises both in respect of general issues of equity and wealth distribution, and also issues of public goods, externalities and common-pool resources that are characteristically associated with use of natural resources and the environment. In recent decades, the thrust of the non-market school has been in research of collective and cooperative private behaviour, perhaps bowing to the general anti-intervention and libertarian emphasis of modern economics, but nevertheless seeking alternative institutional structures to atomistic markets.

The research leading to this book commenced in much the latter vein, seeking to investigate the potential role for collective action and common property in the use of water resources for irrigation in eastern Australia. However, it soon became apparent that there was little value in holding a view of institutional structures as a dichotomous choice between market and non-market allocation mechanisms. The reason for this was an apparent coexistence of both institutional forms in governance structures for allocation and use of a single water resource. Existing institutional theory was found to be inadequate in positive or normative investigation of such situations.

The focus of the research thus shifted to extending the conceptual framework of institutional theory to accommodate a recalcitrant reality. This book is both an exposition of the perceived deficiencies in institutional theory and a presentation of extensions (and, it is hoped, improvements) to institutional theory that will assist in improving insight and policy design for management of natural resources and the environment.

This book is the product of postgraduate research. I am grateful to faculty and fellow students in the Agricultural and Resource Economics Group of the University of Western Australia for providing a stimulating environment within which to study. Particular thanks are given to Steven Schilizzi and Greg Hertzler for many useful discussions on central ideas of the work, Bob Lindner for encouragement to commence the research, and Rob Fraser and Laura McCann for reading and commenting on a draft of the then PhD dissertation. I am especially grateful to Rob Fraser for his commitment to postgraduate students within the Agricultural and Resource Economics Group that results in provision of facilities and a level of integration into the faculty that would undoubtedly be the envy of postgraduate students elsewhere.

Financial assistance for the research on which this book is based was made available through an Australian Postgraduate Award provided by the Australian Commonwealth Government, and additional sponsorship from the Water and Rivers Commission of Western Australia. I am grateful to Paul McLeod, Ian Loh and Roy Stone for their assistance in securing financial support.

Several people provided assistance in obtaining information and data relating to the Murray–Darling Basin of eastern Australia. I am grateful for the assistance provided by all these people and their respective organisations, but particularly Anthony Petch, Jeff Parish, Reg Bristow and Bob Newman.

Finally, sincere thanks are offered to Sally Marsh without whom the experience would not have been the richly rewarding one that it was.

1.   Introduction

INSTITUTIONAL CHANGE IN USE OF WATER RESOURCES

The 1980s and 1990s have seen massive reforms in economic institutions both in Australia and throughout the world. At a world level, there has been the collapse of communist regimes in countries of eastern Europe, steady growth in institutions of market capitalism in China, reduced barriers to international trade, and freeing up of world capital markets. Substantial institutional change of a conceptually similar nature has occurred on a domestic scale in Australia under the banner of National Competition Policy. This reform has sought to reduce constraints on economic activity where such constraints do not satisfy criteria of broad public interest, and generally to make greater use of competitive markets in allocation of productive resources and consumer goods and services.

The same policy motivations that have given rise to institutional reforms under National Competition Policy have trickled down to institutions governing the use of natural resources. Further motivation for institutional change in use of natural resources has arisen from emerging resource scarcity and greater competition for rights of access and exploitation. Such change has been most evident in respect of fisheries and water resources, where new institutions have been created that enhance private rights to the resources and which place greater reliance on markets for the allocation of these rights amongst potential resource users.

The current wave of institutional reforms for regulation of use of water resources was initiated in the eastern states in the late 1970s as a result of increasing scarcity of water resources in the Murray–Darling Basin of eastern Australia, and an emerging inadequacy of institutions that had been put in place in the early part of the century to facilitate development of irrigation industries. By the early 1990s the impetus for reform had become coupled with National Competition Policy and led to the establishment of national agendas for reform. Reform agendas were established in 1994/95 by an agreement of the Council of Australian Governments (COAG) and included:

- pricing of water to reflect all costs of supply and service;
- specification of resource entitlements and property rights;
- allowing and facilitating exchange or trading of water entitlements to allow water to be used in higher-value uses;
- reform of regulatory agencies and water-service utilities; and
- involving users of irrigation water in the water-reform process and in water management (National Competition Council, 1997; Working Group on Water Resource Policy, 1995).

The underlying intent of the COAG agreement was to remove government subsidisation of water supplies and management of water resources, and to increase reliance on market mechanisms for the allocation of increasingly scarce water resources amongst alternative uses and users. These objectives were to be achieved by means including the definition of property rights to water, in accordance with a premise that such specification of rights would motivate trading in water markets and socially optimal allocations of resources. What was not made clear, however, was the exact form that these property rights should take and how such institutional change should be implemented.

In view of the lack of detail in the COAG agreement, the Federal Government's Standing Committee on Agriculture and Resource Management commissioned a study to develop a framework for property rights in water. The result was a text-book specification of private property rights centred on establishing rights to water resources that are vested in individual water users, and minimising impediments to trading in these rights (Standing Committee on Agriculture and Resource Management, 1995). There was an implicit assumption that conferral of private property rights to water would give rise to markets for water that were very similar to markets in land. This would presumably result in a self-maintaining system of resource allocation that would not only ensure that water resources were continually being re-allocated to their highest-value use, but also that there would be very little future need for government involvement in resource allocation.

However, in a slip 'twixt cup and lip the plans for specifying property rights were modified substantially in processes of implementation. Almost contradictory to recommendations for development of private property rights were components of a new institutional framework that would significantly attenuate private rights. These included limiting the private rights to usufructory rights in water rather than ownership rights of the resource itself; variability in the actual interest conferred in the rights, such as with respect to supply reliability and constraints on transferability; restrictions on who could participate in a water-rights market; and strong regulation of trading in water rights to account for constraints imposed by infrastructure, environmental considerations and impacts of transfers on other water-right holders. On the one hand, proponents of reform were saying that strong private property rights would resolve all allocation problems, yet on the other, there seemed to be an unwillingness to make a full commitment to such an institutional initiative, as if the policy makers wanted to have a foot in two regulatory camps. As a consequence, the property-right reforms for water resources have fallen well short of the unattenuated rights upon which predictions were made of the benefits of market allocation of water over other allocation mechanisms. Partly as a result of this, the re-allocations of water rights through trading have been far more limited than initially envisaged by the pro-market reformists. Private decision making for water allocation is a long way from supplanting a historically centralised system of government regulation of water use.

The overall impression of property-right reforms for water allocation in Australia is that there is a large gap between economic analysis and practical institutional reform. It is proposed that, in a general sense, this is symptomatic of an inability fully to address problems of institutional reform within the analytical perspective of neoclassical economics. Policy analysis for institutional reform in the area of water-resources regulation requires an evaluation framework that can clearly address practical constraints and opportunities for institutional change.

DEFICIENCIES IN ECONOMIC ANALYSIS OF INSTITUTIONS

Recognition and investigation of institutions largely lies outside the bounds of conventional economic analysis. A readily observable symptom of this occurs in the generally simplistic and polar views amongst economists as to the roles of markets and governments:

> When economists and other analysts of public affairs think about economic policy, they often pose the basic question as a confrontation between markets and governments. On the one side are those who believe that markets are prone to failures, that governments emerge to correct the failures of markets, and that on the whole they are capable of doing so. On the other side, we find those who believe that markets perform well and that governments are the problem, not the solution. ... As usual, reality is much more complex and defeats any attempts to fit into such neat dichotomies (Dixit, 1996 p. 1).

The complexity that is allegedly not recognised by conventional paradigms of economic analysis relates to the role of institutions in economic activity, not least in the operation of markets. No economist, regardless of how much they favour and promote markets for the allocation of resources, would seriously question the need for strong government. Markets require institutions established by government, including defined property rights, general protocols of contracting, and providing the means for policing and enforcing contracts. Indeed, to the extent that such institutions are necessary for any private trading to take place and that it is generally governments that provide these institutions, it can be argued that no market will exist without public subsidisation of trading activities through establishing the necessary institutional framework.

The role of institutions goes well beyond that of supporting markets, however. A vast range of decisions for resource allocation are made under institutional arrangements other than those providing for private decisions and market trading. A view of economic behaviour that fails to recognise and explain this diversity of institutions is incomplete. Examples of this diversity range from institutions for allocation decisions of international and national significance, such as with the recently topical allocation issues of international emissions of greenhouse gases and allocation of native land title in Australia, to relatively mundane decisions such as the control of pollution on a local scale and specifying permissible uses of land in suburban backyards. Whilst some of these decisions are made by governments for readily recognisable reasons of market failure, for others there has never been any market, nor is it generally conceivable that market processes should be utilised for such decisions.

The growing field of new institutional economics (described later in this chapter) suggests that the lack of attention given to institutions by economics is probably due more to a historical reluctance to address the subject rather than methodological difficulties. Institutions have been outside the bounds of most analysis:

> Price theory or microeconomics, in its conventional form, treats organisations and institutions the same way as it treats the law of gravity: these factors are implicitly assumed to exist but appear neither as independent nor as dependent variables in the models (Eggertsson, 1990 p. xi).

Eggertsson (1990) suggests that the neoclassical view of the world is reasonable for many problems addressed by economics. In particular, the approach allows for the abstract consideration of critical relationships and facilitates the use of mathematical tools in the analysis of these relationships. However, by limiting analysis in this way, economists of the neoclassical mould limit the economic problems that they can usefully examine. Kay

(1997 pp. 9–10) suggests that neoclassical economics has agendas that relate to a simple question relating to optimal product-market price: 'does price (P) equal marginal cost (MC)?' Kay argues that this is a highly limited and simplistic view of human behaviour and decision making. Whilst some types of behaviour can be usefully examined within the bounds of conventional neoclassical economics, such as short-run pricing behaviour in commodity markets, difficulties are encountered in examining broader patterns of economic behaviour.

The narrow bounds of analysis have resulted in conventional microeconomics being rather a blunt instrument in examining economic institutions, either as exogenous or endogenous variables in economic models. This may explain some of the difficulties encountered in reforming institutions of water use where policy analysis has been limited almost entirely to modelling short-run decisions for allocation of water resources in perfectly competitive markets for these resources. Very little attention, particularly in practical policy analysis, has been given to the economic history of water-resource use or comparative assessment of alternative institutional structures for resource allocation. This book addresses this area of neglect.

THE ROOTS OF AN APPROACH TO INSTITUTIONAL ANALYSIS

Despite the predominance of neoclassical theory in twentieth-century economics, some attention has been given to examining institutional issues and a substantial body of relevant theory has been developed. The study of institutions as a sub-discipline of economics dates back to a reaction in the early twentieth century against the mechanistic abstractions of the neoclassical paradigm. The original 'Institutionalists' such as Thorstein Veblen and John R. Commons, and later John Kenneth Galbraith, tended to reject forms of atomism and abstraction and instead assume approaches of investigation and writing that were descriptivist, anti-formalist, holist, behaviourist, collectivist and fairly interventionist (Kay, 1997 p. 18). These 'Old Institutionalists' or 'American Institutionalists' employed case-study methodologies very heavily and would not have had 'any truck with concepts of equilibrium, rational behaviour, instantaneous adjustments, and perfect knowledge, and they all favour the idea of group behaviour under the influence of custom or habit, preferring to view the economic system more as a biological organism than as a machine' (Blaug, 1992 pp. 109–10). The Old Institutionalism ultimately failed to develop as a school of thought, perhaps due to a failure to develop a research strategy with a clear direction and methodology (Williamson, 1993).

In the 1960s and 1970s, a new approach to the study of institutions developed, variously referred to as the 'New Institutional Economics' or 'Neoinstitutional Economics' (Eggertsson, 1990). The approaches used for the study of institutions were derived from various sub-fields within economic history, the theory of the firm and industrial organisation, law and economics, and the sub-section of political science employing the rational choice model as a basis for analysis (Eggertsson, 1990 p. xii). The contributions used research methodologies derived from neoclassical economics but gave particular attention to transaction costs. Drawing on the seminal works of Ronald Coase ('The nature of the firm', 1937; 'The problem of social cost', 1960), a great deal of emphasis was given to alternative institutional arrangements for allocating resources, particularly at the level of the firm. Apart from recognising transaction costs and institutional arrangements other than markets, methodologies of the new institutional economist still reflect neoclassical influences in many other respects (Kay, 1997 p. 19) that would include the central assumptions of motivation and rationality.

Theoretical concepts of the new institutional school will be used in this book in arguing that consideration of institutions for regulating the allocation and use of natural resources is best undertaken by studying decisions for resource allocation and the costs of making these decisions under alternative institutional arrangements. The starting-point of investigation is in the seminal works of transaction-cost economics: examining similarities of institutional choice with questions of decision making for resource allocation outside of and within firms. Outside the firm, resource allocations are made through markets on the basis of relative willingness to pay. Within a firm, resource allocations are made by unilateral individual or collective decisions within a usually hierarchical management structure (Hay and Morris, 1991 p. 281). At the level of the firm, the important question is which allocation decisions should be made at the different levels within a management structure, and which by market transactions? Transaction-cost theory and related organisation theory suggest that the answer lies in considering costs of decision making. Transaction costs may dictate that there are some allocation decisions that are better made internally within firms rather than by a market. In other situations, transaction costs will favour allocation by a market. Thus the boundaries of firms are defined.

Similar reasoning can be applied to alternative institutional structures for allocation of water resources. The choice between the alternative systems for decision making for resource allocation may vary according to the transaction costs for making particular classes of decisions under different institutional arrangements.

Theoretical studies of production costs and transaction costs in alternative organisational structures indicate that the question of which structure is best suited to a particular situation is an empirical one, dependent upon values of the relevant cost parameters and the constraints on allocation processes (Baumol *et al.*, 1982; Quiggin, 1995; Williamson, 1979). Economic analyses of institutions for regulating the use of water and other natural resources has tended to ignore this perspective on institutional choice.

STATIC AND DYNAMIC DIMENSIONS OF INSTITUTIONAL ANALYSIS

It has been indicated that analysis of alternative institutional structures can be undertaken by comparing transaction costs of decision making under alternative structures, drawing on transaction-cost theory and organisational theory. These are essentially static analyses and indeed have a strong similarity to comparative-static analyses in more conventional neoclassical analyses of production where the central problem is one of cost minimisation. It is just that in one case attention is given to transaction costs and in the other attention is given to production costs.

There is, however, another aspect to institutional analysis that is important. This is also a transaction-cost consideration but is a dynamic issue relating to the process of institutional change. Transaction costs arise in institutional change in the form of transition costs, that is, the costs of decision making for institutional change and the costs of implementing institutional reforms.

Recognition of these dynamic transaction costs has developed out of the work of economic historians such as Douglass North, who observed path-dependencies in institutional change (North 1981, 1990). Path-dependencies were broadly defined as occurring where opportunities for institutional reform are constrained by the current institutional structure. The constraints arise through a current institutional structure determining the costs of transition to alternative structures. An institutional *status quo* determines the processes for institutional change and also creates vested interests for certain groups within society who resist institutional changes that threaten these interests. Where the holders of these interests have the ability to impose costs on the political decision makers for institutional reform, they can influence the costs associated with certain options for reform and hence the relative appeal to political decision makers of the different options.

The consequence of transition costs and path-dependencies for institutional analysis is that institutional history influences practical opportunities for institutional change in the present. By extrapolation, institutional changes in the present will influence the costs of institutional change in the future and hence the opportunities and options for change in the future. In this book, it is argued that these intertemporal effects are important in consideration of institutional reforms in that there may be intertemporal opportunity costs associated with institutional changes in the present. In some instances there may be a value to adopting or retaining institutions that minimise these intertemporal opportunity costs through maintaining institutional flexibility to respond to altered parameters or new knowledge in resource systems.

These intertemporal considerations may be of particular importance in considering institutional reforms for regulation of water resources. With the Murray–Darling Basin in Australia, for example, there is still very imperfect knowledge about the ecology of the river system and the environmental consequences of current rates and patterns of water use. Also, future demands for environmental quality and sustainability in resource use are uncertain. Learning will occur in both these areas and society may require institutional change for water use to respond to new information and knowledge. Some institutional reforms in the present, particularly those that strengthen private property rights, may reduce the flexibility of governments to respond to new knowledge and changing parameters. There may be value in maintaining institutional flexibility, albeit possibly at the expense of present benefits from resource use.

Path-dependencies in institutional change have received very little attention in existing literature. Some study has been made by economic historians, for example consideration by North in relation to opportunities and constraints on institutional development in England and Spain and their respective dominions (North, 1990 pp. 112–16). Almost certainly, there has been no rigorous consideration of path-dependencies in institutional change in the context of *ex ante* policy analysis. In this book, the potential benefit of minimising transaction costs in future institutional change, and hence maintaining flexibility for future institutional change, is considered in terms of option values. This draws on previous work on flexibility and option values in the contexts of irreversible investments by business firms (Dixit and Pindyck, 1994) and decisions of conservation versus irreversible development of environmental resources (Arrow and Fisher, 1974; Henry, 1974; Fisher and Hanemann, 1985; Fisher, 1997).

CONTRIBUTION TO ECONOMICS

This book is not proposing that any particular institutional structure or structures be adopted to solve the world's problems in allocation of water and other natural resources. Indeed, it will be argued that a whole range of institutional structures is necessary for the efficient allocation of resources, ranging from private-property and market systems of allocation, through to institutions that provide for highly centralised allocation decisions by governments. Rather than proposing any institutional structure as a panacea to allocation problems or prescribing institutional remedies to particular allocation problems, the objective underlying the book is to explore the complexity of institutions and the way that they affect economic activity. The particular emphasis is on institutions governing the use of natural resources, although the findings make a more general contribution to the relatively new but rapidly growing body of knowledge on institutional analysis and institutional choice.

It is in the area of *ex ante* policy analysis that this book contributes to economic knowledge. The application by the new institutionalists of transaction cost theory to the investigation of alternative institutional arrangements has been extraordinarily successful in *ex post* studies of historical institutional structures and paths of institutional change. However, there has been very little work undertaken and progress made in applying the theoretical developments and historical insight to *ex ante* analysis of proposals for institutional change. This is exemplified in the work of Ostrom (1990) where prediction of success or failure in common-property arrangements for the use of natural resources was hindered by the lack of appropriate theory for incorporating transaction costs into analysis of particular institutional structures and determining prospects for institutional change.

In this book, a conceptual model is developed for framing policy problems of institutional choice. Whereas existing economic analysis of institutions tends to focus on comparative analysis of institutions as if alternative property right institutions are mutually exclusive, the model developed in this book allows for the simultaneous existence of multiple regimes of property rights and associated institutions, organised in an institutional hierarchy. With this model the emphasis of institutional analysis shifts from assessing the benefits of particular property right regimes or allocation mechanisms in isolation, to considering at which level of an institutional hierarchy particular allocation decisions can best be made.

A methodology is suggested for analysing problems of institutional choice. This is based on transaction cost considerations as the major parameter in institutional choice, but extends the scope of analysis by considering both static and dynamic dimensions to these costs. The static dimension is the conventional application of transaction-cost theory to institutional analysis: selecting an institutional structure to minimise transaction costs of decision making to achieve particular objectives in resource allocation. The dynamic dimension relates to the transaction costs incurred in institutional change. These costs are manifest as transition costs and create path-dependencies in institutional development. Institutional choice is framed as a cost-effectiveness problem of minimising a sum of static and dynamic transaction costs.

The methodology developed in this book is not 'complete' in the sense of being able to prescribe particular institutional solutions to problems in allocation and use of natural resources. Neither, at least to the level of development in this book, does it provide a means of rigorously and quantitatively modelling institutional choice. What the methodology does contribute to policy analysis is a new approach to framing problems of institutional choice that takes into account variables that have previously been addressed only in an *ad hoc* manner in policy analysis. In particular, the influences of history and future uncertainty are brought into a model of institutional choice to be considered in a consistent metric with conventional considerations of the economic benefits of an institutional change.

BOOK OUTLINE

This book comprises four general parts. The first part is Chapter 2 which comprises a literature review of past work in institutional economics and the application of transaction-cost theory to institutional analysis. The existing literature is drawn on to develop a general model of regulatory institutions for the use of natural resources. This model uses concepts of institutional hierarchies that have previously been touched on in the literature to frame a problem of institutional choice to which transaction-cost theory can be applied as a methodology for analysis. A distinction is made between static and dynamic dimensions in institutional analysis.

The second part of the book comprises Chapters 3 and 4 and describes investigations of the static dimensions of institutional analysis. This is undertaken with application to institutions of water use for irrigation in the Murray–Darling Basin of eastern Australia. Chapter 3 provides background information on the irrigation industries in two states of the Murray–Darling Basin: New South Wales and South Australia. Institutions of water use in these states are described in accordance with the model of institutional hierarchies developed in Chapter 2. Chapter 4 describes an investigation into whether static transaction costs are really an issue of importance in considering institutional reform. The investigation centres on transaction costs associated with the principal area of institutional reform in the regulation of water use: market allocation of water entitlements. On the basis of this investigation, more general comments are made on transaction costs arising in other parts of the institutional hierarchy governing water use, and how static transaction costs have created, and continue to create, incentives for institutional change.

The third part of the book comprises Chapters 5 and 6 and focuses on dynamic considerations in institutional change and how dynamic transaction costs influence institutional choice. Chapter 5 establishes the importance of the transaction costs in institutional change through a historical examination of institutional development for regulation of water resources in the Murray–Darling Basin. In Chapter 6, a methodology is proposed for incorporating path-dependencies of institutional change into the policy problem for institutional choice.

The fourth part of the book comprises Chapters 7 and 8, in which the concepts of static and dynamic transaction costs are incorporated into a general policy problem for institutional choice. In Chapter 7 the implications of static and dynamic transaction costs for institutional change are examined, a general policy problem defined, and the practicalities of policy analysis according to this statement of the policy problem are explored. In Chapter 8, conclusions are drawn on the contribution of this formulation of the policy problem to policy analysis and on the implications for future research in institutional analysis and choice.

2.   Institutions and Use of Natural Resources

INTRODUCTION

The purpose of this chapter is to establish a paradigm for looking at problems of resource allocation from an institutional perspective. This paradigm will be used in subsequent chapters to examine institutional structures in case studies of water-resource allocation, and ultimately to develop a framework for policy analysis in institutional change.

A study of institutions focuses on the laws and conventions of society that either directly allocate resources, or establish the processes and constraints for agents in an economy to make allocative decisions.   As discussed in Chapter 1, neoclassical economics has historically ignored this aspect of resource allocation. It is, however, an aspect that is central to either normative or positive examinations of resource allocation and determining whether the characteristics of a resource allocation are likely to meet social objectives. Taking even a narrow objective of society with respect to resource allocation, that of economic growth: 'institutions may benefit one group more than/at the expense of another, they may outlive their usefulness, and – through being hard to alter – lock a society onto a historical path which may or may not favour economic development' (Hubbard, 1997 p. 240).

Where the neoclassical literature on allocation of natural resources does address institutional issues, these issues tend to be addressed in terms of very broad institutional categories. Often only two categories are considered: private property and common property, where private property comprises an individual owner and common property comprises all else.   At best, classification schemes extend to four categories: open access or non-property, state property, common property and private property.

The simplistic classification schemes for institutions and property rights cause ambiguity in the description of institutional structures. It is argued in this chapter that this ambiguity arises as a result of the classification schemes being so broad that there is inconsistency in the criteria used for classification, overlap between the classifications, and a loss of important detail. This ambiguity can be avoided by using a more detailed system for classification and description that recognises institutional hierarchies and the functional roles of institutions in specifying the basis for physical division of a resource amongst multiple users, the nature of entities with property rights or decision-making powers over the resource, and the nature of mechanisms for allocation and re-allocation of the resource amongst potential users.

This chapter commences with a general discussion of economic institutions and property rights, their function in an economy and existing classification schemes for different institutional structures relating to property rights over natural resources. The institutional structures for regulation and allocation of natural resources are then discussed in more detail, concentrating on the influence of transaction costs on choices of particular institutional structures.

ECONOMIC AND SOCIAL INSTITUTIONS

Institutions, as the term is usually used in economics, are the humanly devised rules of behaviour that shape human interaction (North, 1990 p. 3). The purpose of institutions is to provide a set of rules for cooperation and competition and thereby adjust conflicting claims of different individuals and groups for scarce resources. Other definitions of the term 'institutions' are used in other disciplines of the social sciences (Goodin, 1996 pp. 2–16). Alternative uses of the term will not be described here, but it is worth noting a distinction between institutions and organisations. Within the context of economics, the term institutions is not used to refer to organisations or groups of people such as 'financial institutions', business corporations, churches, family units or government agencies. These organisations are, however, usually founded on and operate according to formal or informal rules of behaviour. These rules do fall within the definition of institutions as the term is most commonly used in economics.

The general characteristics of institutions are as follows.

* They are socially organised and supported (Scott, 1989a), which distinguishes institutions from other constraints on human behaviour, for example biological and physical constraints.
* They include formal rules as well as informal conventions and codes of behaviour (North, 1990 pp. 3–4).
* They are slowly changing relative to the activities that they guide and constrain (Scott, 1989a).

- They prescribe prohibitions as well as conditional permissions (North, 1990 pp. 3–4).

Bromley (1989, p. 42) provides a broad description of institutions in terms of the two categories of conventions and entitlements.

- Conventions are 'regularities in human behaviour [R] in which everyone prefers to conform to R on the expectation that all others will also conform to R. A convention is a structured set of expectations about behaviour, and of actual behaviour, driven by shared and dominant preferences for the ultimate outcome as opposed to the means by which that outcome is achieved.' An often-used example of a convention is that of driving motor vehicles on a particular side of the road. There is a strongly preferred outcome for vehicles to be driven uniformly on one or other side of the road. Questions of which side of the road, and the means by which vehicle drivers are persuaded to comply with a determination of one side of the road or the other are relatively unimportant.
- Entitlements are 'socially recognised and sanctioned sets of expectations on the part of everyone in society with regard to de jure or de facto legal relations that define the choice sets of individuals with respect to the choice sets of others'. An example of an entitlement is the concept of ownership of object. Ownership implies an expectation on the part of the owner of the object that he can maintain possession of the object and can use the object in certain ways without interference by other individuals.

In a more functional sense, institutions provide *pro forma* roles for interacting individuals. Drawing on the works of Hohfeld (1913, 1917) and Commons (1968), Bromley (1989 pp. 44–6) describes institutions as a set of correlative legal relations amongst individuals in a society. In a static sense of a constant institutional structure, institutions comprise dual correlates of rights and duties, and of privileges and no rights, defined for two parties *Alpha* and *Beta* as follows.

- A right means that *Alpha* has an expectation or assurance that *Beta* will behave in a certain way towards *Alpha*. *Beta* has a corresponding duty to behave in a specific way with respect to *Alpha*.
- A privilege means that *Alpha* is free to behave in a certain way towards *Beta*. *Beta* correspondingly has no right of recourse if *Alpha* behaves in a manner consistent with that privilege.

Over time, the institutional structure may be altered and these concepts can be extended to the dual correlates of power and liability, and immunity and no power, as follows.

- Power means that *Alpha* may voluntarily create a new legal relation affecting *Beta*. *Beta* has a corresponding liability to the new legal relation voluntarily created by *Alpha*.
- Immunity means that *Alpha* is not subject to an attempt by *Beta* to create a new legal relation affecting *Alpha*. Correspondingly, no power means that *Beta* may not voluntarily create a new legal relation affecting *Alpha*.

Institutions thus form the basis for relationships between individuals within a society, with formal or informal institutions existing to govern almost all situations of interaction.

A study of institutions within economics is concerned with one particular subset of human interactions: that of economic exchange and the allocation of resources and consumer goods and services. Of particular importance in this regard is a subset of institutions that define property rights. These are defined and described in the following section.

PROPERTY RIGHTS

Property Rights as Institutions

Property rights are the subset of institutions for regulation of behaviour and social interactions with respect to objects of value. In an institutional context, property refers to the rules of behaviour rather than the object. Bromley (1989 pp. 202–3) describes property as a social relation amongst individuals within a society rather than a relationship between an individual and a particular object of value. Alchian (1988) relates the social relationship represented by a property right to scarcity of the valued object: if an object is available in insufficient quantity to meet the objectives of all individuals within a society, then discrimination is necessary to determine the extent to which each individual's objectives will be satisfied. Property rights are the constraints and permissions that enable such discrimination to occur in a manner that is consistent, predictable and socially acceptable.

Three sets of variables can be used to characterise property rights in terms of the legal relations established by institutions (Hallowell, 1943, cited by Bromley, 1989 pp. 202–3).

i. The nature and kinds of rights that are exercised, and their correlative duties and obligations.

ii. The individuals or groups in whom these rights and duties are vested, and those who play the correlative roles.
iii. The objects of social value to which the property relations pertain.

Extending the conceptualisation of property rights to a description in terms of the dual legal relations of institutions, Bromley (1991a pp. 42–5) distinguishes between three types of entitlements conferred by property rights.

i.   Property rule: where one party has a right to undertake certain actions without regard for another party, or conversely where one party may not take actions that interfere with another party without the latter's consent.
ii. Liability rule: where a party may proceed with an action that may interfere with a second party, but the second party must be compensated for any interference, or conversely where the second party must compensate the first party if they want the action to be halted.
iii. Inalienable entitlement: where a party may proceed with an action and no other party may interfere, or conversely where the first party has no right under any circumstances to undertake certain actions that interfere with the second party.

A property right thus provides an entitlement to behave in a manner that may impose costs on another party. This raises the question of how societies justify the creation of institutions which confer property rights. Bromley (1989 pp. 191–202), drawing mainly from Becker (1977), reviews the philosophical basis of property rights. The five major arguments commonly used to support the concept of property rights over valuable objects are first occupancy; the labour theory; the utility theory; political theory; and moral enhancement.

The *first-occupancy* argument is based on the premise of first in time, first in right. Whilst in some instances this principle has some application in the distribution of property rights, it does not contribute to the more general question of whether an institution of property ownership should exist in the first place. Possession does not necessarily imply a socially recognised right to possess. There are also legal and moral implications to this principle: to assume first in time is first in right is 'to impart great social and economic significance to events of great luck and serendipity, or the providence of having been born earlier than most of the others in the world' (Bromley, 1989 p. 195).

The rationale to the *labour* argument is that individuals are entitled to hold as property whatever they produce by their own initiative, intelligence, risk-taking and labours. This is complicated, however, by such issues as ownership of children and labour undertaken under employment relationships.

'Once it is acknowledged that some labour is expected to yield property rights in the very thing laboured on, while other labour is not, the root idea of a labour theory must be seen as a poor choice for a fundamental principle' (Becker, 1977 p. 47, cited in Bromley, 1989 p. 196). Alternatively, labouring may carry with it an implication of psychological appropriation, where the individual is entitled to a benefit proportional to the value created by his labour, or to a cost proportional to the value destroyed.

Under the *utility* argument, property rights in some objects may be justified by the contribution of these rights to orderly use or proper care of the object in accordance with certain objectives of society. This appeals to a general argument of a property-right system being justified by the socially desirable patterns of use of the valued objects that such a system produces.

Political-liberty arguments focus on the innate characteristics of humans that have them acquiring, accumulating, controlling, using and modifying valuable objects. It is argued that denying these behavioural tendencies is to violate fundamental precepts of human expression and therefore liberty. This same argument can, however, be used to justify restrictions on property ownership if such ownership can be construed as infringing upon other individuals' liberty.

The *moral-character* argument supports property rights on the basis that they are necessary to develop good moral character in the holder of the rights. Further, if the existence of property rights is justified, then the distribution of these rights should be on the basis of which parties will use the rights to 'good' or beneficial effect, will manage the object well, or who are otherwise virtuous. Bromley (1989 p. 199) argues that there is no evidence that property rights produce good or bad moral character and the development of moral character cannot be used to justify the existence of property-right institutions. Thus the relevance of the moral-character argument is limited to forming a principle by which rights may be distributed and in this regard it resembles the utility argument inasmuch as the merits of the rights distribution are related to the resultant social outcome.

The justification for property rights implicit in modern economic theory is a combination of the utility, labour and moral arguments. The most common justification is utilitarian, as evidenced by a social tendency to judge the value of property rights on the basis of the contribution of these rights to production or wealth generation (Bromley, 1989 p. 202). Essentially, property rights are justified by their economic function: to create incentives to use resources in their highest-value use (Posner, 1972 pp. 10–11). This philosophical basis to property rights and their allocation is particularly evident in regulatory policies for natural resources whereby rights of access to resource stocks are granted on the basis of beneficial use, where this is loosely defined as use of a productive asset for the purposes of wealth generation. In some instances where the beneficial-use criterion has not been used as a criterion for assigning property rights, considerable social opposition to the rights assignment has arisen. For example, native title of land by Australian aborigines has been opposed on the basis that private control of the land and use for agricultural or pastoral purposes will generate greater economic wealth (National Farmers' Federation, 1998).

That the justification for property rights is not based solely on utilitarian arguments is evident from inconsistencies in application of the 'beneficial-use' principle. For example, purchase of vacant land with the intention of holding it idle for future development or sale is a common and generally accepted property transaction.   However, securing rights for similar speculative purposes in other assets such as rights to water resources or to radio broadcasting frequencies is generally not regarded as socially acceptable due to the lack of beneficial use (Posner, 1972 p. 14). In these examples there appears to be an inconsistently applied justification for property based on a political-liberty argument that property-right institutions should in some circumstances allow individuals to accumulate wealth without regard for wider effects on society.

Despite some inconsistencies, the philosophical justification for property rights in modern societies remains essentially utilitarian and gains credibility by the increasing need of societies to cope with resource scarcity. The role of property rights in this sense is succinctly described in relation to natural resources by Seabroke and Pickering (1994 pp. 161–2):

> the framework of property rights operates alongside ... other institutions designed to facilitate the exchange or transfer of property, to control the effect of the utilisation of natural resources on society at large, and to resolve conflicts arising from the exploitation or neglect of property with other competing interests.

Characteristics of Property Rights

In economics, the term 'property right' is generally used synonymously with the term 'institution' to define all the rules, privileges and duties that accompany 'ownership' of a physical object. It will be argued later in this chapter that this use of the term is too broad to enable property rights to be adequately addressed in the investigation of institutions for use of natural resources and an alternative definition will be offered. For the time being, however, a description will be offered of property rights as the term is used throughout much of the relevant literature.

A property right is usually considered to convey power to manage the object that is the subject of the right, a power to receive income derived from the object, and a power to alienate or sell the object (Scott, 1989a, 1989b). Bromley (1991a pp. 27–8) is one of many authors who use the term synonymously with institutions and suggests that property regimes refer to more than simple assignment of an ownership title: they also include use rights, exchange rights, distribution entitlements, management systems and systems of authority and enforcement. That is, property rights encompass the full set of institutional rules that govern an individual's rights and duties with respect to the relevant physical asset.

Honoré (1961, cited in Bromley, 1989 pp. 187–90) lists eleven characteristics that are said to be present in a full, or liberal, property right over an object.

i.   Right of possession, constituting a right to exclude other parties from use of the object.
ii.   Right of use of the object.
iii.   Right of management, incorporating the right to allow others to use the object.
iv.   Right to capture income or the benefit stream arising directly or indirectly from the owned item.
v.   Right to the capital of the object, that is, the right to alienate, consume or destroy the object.
vi.   Right of security, providing protection from arbitrary appropriation by another party.
vii.   Right to transfer ownership to another party.
viii. Absence of term, meaning that ownership is perpetual.
ix.   Prohibition of harmful use, meaning that ownership does not include the ability to harm others.
x.   Liability to appropriation of the object to settle debts.
xi.   Rights to residuary character are specified; that is, social rules exist to govern situations in which ownership rights lapse.

In most cases, these rights associated with property are incomplete or attenuated as a result of restrictions imposed by society. Scott (1989a, 1989b) recognises this in a model of a property right where the right is described in terms of the degree to which each of the following six parameters are conferred by the right.

i.   Duration – the period over which the right exists.
ii. Exclusivity – the extent to which other parties can be excluded from the item or from the flow of benefits arising from the item.
iii. Transferability – the extent to which the right may be transferred between parties and the ease with which it may be transferred.
iv. Divisibility – the degree to which the property right can be subdivided.
v.   Quality of title – the extent to which the property right describes the item

covered by the right, the related rights and duties of the rights holder and other parties, and the penalties for violation of rights or non-performance of duties.
vi. Flexibility – the extent to which the owner of the property right can alter patterns of use of the item to meet his own objectives.

Scott (1989a, 1989b) summarises this model in a graphical representation (Figure 2.1) and suggests that characteristics of one property-right structure can be compared with those of an alternative structure by plotting some measure of each parameter on the relevant axis. To the extent that any characteristic of a property right is not 'complete', the right can be said to be attenuated and in Figure 2.1 the ray representing that characteristic would be shorter.

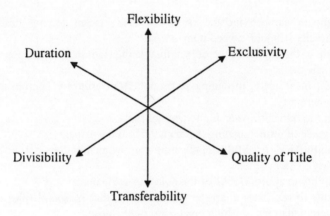

Figure 2.1: Characteristics of Property Rights

INSTITUTIONS FOR ALLOCATION OF NATURAL RESOURCES

Property-Right Regimes

In the discussion of institutions and property rights so far, only a generic distinction has been made between the party holding the right and all other parties. Alternative property-right regimes differ in terms of the nature of the entities holding the rights. The most usual classification of property rights is a distinction between private property and common property, derived from Gordon's (1954) seminal work on property rights in fisheries and popularised by Hardin's (1968) classic article 'The tragedy of the commons'. 'Private property' was used to refer to exclusive control of a resource by a single agent, and 'common property' to refer to an absence of exclusive rights.

This dichotomous classification of property rights was rejected by many writers in the 1970s and 1980s due to the failure to recognise property rights exercised by governments and collectively by finite groups of people (Lindblom, 1977; Ciriacy-Wantrup and Bishop, 1975; Dahlman, 1980). This resulted in a now widely accepted description of four classes of property-right regimes as described by Bromley (1989 pp. 204–6) in terms of the holders of rights and the corresponding duties of the rights holders and other parties.

i.   State property: individuals have a duty to observe use/access rules determined by a controlling/managing state agency. State agencies have a right to determine use/access rules. An example is where a government regulatory agency establishes rules for use of land in national parks or state forests.

ii. Private property: individual owners have a right to undertake socially acceptable uses and have a duty to refrain from socially unacceptable uses. Others (non-owners) have a duty to refrain from preventing socially acceptable uses and have a right to expect that only socially acceptable uses will occur. For example, ownership of freehold land can be regarded as a private property right enabling the owner to make use of the land in certain ways and without interference by other persons.

iii. Common property: a management group of owners has a right to exclude non-members, and non-members have a duty to abide by exclusion. Individual members of the management group (co-owners) have both rights and duties with respect to use rates and maintenance of the object owned. Examples exist in group irrigation schemes where members of the groups utilise water according to certain rules of supply, and pay rates for the purpose of maintaining collectively owned infrastructure.

iv. Non-property (open access): no defined group of users or owners exists and the benefit stream from use of the object is available to anyone. Individuals have a privilege with respect to use of the object and 'no rights' with respect to use of the resource by others. Commonly cited examples are ocean fisheries, over which no nation or group of resource users has jurisdiction.

Since the essence of property is discrimination in rights of access and use of an object, the definitions can be reworded in this context. A classification of property-right regimes based on the classification schemes of Bromley (1989) and Stevenson (1991 p. 58) is shown in Table 2.1.

Table 2.1: Classification of Property-Right Regimes

	Property-Right Regime			
	State Property	**Common Property**	**Private Property**	**Open Access**
User Limitation	As determined by state agency	Finite and exclusive group	One person	Open to anyone
Use Limitation	Rules determined by a state agency	Rules determined by mutual agreement	Individual decision	Unlimited

Within relevant economic literature there is considerable inconsistency and ambiguity in the terminology used to describe property-right regimes, particularly in distinctions between open access and common property, and between private property and common property. The term 'common property' has been used to refer to almost all situations where a resource is subject to joint exploitation, ranging from well-defined joint ownership and management by a finite set of individuals to open access. Consequently, the term is ambiguous. Bromley (1991b) suggests that the ambiguity in terminology has arisen due to widespread misunderstanding or ignorance of the meaning of property rights. As already indicated, seminal literature on the joint use of natural resources by multiple parties (Demsetz, 1967; Gordon, 1954; Hardin, 1968) failed to recognise the institutional characteristics of property-right regimes and consequently did not distinguish between common property (*res communes*), where property rights reside with an exclusive group of co-owners, and non-property (*res nullius*), where no property rights have been defined and enforced (Bromley, 1991b). This conceptual and definitional oversight has been perpetuated in subsequent literature and has led to errors in description and economic assessment of actual and historical common-property situations (Bromley and Cernea, 1989; Bromley, 1991b; Quiggin, 1988).

A second set of definitional problems has arisen from the very broad definition of property rights as encompassing all institutions relating to use of a physical asset. Such broad definition masks subtleties in the characteristics of property regimes in the four categories as defined above. Examples of conceptual difficulties in classification schemes are described as follows.

- Property rights to a resource may formally be held by one entity such as a state or national government, but many decisions for the allocation and use of the resource are made by different entities such as collective groups of resource users and individual resource users. Examples of such situations are common with fisheries and water resources in Australia where the resources are legally 'owned' by the state, but regulatory decisions are made by committees that include representatives of the state agency and the resource users, and individuals may 'own' entitlements to utilise the resources. *Ad hoc* classifications of property-right structures have been developed in some investigations to cope with such complexities in property-right distributions (for example, Santopietro and Shabman, 1992).

- A resource that is owned and controlled by a corporation resembles private property inasmuch as the corporation exists as a single legal entity, but also may resemble common property if allocative decisions are made by a group of directors representing multiple company shareholders that collectively own the resource.

- Institutions for resource allocation may comprise a combination of private rights and communal constraints, making it difficult to categorise the property-right system as one of private property or common property. Bromley (1991a p. 26) considers that under common property the rights to resource use held by any individual are usufructory rights only and the individual user does not have the power to transfer those rights to another resource user. In contrast, Stevenson (1991 pp. 66–7) considers that tradable or transferable rights can be considered common property if the institutional system for allocation and transfer is applied by a collective group of resource owners.

- Where adequate rules have not been established under state-property or common-property regimes, or where existing rules are not adequately enforced, patterns of resource exploitation may resemble open-access situations. Ostrom (1990) describes several examples of this situation in the exploitation of fisheries and water resources.

These difficulties with descriptions of property-right regimes in practical applications are due to the broad definitions of property rights which include all institutions relating to resource use. A more useful scheme for describing these institutions may be derived if use of the term 'property right' is restricted to describing the nature of the decision-making entity holding the rights pertaining to use of a resource. Thus private property corresponds to a single decision-making entity such as an individual person or firm; common property to a finite collective entity such as a cooperative group; state property to a government entity; and open access to the absence of any entity with decision-making power over a resource.

Limiting the definition of property rights in this way allows consideration of situations where multiple types of parties simultaneously hold decision-making power over a resource. This can be accomplished by a conceptual model of a property-right hierarchy or a system of 'nested' institutions (Ostrom, 1990 pp. 50–51). For most resources there are multiple levels of property rights, starting with broad powers of state or national governments to control use of resources, and ending with powers of individual resource users to make investment and production decisions for resource harvesting and exploitation. In between these extremes may be more decision-making levels, all relating to some individual or collective entity with property rights over the resource. Parties at each level within a hierarchy have their own peculiar objectives in resource management and may make fundamentally different types of decisions, all of which ultimately produce a pattern of resource use.

As a conceptual example, consider the property-right hierarchy that may exist in an ocean fishery. The highest and most general form of property right can be conceptualised as common property amongst all nations of the world and an allocation institution might be an international agreement which establishes zones of 'territorial waters' within which each nation has exclusive rights to fish stocks. The next level in the property hierarchy may be state property, wherein a state or national government may allocate common property rights to fish stocks in particular regions to, for example, coastal communities with a historical reliance on a fishing industry. The local communities may then allocate rights to the fish stocks to individual fishermen who in turn make production decisions individually within a private-property framework. This conceptual example is summarised in Table 2.2.

In the conceptual example of the ocean fishery, each level of the institutional hierarchy solves a resource-allocation problem by establishing allocative institutions for the next level down, until the final level is reached where decisions are made in regard to use of the resource in a production process. A point to note is that the property-right regime at any level in the hierarchy relates to the nature of the entity making the allocative decisions and is distinct from characteristics of the allocation decisions. Thus, for example, a group of resource users holding common property rights to a resource may implement an allocation system based on individual rights to shares of the resource and relative freedom of the individuals in production decisions and transfer of the rights to other users. What has essentially happened in such a case is that an additional level in the property-right hierarchy has been created, in this case one of private property. This exemplifies an important feature of a property-right hierarchy: the hierarchy comprises a system of nested rules where each successive level is legally supported and maintained by the superordinate level.

Table 2.2:   Conceptual Example of a Property-Right Hierarchy in an International Fishery

Scope of Allocation Problem	Parties to Decision Making	Conceptual Property-Right Regime	Allocation Decision
Allocation of fish stocks amongst nations	Multiple national governments	Common property	Definition of territorial waters
Allocation of fish stocks amongst regional communities	National government	State property	Exclusive community rights to fishing areas
Allocation of fish stocks amongst individual fishermen	Community members or representatives	Common property	Individual transferable quota issued to fishermen
Allocation of quotas to fishing effort or sale to other fishermen	Individual fishermen	Private property	Private production and investment decisions

Previous empirical studies of property-right regimes have generally not given attention to the nature of decision-making entities or recognised property-right hierarchies when classifying property-right regimes, leading to ambiguity in the classifications. For example, in a study of grazing commons in Switzerland, Stevenson (1991 pp. 67–8) categorises systems of transferable grazing rights as common property if the rights system is administered by a collective of owners of the grazing lands but as private property if the system is administered by a private owner of the grazing lands. In doing so, he is failing to recognise multiple levels of a property-right hierarchy and not distinguishing between the entities making decisions with respect to allocation systems and the allocation systems themselves. The transferable-rights system is in both cases private property since many decisions as to the use of the rights are made individually by the owners of the rights. It is in the superordinate level of the hierarchy that the property-right regimes differ. In the first case, decisions on the allocation of grazing rights are made under a regime of common property. In the second, the decisions are made under a regime of private property.

There are, of course, aspects of institutions for regulation of natural-resource use other than the property rights held by different entities. These relate to the manner in which entitlements to the resource are defined and allocated to the holders of property rights. Three broad types of institutions are important in this regard: the system of entitlements by which the resource is physically divided amongst holders of property rights; the means by which the entitlements are initially allocated amongst the holders of property rights; and the means by which the entitlements may be re-allocated amongst holders of property rights according to changes in the socioeconomic or biophysical parameters of the resource system. These other aspects of institutions for regulating use of natural resources are described below.

Entitlement Systems

Allocation of a resource necessitates physical division of the resource between potential users. The rules and procedures for physical division of a resource may be referred to as an entitlement system.

An entitlement system can be conceptualised as a quota system which provides an exclusive right of access to a resource. Stevenson (1991 pp. 63–7) differentiates between two generic types of quota: output quota and input quota. An output quota places a direct limit on the amount of the resource that the owner of the quota may use or consume. An example is a catch quota in a fishery that sets a quantitative limit on the amount of fish that the quota holder may harvest in a given time period. A further example is an irrigation right that sets a quota on the volume of water that an irrigation farmer may utilise in a given time period. An input quota restricts use of a resource by establishing limits on one or more of the inputs, other than the resource itself, to the production process within which the resource is utilised. Examples include the use of equipment restrictions to limit harvests in fisheries, and restricting use of irrigation water by limiting areas of land that may be irrigated.

The term 'output quota' can be confusing since it refers to a restriction on use of the resource that may not necessarily be an output from a production process. For the sake of clarity, the term 'resource quota' will henceforth be used to refer to a quota placed directly on the resource.

An allocation mechanism may have aspects of both input and resource quotas: for example, a fishery regulated by resource quotas may also have restrictions on inputs such as the period of the fishing season, restrictions on areas of fishing and restrictions on fishing equipment.

Mechanisms for Initial Allocation of Entitlements

An initial distribution of entitlements between competing parties can occur in two generic ways. Firstly, entitlements may be distributed according to administrative decisions by resource managers. Examples of initial distribution of resource entitlements by administrative decisions are the 'first come first served' rule implicit in the prior appropriation doctrine for allocation of water resources in western states of the USA, and allocation on the basis of historical use prior to the entitlement system being introduced, such as with the allocation of catch quotas in New Zealand fisheries. The second general means of distributing entitlement is the use of a market whereby the resource managers sell units of entitlement to competing resource users. Examples include use of tender systems to allocate logging rights in public forests to private timber companies.

Mechanisms for Adjusting Allocations

With changing economic and social circumstances for a group of resource users and changes in condition of the resource itself, social benefits may be gained by altering the allocation of the resource amongst users within any particular level of a property-right hierarchy. It is therefore common for the specification of any allocation system to include procedures whereby resource entitlements may be redistributed.

As with the procedures for determining an initial allocation of entitlement, the procedures for altering allocations may be broadly categorised as administration-based or market-based. An administrative system of re-allocation would adjust allocations by either specific decisions for particular circumstances, or by establishing a set of rules that specify the circumstances under which a re-allocation of entitlements may occur and the basis for altering the allocation. Such rules may vary from highly simplistic and general 'use it or lose it' conditions, such as are part of the prior-appropriation system of water allocation in the western states of the USA, to complex rules such as those of the Spanish irrigation huertas described by Maass and Anderson (1978) which make detailed provisions for re-allocation of water resources in times of drought. Market-based systems allow for trading of entitlements between resource users, often subject to constraints on who may participate in the market and the nature of transactions that may occur. Examples are *individually transferable quotas* in fisheries, *transferable water entitlements* for water resources, and *tradable pollution permits* for regulating water and atmospheric pollution.

An allocation-adjustment system may have aspects of both administrative and market systems to accommodate different changes in the environment of resource use. An example is an irrigation system with rules to alter water entitlements in response to seasonal water availability, and a market to allocate water entitlement between users in response to fluctuating economic conditions.

INSTITUTIONAL ANALYSIS AND INSTITUTIONAL CHOICE

Institutional Decisions and Transaction Costs

In the previous section, four aspects of institutions for regulation of use of a natural resource were defined and described. These were (i) property-right regimes that define the entities with decision-making power over the way in which the resource will be used; (ii) entitlement systems that define the physical basis for dividing the resource amongst users; (iii) mechanisms for making an initial allocation of entitlements amongst competing resource users; and (iv) mechanisms for making changes to the allocation of entitlements. Within the context of a property-right or institutional hierarchy, these four types of institutions exist at each level of the hierarchy. An institutional hierarchy forms a nested set of institutions inasmuch as the institutions at any particular level are legally supported by a superordinate level, with the exception of the top level that must be self-supporting.

It was also noted in the previous section that within each of the four subsets of institutions there are alternative institutional structures: different property-right regimes, different systems of entitlements, different mechanisms of initial allocation of entitlements; and different mechanisms for re-allocating entitlements. In establishing or modifying an institutional structure, decisions need to be made about the form that each of these subsets of institutions will take.

The central issue in examining alternative institutional structures is that of transaction costs. The concept of transaction costs is introduced below. Alternatives for each of the four types of institutions relating to the use of natural resources are then described and criteria for institutional choice developed using considerations of transaction costs.

In the most general sense, transaction costs are the costs incurred in organising and coordinating human interaction. Coase (1960 p. 15) has described the nature of this interaction in the context of economic exchange in a market:

> In order to carry out a market transaction it is necessary to discover who it is that one wishes to deal with, to inform people that one wishes to deal and on what terms, to conduct negotiations leading up to a bargain, to draw up the contract, to undertake the inspection needed to make sure that the terms of the contract are being observed, and so on.

Transactions costs are the costs of undertaking these activities.

The above description of interaction and definition of transaction costs is centred on an individual making a trading decision in a market place, but not all economic decisions are made in such a manner. The description can be broadened to include a wider diversity of economic decisions. Thus, in words similar to those of Coase: in order to make *an allocative decision* it is necessary to discover who has interests in the decision; to discover who it is necessary to include in the decision-making process; to exchange information between parties to decision making; to conduct negotiations leading up to a decision; to monitor subsequent behaviours to ensure that these are consistent with the decision; and to bear some uncertainty with respect to the outcome of the decision. Again, transaction costs are the costs of undertaking these activities. More briefly and more generally, transaction costs have been defined as 'the costs of arranging a contract ex ante and monitoring and enforcing it ex post' (Matthews, 1986, cited in Hubbard, 1997); the 'costs of running the economic system' (Arrow, 1969, cited in Hubbard, 1997); and 'the economic equivalent of friction in physical systems' (Williamson, 1985, cited in Hubbard, 1997).

What is the relationship between transaction costs and institutions, including property rights? It has already been indicated above that the role and principal philosophical justification of institutions, and especially of property rights, is to facilitate interaction and exchange. The 'new institutional economics' holds that the way that institutions provide facilitation is through the reduction of transaction costs (Hubbard, 1997). Property rights define the rights and duties associated with ownership of an object and other institutions establish paradigms for the exchange of property rights so that there is a reduction in uncertainty in interactions between parties with respect to objects of value. Well-defined property rights and supporting institutions reduce the transaction costs of negotiated decisions by reducing the amount of information that must be collected, by providing paradigms for negotiation, and by providing mechanisms for enforcing contracts.

The down side of property rights and institutions is that resources are required for their establishment and maintenance: 'there are costs of establishing and protecting ownership rights and of policing compliance with socially determined attenuations of decisionmaking [*sic*] rights' (Dahlman, 1980 p. 83). Alternative institutional arrangements will differ with respect to (i) the transaction costs of decision making and exchange to achieve a particular objective with respect to resource allocation; and (ii) the costs of institutional establishment and maintenance. A new institutional structure will be of benefit to society where the reduction in transaction costs of allocation decisions exceeds the costs of establishing and maintaining these institutions. This introduces a concept of institutional efficiency: the efficient set of institutions for governing a particular set of allocation decisions will be that which minimises the sum of transaction costs incurred in making the decisions and in establishing and maintaining the institutions.

The scope of a transaction-cost analysis of institutional structures is the examination of institutional efficiency within a cost-effectiveness framework. This is neatly described by Williamson (1979): '[t]he overall objective of the exercise essentially comes down to this: for each abstract description of a transaction, identify the most economical governance structure – where by governance structure I refer to the institutional framework within which the integrity of a transaction is decided.'

In the remainder of this section, the concept of transaction costs is used to examine choice between alternative institutional forms for regulating the use of natural resources.   This is undertaken in turn for selecting amongst alternative property-right regimes, entitlement systems, mechanisms for initial allocation of entitlements, and mechanisms for re-allocation of entitlements.

Property-Right Regimes

Within a property-right hierarchy the nature of the property-right regime at any level is determined at least in part by institutional decisions at the superordinate level which must provide institutional support for whatever property-right regime will be adopted. The choice of property-right regime is to a large extent independent of the decisions made with respect to entitlement allocations, a point often confused in the literature. For example, a state agency may choose to allocate resource entitlements to cooperatives of resource users in local areas, but also to allow trading of these entitlements between the cooperatives. Thus common property is quite consistent with a market system for re-allocation of resource entitlements.

The top level in the hierarchy of property rights for resource allocation can be considered as exogenous to the system of resource use. Either there will be a situation of open access or a property-right structure will be determined by the nature of the resource and institutions that lie outside of the resource-allocation problem. Consider the conceptual example of the international fishery, the property-right hierarchy for which was earlier described in Table 2.2. Prior to any decisions about allocation of the fish resource, existing institutions have created nation states with potential claims for access to the resource. There is no overlying 'world government' that could hold state ownership, nor any individual powerful enough to grasp private ownership. The only possible form of ownership of the resource (other than having no ownership at all) is that of common property between the nation states, as has occurred in one example with cooperation between Norway and Russia (Armstrong, 1994). As another example, consider any terrestrial natural resource. Property-right and allocation systems that are to be implemented for a resource depend ultimately on institutional support from the government or governments that have jurisdiction over the area in which the resource occurs and is used. The top level of a property-right hierarchy for the resource must therefore be one either of open access, state property, or common property between multiple national or sub-national states where the particular resource occurs across political boundaries.

The bottom level of any property-right hierarchy generally constitutes a private-property regime, although theses private rights may be strongly attenuated. In most cases of natural resources it is ultimately individuals or private corporate entities that have a right to extract benefits from entitlements to resource use. This includes many resource situations described as common property: it is just that in these cases the bottom hierarchy level of private property may comprise strongly attenuated rights and the investigator making the description has directed attention to the superordinate common-property level in the hierarchy where most decisions relating to resource use are made. For example, in the Swiss Alpine grazing systems examined by Stevenson (1991), grazing lands are often owned and managed by groups of graziers, and the property-right regime in these situations was described as common property. With the common-property system, however, there was a subordinate level of private property rights in the entitlements of individual graziers to run cattle on the commonly owned land.

The choice between alternative property-right regimes can be considered as a problem of minimising transaction costs associated with the making of decisions over the use of a resource. That is, given the need to make certain management decisions for use of a resource, under which type of property-right regime (state property, common property or private property) might the costs of making these decisions for a resource be minimised? The influence of transaction costs in determining the optimal type of property-right regime can be demonstrated by considering some conceptual examples of different situations of resource use where one property-right regime may be preferred over another.

Consider first the choice between a private-property regime and some form of collective property-right regime, the latter being either common property or state property. The choice is between having certain decisions made by individual holders of entitlements to resource use, or having these decisions made by a collective. A conceptual analysis based on the well-known prisoners' dilemma game can be used to examine this choice. Table 2.3 shows a payoff matrix for a prisoners' dilemma game applied to a hypothetical grazing 'commons'. In this case, two cattle owners each graze ten cattle on a common pasture. The quantity of pasture is scarce relative to the number of cattle and thus if the number of cattle is increased, there will be a lower return on all cattle. Each owner must decide whether to add an additional beast to the common pasture. If neither owner adds an extra beast, they will maintain a net return on their grazing activities of $10 per head, or a total of $100 each. If either owner adds another beast to the pasture, he will accrue the extra revenue for that beast, but due to degradation of the pasture the return on all existing cattle will be reduced by 5 per cent. Thus the expected return to the farmer adding the extra beast is $(100 + 10) \times 0.95 = \$104.5$. The expected return to the other farmer is $100 \times 0.95 = \$95$.

Table 2.3: Payoff Matrix for Two Graziers of a Common Pasture Faced with a Decision of whether to Increase Stocking Rates

		Owner 2	
		Do Nothing	**Add 1 Cow**
Owner 1	**Do Nothing**	$100, $100	$95, $104.5
	Add 1 Cow	$104.5, $95	$99, $99

The conventional interpretation of a payoff matrix such as this is that each grazier makes his decision individually and with uncertainty as to the decision made by the other grazier. It is easy to show in this case that each grazier has a dominant choice strategy of adding an extra cow to the pasture with the result that the common pasture is degraded and the expected return for each owner is reduced from $100 to $99. More complex models, such as used by Stevenson (1991 pp. 8–38), can be used to show that the process of adding extra cows will continue under these decision-making arrangements until payoffs are reduced to zero for both graziers; that is, the economic rent from the resource is totally dissipated. Such analyses have been the basis of many criticisms of open access and, erroneously, of common property.

Several investigators of property-right regimes have, however, interpreted the prisoners' dilemma game in terms of incentives for collective decision making, in which case a different solution is obtained (Bromley, 1989 pp. 87–8; Ostrom, 1990; Ostrom *et al.*, 1993 pp. 294–7). If the grazing decision is made within an institutional environment of collective decision making and coordination, then an equilibrium can be achieved with the maximum economic rent (the top right-hand corner in Table 2.3). Assurances, enforcement mechanisms and threats can provide incentives for restraint on individual behaviour and allow effective implementation of collective decisions that maximise the total benefits to the group of resource users and, in the long run, the benefits to individual users.

In the example shown in Table 2.3 it can thus be seen that there are benefits to collective decision making in regard to resource use. The reason that such benefits exist is that there are external costs and benefits to individual decisions that can be incorporated into collective decisions. When the costs of engaging in collective decision making are also considered, the choice between private decision making and some form of collective decision making can be stated as: if the benefits of collective decisions exceed the additional costs of collective decision making, then the associated regime of collective property rights is more efficient than a regime of private property rights. It is conceivable that in some circumstances the costs of collective decision making would exceed the benefits, resulting in private property and individual decision making being the optimal property-right regime. An example of such a case may be where allotments of farming land are owned and managed individually, with degradation of land being a cumulative and external effect of farming decisions made individually. There may well be benefits to restraining land management by individual farmers, but the costs of making and enforcing collective decisions may exceed these benefits.

If some form of collective action is an efficient means of management of the resource, then a choice still needs to be made between state property and common property. This choice can also be considered in terms of the benefits and costs of decision making under each regime. The types, and hence benefits, of decisions made under each regime and the costs of decision making may differ due to such factors as different information, different objectives and different decision-making procedures. Ostrom (1990, 1992), for example, lists several factors which influence benefits and costs of decision making under a common-property regime. These include existence of supportive institutions from superordinate levels in institutional hierarchies, clear definition of rights to participate in decision making, precedents of successful collective decision making, and information about the state of the resource and the impacts of resource. Similarly, there will be many factors which influence the costs and benefits of decisions under state property, for example the characteristics of information available to decision makers, efficiency losses in taxation schemes, the nature of political decision-making processes, and the extent of rent seeking by officials of government agencies.

One further question that can be asked about the relationship between choices of property-right regimes and transaction costs is why do hierarchies of allocative institutions, including property-right regimes, develop? Why are allocative decisions not all made at the top level of an institutional hierarchy? A possible answer from the theory of transaction costs is that there are net benefits to be gained by retaining some allocative decisions at particular levels in a hierarchy and by delegating power to make other allocative decisions to subordinate and decentralised decision-making entities. The potential for net benefits by so doing arise where there are multiple decisions that need to be made for use of a resource. Each type of decision is associated with particular information requirements and patterns of interest amongst individuals or groups in a society. Consequently, transaction costs in decisions of resource management may be minimised by assigning powers to make particular decisions to different levels in an institutional hierarchy. As an example, consider again the institutional hierarchy described for the international fishery in Table 2.2. For a decision of allocation of fish stocks amongst nations, it may readily be imagined that the transaction costs associated with a negotiated decision between national governments, supported by bioeconomic information collected by state agencies, would be substantially lower than if the same decision were to be made by agreement amongst individual fisherman from multiple countries, each with very limited knowledge of the total fishery. Conversely, decisions about investment in equipment to catch fish may be made at lower cost by individual fishermen who hold information on market conditions and the efficacy of different technologies than by government agencies who do not hold this information and for whom the process of decision making is relatively inflexible and time-consuming.

Entitlement Systems

Allocation of a resource amongst users involves defining entitlements or shares in the resource to which property rights pertain. An entitlement system is defined as a mechanism for physically dividing a resource between potential users. As previously described, entitlement systems can be broadly categorised into 'resource quota' and 'input quota', depending upon whether an entitlement is specified on the basis of a physical quantity or share of the resource itself, or on the basis of a right to use certain quantities or types of inputs to the production processes that utilise the resource.

The transaction costs in establishing an entitlement system based on either input or resource quotas can be divided into two categories: (i) the costs incurred in determining and adjusting the quantitative size of the quota and, for the input quota, determining the particular inputs to the production process to which the quota will be applied; and (ii) the costs incurred in monitoring and enforcement of the quota limits. It will be argued below that the relative transaction costs incurred by use of an input quota or resource quota vary according to the characteristics of the resource, the technology of use, and characteristics of the resource users.

Development and effective implementation of an input-quota scheme require that the following conditions hold (Stevenson, 1991 pp. 63–4).

- Regulators have knowledge of at least the principal components of the production function by which the resource is utilised.
- The production function is consistent across users of the resource.
- The production function is 'rigid' inasmuch as there cannot be substitution of other inputs for the regulated inputs and the production function is slowly changing over time.

The information requirements and therefore the transaction costs of establishing an input-quota system will be proportional to the extent that these conditions do not hold. If the production function is complex, with many possibilities of substitution between inputs, then substantial information may be required to define the function and to determine which inputs should be regulated so as to limit use of the resource to the desired level while allowing a technically efficient input combination. If the input-quota scheme prevents the resource users from adopting a technically efficient combination of inputs, then the resultant dead-weight loss of welfare may also be regarded as a transaction cost of the regulatory action. If the technology of production is changing rapidly over time, then high transaction costs would be incurred in frequent revisions of the quota system to accommodate new inputs or production relationships and thereby maintain limits on use of the resource.

Monitoring and enforcement of an input-quota scheme require measurement of the level of use of regulated inputs in the production process. Transaction costs of measurement and enforcement will be proportional to the number of inputs that have to be monitored and difficulties in measurement.

An input quota may avoid some transaction costs in establishing and administering a quota system. For a flow resource, it may be desirable to alter restrictions on resource use according to the availability of the resource in any given time period. A potential advantage of input quotas is that if the productivity of the inputs is proportional to the total availability of the resource, then there may be an inherent self-adjustment mechanism within the input-quota scheme which allows use of the resource to vary according to its availability.

Input quotas have been commonly used for the regulation of fisheries. These quotas typically include limitations on a range of inputs such as boat numbers and dimensions, net dimensions and on-board storage capacities. Restrictions on lengths of fishing seasons and on access to favoured fishing locations may also be considered as input quotas. Campbell and Lindner (1990) demonstrated both graphically and with a numerical example that input quotas could restrict fish harvests without substantial compromise of technical efficiency if other inputs could not be readily substituted for the regulated inputs. Input quotas have been the dominant schemes used by self-governing groups of fishermen and this has been attributed to the greater ease, and hence lower cost, of measurement of inputs over measurement of fishing catch (Schlager, 1990, cited in Scott, 1993).

The transaction costs of establishing a resource quota arise only from establishing the size of the total allocation to achieve the desired level of resource use. The same transaction costs apply under an input quota and are not a point of difference between the two alternative schemes. Unlike an input quota, however, a resource quota would not have a self-adjustment mechanism to allow changes in resource use in response to changes in resource availability. Thus if such changes to the level of resource use are desirable, then transaction costs would have to be incurred in monitoring availability of the resource and altering the quota entitlement.

The transaction costs of monitoring and enforcement of an output quota depend upon the ease of direct measurement of resource use. The more difficult the level of resource use is to measure, the higher the associated transaction cost of enforcement of the quota system. Returning to the example of regulation of catch in fisheries, Scott (1993) concludes that resource quotas are relatively uncommon in self-governed fisheries due at least to a perception amongst fishermen that reliable measurements of catch are difficult and costly to obtain. Resource quotas have, however, been increasingly favoured in fisheries managed by state agencies, as for example in several fisheries of New Zealand where the state agency itself undertakes the measurement and enforcement role (Lindner, 1990).

Resource quotas have also been used in the regulation of water resources where quantities of water used for irrigation are readily measured by use of flow meters in channels or pipelines. Technological advances in construction of flow meters, as well as increasing scarcity of water resources and greater economic benefits of regulation, have contributed to the replacement of input quotas to restrict use of irrigation water (limits on areas of irrigated land) with resource quotas (volumetric allocations of water). This example will be returned to in later chapters describing institutional structures for irrigation systems.

A summary of how factors causing transaction costs affect the choice of institutional arrangements for physical allocation of a resource is shown in Table 2.4.

Mechanisms for Initial Allocation of Entitlements

An initial allocation of entitlements to a resource between competing parties can occur in two generic ways: (i) allocation by administrative decisions by resource managers; or (ii) allocation by a market process whereby the resource managers sell units of entitlement to competing resource users.

*Table 2.4: Efficient Institutional Structures for Physical Allocation of a
Resource under Different Conditions of Transaction Costs*

		Resource Monitoring Costs	
		LOW	HIGH
Production Function Complexity and Instability	LOW	Input or resource quotas	Input quotas
	HIGH	Resource quotas	Neither input nor resource quotas may provide a suitable system of entitlements

The initial distribution of resource entitlements by administrative decision
is frequently regarded with disdain by economists. For example, Hartwick
and Olewiler (1986 p. 302) criticise this means of distribution on the basis of
'[t]he arbitrary nature of these types of distribution schemes can politicize the
fishery and create high administrative costs. ... There is no guarantee that the
firm receiving the quota is the one with the lowest costs of harvest.' The
corresponding argument for use of a market system of allocation, such as by
auctioning off entitlements to the highest bidder, is that the prices offered by
potential users of the resource will equal the present value of the resource
rents that each user will be able to generate by use of the resource. Thus the
resource is allocated to users in such a way as to ensure its maximum-value
use (Hartwick and Olewiler, 1986 p. 302).

There are, however, two major flaws in this argument for a ubiquitous
superiority of market allocation over administrative allocation. Firstly, the
reasoning implicitly assumes that there will be no large transaction costs in the
market that will cause prices to diverge from the rent value of the resource.
Secondly, the reasoning fails to take into account potential spillover effects
and associated transaction costs arising in implementation of a distribution
mechanism. These two considerations make the choice of distribution
mechanism an empirical issue.

The proposition that an auction system of entitlement distribution will
result in a pricing of quotas equal to the discounted stream of resource rents is
based on the usual assumptions of competitive markets. It is assumed that any
market operates in a long-run equilibrium with no distortions to the price of
quotas arising from imperfect information or imperfect mobility of other
factors employed in a production process. That is, it is assumed that there are
no transaction costs that prevent markets instantaneously reaching equilibria.
This could be an unrealistic assumption. In discussing pricing of resource
quotas in fisheries, Lindner (1990) demonstrated that prices offered for quotas

would not reflect the economic rent attributable to the quota if factor markets are not in a long-run equilibrium, that is, there is under-capacity or over-capacity in the fixed inputs to the production process in which the resource is used. If there is excess capacity in fixed inputs for resource utilisation relative to the total amount of quota to be distributed, then an investment decision for purchase of quota will take into account the sunk costs of fixed assets. The willingness to pay for quotas will equal the expected value of resource rents pertaining to the quota plus part of the sunk costs of fixed inputs. Conversely, a situation of under-capacity in fixed inputs may result in the quota being underpriced relative to resource rents.

Transaction costs also arise in the initial allocation of resource entitlements as a result of the redistributions of wealth that are inherent in such allocation exercises and the consequent social disruption and political implications for the decision makers. The choice of an administrative system of allocation can often be interpreted as minimising these transaction costs. For example, in most fisheries for which catch quotas have been introduced, the initial distribution of quotas has been on the basis of historical catches by each resource user. Such a system minimises the redistribution of wealth resulting from the implementation of the quotas and consequently minimises the transaction costs to the resource managers arising from opposition to such redistributions. It may also be envisaged that where quotas are to be issued for a resource that has not previously been exploited, there is no redistribution effect and a market system may be the more appropriate means of quota allocation.

The use of an administrative means of quota allocation is therefore not necessarily as arbitrary as some economists would argue. Instead, the use of administrative systems may be a carefully considered decision, taking into account the transaction costs of implementing an allocation mechanism. Where there is a history of resource use prior to introduction of regulation, there are factors other than a narrow definition of resource rents to take into account in deciding what is an efficient allocation and how an efficient allocation should be achieved.

The resultant choice of mechanism for initial allocation of resource entitlements is thus summarised in Table 2.5.

Mechanisms for Adjusting Allocations

As with the procedures for determining an initial allocation of entitlement, the procedures for altering it can be broadly categorised as administration-based or market-based. The choice between these two institutional mechanisms for re-allocation can be examined by drawing on literature relating to allocation of resources outside of and within firms. Outside the firm, resource allocations are made through markets on the basis of relative willingness to pay. Within a firm, resource allocations are made by unilateral administrative decisions (Hay and Morris, 1991 p. 281). The important question is when should allocations be made by unilateral decision, and when should allocations be determined by a market?

Table 2.5   Efficient Institutional Structures for Allocation of Resource Entitlements under Different Conditions of Transaction Costs

		External Transaction Costs of Market Allocation	
		LOW	HIGH
Potential Efficiency Gains of a Market	**LOW**	Administrative or market	Administrative
	HIGH	Market	Administrative or market

The division of allocation decisions between the market and firms is counter-intuitive to the efficiency properties of market allocations extolled by neoclassical microeconomics. Organisational theory suggests two reasons why administrative allocation within firms may have a cost advantage over allocation of resources by a market.

- Participation in a market confers transaction costs on participants that can be avoided or reduced by using internal decision making for resource allocation. Transaction costs occur as a result of (i) obtaining information on prices, market participants and processes of exchange; (ii) negotiating and concluding contracts; (iii) divergence in interests of market participants and consequent market externalities; and (iv) requirements for contract enforcement and conflict resolution (Coase, 1937; Hay and Morris, 1991 pp. 282–4; Williamson, 1971).
- Internalisation of production activities and decision making may confer cost savings arising from economies associated with sub-additivity of production costs: (i) scale economies, resulting from production of a larger amount of a particular output; and (ii) scope economies, resulting from production of two outputs within one enterprise rather than two separate enterprises (Baumol *et al.*, 1982).

Conversely, there are reasons why allocations by internal decision may prove inferior to market allocations.

- Internalisation of decision making may result in a loss of control over resource allocation due to either (i) loss or distortion of information as it passes through an organisation; or (ii) problems and costs associated with monitoring (Hay and Morris, 1991 p. 286).
- There is a potential for erroneous or sub-optimal decisions when decision-making responsibility is concentrated in individuals of limited decision-making ability. This potential arises from an inherently limited capacity of decision makers to process information in relation to objectives. The consequence is that the decision-making process may be aimed at obtaining satisfactory rather than optimal outcomes (Hay and Morris, 1991 pp. 286–7; Simon, 1979).
- As a result of rent-seeking behaviour, the objectives of individuals within an organisation, and hence the allocation of resources determined by these individuals, may deviate from the objectives of the organisation itself and the optimal resource allocation for the organisation (Hay and Morris, 1991 p. 287).

With regard to allocation of a natural resource, the choice between 'market' and 'administrative' systems of allocation can be described in terms of two organisational structures and consequences for resource allocation and transaction costs.

- In a market system, re-allocations of a resource between firms would be determined on the basis of voluntary trading in quotas, which would tend to move the resource to uses of greater economic value. Re-allocations by way of the market would, however, be constrained by transaction costs arising in market participation. High transaction costs would result in market failure and reduce the potential of market mechanisms to achieve a desired resource allocation.
- In an administrative system, allocation decisions are made unilaterally by an individual resource manager or a collective management agency. The extent to which the resource would be allocated to its highest-valued use would be constrained by transaction costs arising from (i) restrictions on the availability and processing of information; (ii) problems and costs of monitoring and information collection; and (iii) the need for general consensus to be achieved in allocative decisions. High transaction costs may result in 'administrative failure' or 'government failure'.

Theoretical studies of production costs and transaction costs in alternative allocation systems indicate that the question of which system is best suited to a particular situation is an empirical one, dependent upon values of the relevant transaction-cost parameters and the constraints on allocation processes

(Baumol *et al.*, 1982; Quiggin, 1995; Williamson, 1979). Economic analyses of allocation mechanisms for natural resources have tended to ignore this question. Instead, conventional neoclassical models with assumptions of zero transaction costs have been used to demonstrate a theoretical potential for markets in individual property rights to produce a perfect resource allocation. Whilst there are countless publications describing major and minor variations on this central theme, investigators have ignored the unavoidable imperfections of market systems resulting from the existence of transaction costs.

The effects of transaction costs on outcomes from market allocation can be demonstrated using a spatial equilibrium model. Such models explicitly recognise transfer costs as well as regulatory restrictions on market participation and trade quantities.

A spatial equilibrium model of water trades can be illustrated in a simple form as a static optimisation problem derived from the work of Takayama and Judge (1971). This problem is described as follows.

The market comprises two participants, each with a linear and perfectly inelastic supply curve for resource quotas, and a linear and downward-sloping demand curve for quotas.

$$\text{Demand:} \qquad y_i = \alpha_i - \beta_i p_i, i = 1,2 \qquad (2.1)$$
$$\text{Supply:} \qquad\qquad x_i = \theta_i \qquad\qquad\qquad (2.2)$$

where:

y_i = quantity of quota demanded in region i;
p_i = quota price in region i (a shadow price to the resource user);
x_i = quantity of quota supplied in region i; and
$\alpha_i, \beta_i, \theta_i$ = constants specific to each region.

The welfare of each market participant is defined as the sum of consumer and producer surplus. Due to the assumption of perfectly inelastic supply curves, the area under the supply curve is equal to zero and hence welfare equals the area under the demand curve.

Inverse expressions of demand functions are:
$$p_i = \lambda_i - \omega_i y_i, i = 1,2 \qquad (2.3)$$

Where λ_i, ω_i = constants specific to each region ($\lambda = \alpha / \beta$ and $\omega = 1/\beta$).

The welfare of each participant is thus:

$$W_i = W_i(y_i) = \int_0^{y_i} (\lambda_i - \omega_i y_i) dy_i \qquad (2.4)$$

$$= K_i + \lambda y_i - (\omega_i / 2) y_i^2 \qquad (2.5)$$

where K_i = constant.

The community welfare function is assumed additive:

$$W = \sum_{i=1}^{2} W_i(y_i) \qquad (2.6)$$

$$= K + \sum_{i=1}^{2} (\lambda_i y_i - \omega_i y_i^2 / 2) \qquad (2.7)$$

$$\text{where } K = \sum_{i=1}^{2} K_i. \qquad (2.8)$$

Transaction costs associated with transfers of resource quota from participant i to participant j are treated as a constant: t_{ij}. Net community welfare (NW) is defined as the community welfare minus transaction costs:

$$NW = K + \sum_{i=1}^{2} \left[W_i(y_i) - \sum_{j=1}^{2} (t_{ij} x_{ij}) \right] \qquad (2.9)$$

$$= K + \sum_{i=1}^{2} \left[\lambda_i y_i - \frac{\omega_i y_i^2}{2} - \sum_{j=1}^{2} t_{ij} x_{ij} \right]. \qquad (2.10)$$

The quantity of water consumed in each region, y_1 and y_2, is less than or equal to the quantity supplied internally, plus the quantity transferred from the other participant:

$$y_i \leq x_{ii} + x_{ji}. \qquad (2.11)$$

The quantity of water supplied by each participant is greater than or equal to the effective supply to himself and the other participant:

$$x_{ii} + x_{ij} \leq x_i. \qquad (2.12)$$

All variables are greater than or equal to zero:

$$y_i, x_i, x_{ii}, x_{ij}, x_{jj}, x_{ji} \geq 0. \tag{2.13}$$

Dropping the constant term from the net welfare function, the problem can thus be stated as follows.

$$\text{Max: } NW\left(y_i, x_{ii}, x_{ij}, x_{jj}, x_{ji}\right) = \sum_{i=1}^{2}\left[\lambda_i y_i - \frac{\omega_i y_i^2}{2} - \sum_{j=1}^{2} t_{ij} x_{ij}\right]. \tag{2.14}$$

Subject to:

$$y_i \leq x_{ii} + x_{ji} \tag{2.15}$$

$$x_{ii} + x_{ij} \leq x_i \tag{2.16}$$

$$y_i, x_i, x_{ii}, x_{ij}, x_{jj}, x_{ji} \geq 0. \tag{2.17}$$

In the regular solution to the problem (Figure 2.2), there is a transfer of a resource between participants so as to shift the resource to the higher-value use, in this case from participant 1 to participant 2. Trade is constrained by transaction costs in the form of transport costs, and the marginal value of the resource to each participant differs by the value of these transaction costs. The increase in net welfare as a result of trade is equal to the sum of the areas *abc* and *def* shown in Figure 2.2. 'Irregular' solutions can include corner solutions, where one participant will trade their entire supply of the resource to the other user, and no-trade solutions, where the initial difference in resource value between the two users is less than the transaction cost and hence the existence of a market does not improve the allocation.

It can be concluded from the above model that the extent of trading in a market for resource quotas, and consequently the potential for a market system to improve resource allocation, is dependent upon differences in supply and demand schedules between users, and the magnitude of transaction costs.

For an administration system, re-allocations are made by collective decisions of resource users or by state agencies, either as specific decisions for particular circumstances or as operational rules for recurring circumstances where re-allocation is required. The collective formulation and choice of allocation rules can be interpreted as an issue of transaction costs. It may be intuitively expected that under an administrative system, transaction costs in re-allocation would arise from (i) collection and processing of information, and (ii) negotiations in the decision-making process. These costs will affect the nature of the allocation decisions and rules, and consequently the efficiency and social-welfare characteristics of the resource allocation.

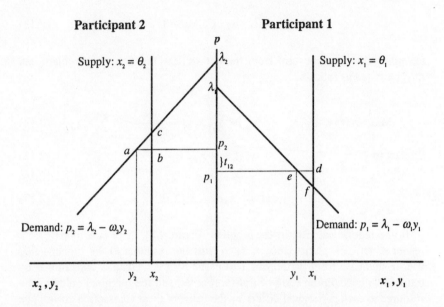

*Figure 2.2 Regular Solution to a Two-Party Trade Model with
          Transaction Costs*

The theory of administrative decision making is not sufficiently developed to enable a quantitative analysis equivalent in scope to the spatial equilibrium model described above for assessment of market allocations. The published literature has not specifically addressed the incidence and magnitude of transaction costs incurred in such decisions. While some studies describe factors considered to influence the magnitude of transaction costs in common-property organisations (e.g. Ostrom, 1990 and 1992), at best these studies only provide a basis for subjective appraisal to indicate whether transaction costs of organisation and administration may be 'high' or 'low'. Attention has focused only on whether or not participants in a common-property system perceive that the benefits of cooperation exceed costs of organisation and decision making.

There has been little study into selection of administrative decision making by common-property organisations or state agencies for altering allocations of resources. The literature reveals two approaches to defining allocation rules: (i) a theoretical approach based on cooperative game theory; and (ii) an empirical approach based on study of existing common-property systems. These two approaches are briefly described below.

A few studies have looked at selecting between allocation strategies using principles of cooperative games and assuming a requirement for unanimous decision making. Staatz (1983) used an analysis based on *n*-person cooperative games to determine conditions which must be satisfied if a set of allocation rules is to maintain incentives for heterogeneous members to remain part of a cooperative. The analysis indicated that maintenance of cooperation required that allocation rules provide a return to each individual member that exceeds the return that that member may obtain individually or in an alternative coalition. In an empirical application, Rosen and Sexton (1993) used a cooperative-game model to analyse the responses of agricultural water-supply organisations in California to potential rural-to-urban water transfers. Programming models were used to estimate the returns to individual farms from alternative water-trade scenarios. The game-theoretic analysis involved subjectively defining four coalitions that may conceivably emerge in response to considering proposals for water trading, and which vary according to the order in which they rank the alternative trade scenarios. A solution was found to the game by comparing the payoffs available to the whole water organisation under the various trade scenarios to the payoffs attainable by each coalition if it formed its own water-supply organisation.

The cooperative-game-theory approach to predicting allocation rules has some major deficiencies as a tool for predicting group behaviour. Firstly, there is no rigorous process for determining potential allocations which can then be tested for unanimous support. The allocations to be tested must be subjectively defined and selected from an essentially infinite number of possibilities. Secondly, the approach seeks only allocations which command unanimous support. This may not be necessary for the working of a cooperative organisation, and indeed may be sub-optimal as a result of high decision-making costs. Empirical surveys of long-established common-property organisations in water and other resources indicate that unanimous or broad support is generally required only for the governing institutions of the organisation and not for specific allocation rules or conflict resolutions (Maass and Anderson, 1978; Ostrom, 1990). Buchanan and Tullock (1962) have demonstrated that once the costs of reaching a decision are taken into account, a unanimity requirement may not be optimal either for the group or the individual.

How then should a policy maker decide between administrative and market systems for resource allocation? Williamson (1979) has examined a conceptually similar problem in terms of the characteristics of the transactions inherent in resource re-allocation, the associated transaction costs, and alternative governance structures for transactions. On the basis of the classification schemes developed by Williamson, two broad types of re-allocation transactions for natural resources can be described: *idiosyncratic* and *non-specific* transactions. In practice the difference between the two types of transaction would be gradational, but it is useful to consider them as discrete.

An idiosyncratic re-allocation is one where the identities of the parties to the re-allocation transaction are important with respect to the benefits of the re-allocation. The most common case of this would be where there are significant external costs or benefits to other resource users arising from a re-allocation. For example, with a groundwater resource, the re-allocation of rights of groundwater extraction between two users has the potential to alter the spatial pattern of groundwater use and hence the availability of groundwater to other users with wells close to those of the two parties undertaking the re-allocation. The extent of the external costs and benefits to other groundwater users, and hence the net benefit of the transaction, will depend upon the identities of the parties undertaking the re-allocation and their previous and planned patterns of resource use.

In contrast, a non-specific re-allocation is one where the identities of the parties are irrelevant with respect to the benefits of the re-allocation. Such a re-allocation would occur where there are no external effects of the re-allocation. Outcomes from the re-allocation are readily predictable and factored into the contract between the parties engaging in the re-allocation.

The two categories of re-allocation transactions have different ramifications for transaction costs and institutional choice. Non-specific re-allocations typically involve low transaction costs. Since the outcomes from re-allocation are readily predictable and there are no external parties with interests in the re-allocation, there is only a low investment required in the transaction in terms of information collecting and the contract process. As a consequence, this type of transaction is ideally suited to being undertaken within a market, and is indeed the type of transaction implicitly assumed to occur in neoclassical models of market trading. Idiosyncratic transactions on the other hand involve high transaction-specific investments. Outcomes are relatively uncertain without investing in information that is specific to each individual transaction and the contracting process would typically be more complicated due to such factors as greater numbers of interested parties or the need to develop complex contracts with provisions that are contingent upon uncertain outcomes to the transactions. The consequently high transaction costs would reduce the efficacy of market processes in efficiently allocating a resource, and re-allocation by administrative decision may produce a more efficient outcome under such circumstances.

INSTITUTIONAL INNOVATION AND CHANGE

The previous section of this chapter described four aspects of institutions associated with use of natural resources and indicated how choices amongst alternative institutions could be examined in terms of a problem of minimising transaction costs. This framework for evaluation of alternative institutional structures is essentially one of comparative statics and ignores processes of institutional change and constraints on change. In this section, processes of institutional change are examined. It will be seen that when processes of change are included in a problem of institutional choice, the costs of change may impose substantial constraints on that choice. The costs of institutional change and effects on institutional development have also been considered within a transaction-cost framework.

The study of institutional change is complicated by the diverse forms of rules and behavioural norms that institutions comprise. This is recognised by North (1990 p. 6) in his statement that 'institutional change is a complicated process because the changes at the margin can be a consequence of changes in rules, in informal constraints, and in kinds and effectiveness of enforcement.' Nevertheless, despite the complexity of the subject there have been several attempts to describe and model processes of change.

Scott (1989a) identifies four means by which institutional change has occurred historically.

i.   Spontaneous and discontinuous change by revolutions and conquest.
ii. Spontaneous and incremental change from the working of custom and common usage.
iii. Incremental change by judicial processes and evolution of common law.
iv. Incremental change created by imperial, bureaucratic or political means.

The last three of these means of institutional change are entrenched in modern democratic cultures. Economic studies have focused on investigating the means by which these changes come about, concentrating on the motivations of the economic agents that promote and produce change.

The first, and still standard, models of institutional change focused on the role of institutions in determining the magnitudes of transaction costs and external costs and benefits accruing to and arising from economic exchange. Demsetz (1967) paraphrases the externality perspective on institutional change:

> Changes in knowledge result in changes in production functions, market values and aspirations. New techniques, new ways of doing the same things, and doing new things – all invoke harmful and beneficial effects to which society has not been accustomed. It is my thesis ... that the emergence of new property rights takes place in response to the desires of the interacting persons for adjustment to new benefit–cost possibilities. ... Property rights develop to internalise externalities when the gains of internalisation become larger than the cost of internalisation. (p. 34)

In a similar manner, institutional change has been considered to occur in response to the existence of transaction costs and opportunities to reduce them (Barzel, 1989; Bromley, 1989 p. 14; North, 1990 p. 125).

These models describe institutional change as essentially a market process with interacting forces of supply and demand producing an efficient level of investment in institutional development and resulting in incremental increases in the 'efficiency' of an institutional framework. Efficiency is regarded in terms of optimal reductions in transaction costs and internalisation of externalities. Thus, 'property rights [i.e. institutions] will be developed over resources and assets as a simple cost–benefit calculus of the costs of developing and enforcing such rights, as compared to the alternatives under the status quo' (North, 1990 p. 51).   Competition between alternative institutional structures would result in the changes being made on the basis of marginal net benefits, and thus institutions would become progressively more efficient.

Studies of the historical development of institutional systems revealed two principal deficiencies in this model of institutional change. Firstly, the model fails to explain empirical evidence for the persistence of inefficient institutional structures and the introduction of inefficient institutions (North, 1981).   Secondly, the model does not specifically recognise a distinction between private economic agents (firms and consumers), from where demand for institutional change may arise, and political organisations which are the source of change in at least formal institutions (North, 1990 p. 7).

In order to accommodate these deficiencies in the basic model of institutional change, North (1990) proposed an alternative model based on two premises.

i.   Institutions are a creation of human beings. They evolve and are altered by human beings, and hence a theory of institutional change must begin with the individual (North, 1990 p. 5).
ii. Incremental institutional change comes from the perceptions of the entrepreneurs in political and economic organisations that they could do better by altering the existing institutional framework at some margin, but perceptions of costs and benefits are imperfect due to imperfect information and transaction costs (North, 1990 p. 8).

An interpretation of North's (1990) model of institutional change is shown schematically in Figure 2.3.

From the perspective that institutional change arises from the actions of individuals, there are two generic types of individuals within the model: private entrepreneurs and political entrepreneurs. Private entrepreneurs are the firms, households, producers and consumers that comprise the typical set of actors in economic models. Political entrepreneurs comprise members of the polities that develop and implement formal institutions of social and economic change.

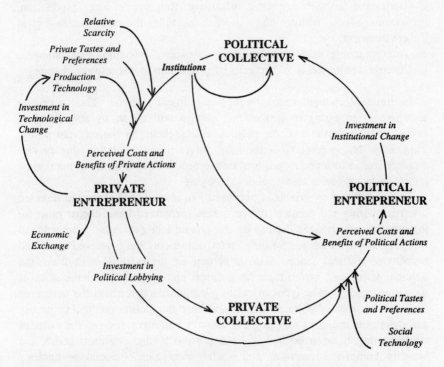

Figure 2.3: Conceptual Model of the Process of Institutional Change

The process of institutional change is a continuous one, hence the model is presented as a cyclic process. For the sake of description, the cycle can be considered as commencing with an existing set of institutions. These institutions comprise a component of both the economic environment of private entrepreneurs and the political environment of political entrepreneurs. These environments present the respective entrepreneurs with benefits and costs of prospective actions which include options of maintaining as well as altering the existing institutions.

The private entrepreneur is a 'typical' economic agent who is interested in maximising an intertemporal utility function. The environment of the private entrepreneur comprises existing institutions, scarce resources, a set of tastes and preferences, and a given state of production technology. These components combine to determine prices and to create perceptions of costs and benefits to the private entrepreneur for all possible actions. In maximising a utility function, the private entrepreneur can select between three generic types of actions.

i.   Undertake normal economic exchange (buying, selling, production, consumption) within the given institutional and technological environment.
ii. Attempt to alter costs and benefits by investment in technological change.
iii. Attempt to alter costs and benefits by investment in institutional change.

Institutional change occurs through a political system. Thus a private entrepreneur investing in institutional change will do so by attempting to influence the behaviour of the political entrepreneurs in the relevant polity. This may be undertaken either by direct investment by the private entrepreneur in influencing political entrepreneurs or indirect investment via a collective group undertaking political lobbying.

The investment by private entrepreneurs in institutional change is directed towards altering the political entrepreneurs' perceived benefit–cost ratio for the institutional changes desired by the private entrepreneurs. The political lobbying is not, however, the only factor influencing the perceived costs and benefits of political action. Also important are the existing institutions, the political tastes and benefits of the political entrepreneurs, and the state of social technology. The types of existing institutions that affect the perceived costs and benefits of political actions are those that define political processes and determine the costs of designing institutional structures and the costs of implementing these structures via a collective polity. Political tastes and benefits comprise economic and social ideologies. Social technology comprises such factors as institutional precedents, and states of political and social knowledge.

On the basis of the perceived costs and benefits of political actions and with the objective of maximising some form of political utility function, the political entrepreneurs will undertake investment in institutional change through the relevant processes of the polity or political collective. As an outcome of the political process, there will be changes to the institutional framework and thus a change to the economic environment of the private entrepreneurs. Thus the cycle re-commences. It can be envisaged, though, that if levels of relative scarcity, levels of technology (both production and social), and tastes and benefits were constant, the institutional systems would reach some form of equilibrium.

This general model has been interpreted in terms of demand for, and supply of, new institutions (Hayami and Ruttan, 1985). Demand for institutions may arise from either private or political entrepreneurs responding to perceived costs and benefits of possible actions. For private entrepreneurs, demand for institutions could be brought about by changes in any of the components of the economic environment, that is, changes in relative scarcity, technology, changes in tastes and preferences, or a change in some aspect of the existing institutional structure. With political entrepreneurs, demand for institutions may arise from the existing institutional structure, political lobbying by private entrepreneurs, changes in social technology and changes in political tastes and preferences. The latter may arise from, for example, change in a political party holding power in a government.

The supply of institutions arises from political entrepreneurs that initiate institutional innovations in accordance with institutional 'power' as defined on p. 15. A supply function for institutional change can be conceptualised as a function of 'transition costs' of moving to a new institutional structure: direct costs of developing an innovation (research, drafting, community consultation, etc.), costs of pushing the innovation through the political collective, and political costs from the innovation not pleasing all of a political electorate. The actual supply decision by political entrepreneurs can be envisaged as arising from the interaction between the entrepreneurs' supply and demand 'functions', with a supply decision equating subjective assessments of the marginal benefit of an increment of institutional change with the marginal transition costs.

The process of institutional change is thus modelled as many transactions between economic and political agents with associated transaction costs.

The existence of transaction costs in institutional change has the important implication of path-dependency in change. Since demand and supply for institutional change occur at the margin of an existing institutional structure, any transaction costs of 'institutional transactions' that arise from the existing structure may favour some options for change over others. The apparent costs and rewards arising from options for institutional change are dependent to some extent on the institutional *status quo*. This may favour the development of new and more efficient institutions, or may impede institutional change and allow relatively inefficient institutional arrangements to persist (North, 1990 pp. 115–17).

North's model of institutional change has been criticised on the basis of a lack of attention to complexities of political processes and potential for new institutions to emerge out of bargaining processes between agents with conflicting interests (Sened, 1997; Knight, 1992). However, such criticism is perhaps unjustified for a model as general as North's. Detailed attention to any part of the model, such as political processes and institutional supply, will deliver additional insights into institutional development and change, as for example with the work on private property rights by Sened (1997). However, this does not necessarily detract from the presentation in North's model of the basic motivations and constraints for institutional change, particularly for economic institutions. Indeed, it would appear to add to the value of the model in so far as it creates a consistent framework within which to make detailed investigation of particular processes.

CONCLUSIONS

This chapter has reviewed previous work on institutional structures, institutional efficiency, institutional choice and institutional change.

The conventional classification scheme for institutions of natural-resource use concentrating on the property-right regimes of open access, state property, common property and private property is too broad to be useful in describing and analysing institutional structures. To avoid ambiguity in description it is necessary to use a more detailed classification scheme that recognises institutional hierarchies and differentiates between the nature of decision-making entities and the decisions made by these entities on institutions of resource allocation.

The framework proposed in this chapter for describing institutional structures involves identifying the institutional hierarchy for the resource situation being studied and then describing the institutions at each level of the hierarchy in terms of four parameters: the property-right regimes existing at the different levels of the hierarchy; the entitlement systems forming the basis for physical division of the resource; the mechanisms by which entitlements are initially allocated amongst holders of property rights; and the means by which allocations of entitlements can be altered over time.

By dividing description of institutions into these four parameters, the theory of transaction costs can be used to speculate on why certain institutional arrangements arise in particular circumstances. There are two components to such an analysis which can be discussed in terms of a classification into static and dynamic concepts of transaction costs.

Static transaction costs are those transaction costs associated with making and implementing decisions for resource allocation under a given institutional structure. Comparative-static analyses of different institutional arrangements can be undertaken to ascertain which arrangements would minimise the static transaction costs in resource allocation. Such analyses can be used to ascertain the desirability of alternative institutions, as follows.

i. Assignments of property rights for particular allocation decisions according to the transaction costs that would be incurred in making these decisions at different levels in an institutional hierarchy.

ii. Use of input or resource quotas for physically dividing the resource between resource users, according to transaction costs of specifying entitlements and monitoring resource use.
iii. Use of market or administrative mechanisms for the initial allocation of entitlements depending upon costs of disrupting existing patterns of resource use.
iv. Market or administrative mechanisms of re-allocation of entitlements to a resource depending upon the 'non-specific' or 'idiosyncratic' characteristics of re-allocation transactions.

Such comparative-static analysis of alternative institutional structures is essentially normative. A more positive analysis of institutions requires consideration of another type of transaction cost: the transaction costs associated with institutional change. These transaction costs can be referred to as dynamic transaction costs and arise where decision making for institutional change is costly. To the extent that the costs associated with decision making for different institutional options are a function of pre-existing institutions, institutional change will be path-dependent. An institutional *status quo* affects the costs that would be incurred by decision makers in adopting different institutional proposals and thus constrains institutional choice.

Subsequent chapters of this book use the frameworks of institutional hierarchies and transaction-cost analysis to examine institutions of water use in the Murray–Darling Basin of eastern Australia and then to suggest a new framework for policy analysis in institutional reform that gives explicit recognition to transaction costs in both the static and dynamic contexts.

3. Institutions of Water Use for Irrigation in the Murray–Darling Basin

INTRODUCTION

In Chapter 2 a review of literature in institutional economics was used to develop a conceptual model for the description of institutions for regulating the use of natural resources. Institutions were modelled as hierarchies: hierarchical relationships between organisations and agents according to the nature of property rights held by each with respect to a resource and the associated institutions of entitlements, allocation and re-allocation that link these organisations and agents. It was then shown how transaction-cost theory could be used in comparative-static analyses to evaluate different institutional arrangements in terms of minimising the transactions costs associated with resource allocation, and in dynamic analyses to examine institutional change though reference to the transaction costs of political decision making and institutional choice.

In this chapter, the hierarchical model of institutions is used to interpret and describe institutions of water use in the Murray–Darling Basin. This description forms the basis for consideration in subsequent chapters of the use of transaction-cost theory as an approach to policy analysis for institutional performance and institutional change.

This chapter is organised into three main sections. Firstly, a brief geographical and historical description is provided of irrigated agriculture in the Murray–Darling Basin, with an emphasis on two case-study areas of southern New South Wales and South Australia. This provides the necessary background information for the description and discussion of institutions for regulation of water resources within a context of the physical, social, historical and technological environments of irrigation and regulation. Secondly, the framework of institutional hierarchies developed in Chapter 2 is used to develop a descriptive model of institutions of water use as they existed in 1997. Finally, general observations and conclusions are made as to the implications of the hierarchical structure of institutions for the assessment of performance of institutions and for policy analysis associated with institutional change.

IRRIGATED AGRICULTURE

Case-Study Regions

Two case-study areas of irrigated agriculture in the Murray–Darling Basin are described below: (i) the Riverland and Lower Murray regions of South Australia, and (ii) the Murrumbidgee and Riverina regions of New South Wales. Locations of these regions are indicated in Figure 3.1. Together, the two case-study areas exhibit most of the institutional characteristics of water regulation relating to the use of surface-water resources for irrigated agriculture in Australia.

The Riverland and Lower Murray Regions of South Australia

Geography

Part of south-eastern South Australia occurs within the River Murray catchment. An approximately 320 km section of the River Murray occurs in this area, flowing west from the Victorian border and then south to the southern coast. The land in the vicinity and catchment of the River Murray is divided for government statistical and administrative purposes into two regions: the Riverland which extends along the east–west-flowing section of the river, and the Lower Murray which extends along the north–south-flowing section of the river.

The South Australian section of the River Murray occurs within an incised valley in an otherwise generally flat landscape (Cole, 1978). In the Lower Murray region the valley comprises a generally steep-sided river channel of approximately 30 m depth and 1 to 2 km width formed by incision of sedimentary rocks to about 60 m depth and subsequent sedimentary infill. This section of the valley originally contained perennial swamps flanking the river, although most of these have been drained for agriculture. Soils within the valley are typically alluvial clays and organic soils with occasional calcareous and sandy soils. Upstream in the Riverland region, the valley formation is similar, but becomes wider (4 to 9 km) and the valley floor is occupied by alluvial and colluvial terraces rather than swamps. Soils are typically medium to heavy clays on low terraces, sands and clays on the high

terraces, and deep sands of aeolian sand hills and alluvial sand bars. The soils
are often saline or underlain at shallow depth by saline groundwater.

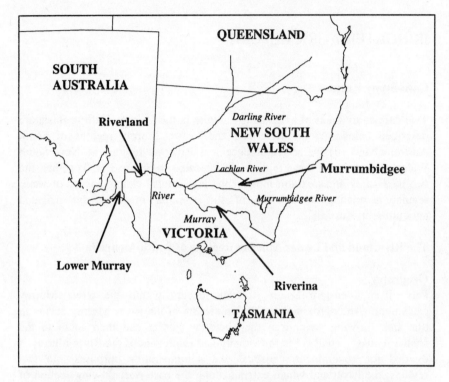

*Figure 3.1: Location of the Riverland and Lower Murray Regions of South
Australia and the Riverina and Murrumbidgee Regions of New
South Wales*

The highland areas outside of the river valley comprise aeolian landscapes
of parallel sand hills and depressions. Soils are extremely variable at a local
scale and range from deep sands in the sand hills to shallow sands overlying
clay and/or calcrete at shallow depth in the depressions. The subsoil materials
in the depressions are often saline (Menzies and Gray, 1983 p. 25).

The climate of the Murray region of South Australia is predominantly semi-
arid with a mean annual rainfall of less than 375 mm that occurs
predominantly in winter. Temperatures are warm to hot in summer and cool
to mild in winter (Menzies and Gray, 1983 pp. 9–11).

Water resources

The entire water resource available from the River Murray to South Australia is derived from river flows from New South Wales and Victoria. There are no significant tributaries or rainfall-runoff contributions to the River Murray within the South Australian section of the catchment. Nor are there significant groundwater resources.

The entitlement of South Australia to water flow of the River Murray is specified by the Murray–Darling Basin Agreement between state and federal governments. This agreement is further described later in this chapter but, in brief, the agreement provides South Australia with an annual water entitlement of 1 850 000 megalitres (ML). Of this, the South Australian state government has allocated approximately 440 000 ML to diversion for irrigation purposes. As a result of the minimum water flows into South Australia being determined by interstate agreement rather than by climatic factors, the water supplies for irrigation have not been subject to year-to-year variation.

History of irrigated agriculture

The first significant development of irrigated agriculture in the Murray region of South Australia commenced in 1887 when an irrigation area was established on the River Murray floodplain by the Californian irrigation developers George and William Chaffey and the South Australian colonial government. An Australian economic depression of the 1890s saw the collapse of the Chaffey enterprise, although the irrigation settlement continued and was later reconstituted as the Renmark Irrigation Trust, which is still in existence.

Several small-scale irrigation settlements were established along the river by the colonial and state governments in the 1890s and early 1900s. Similar to the Renmark Irrigation Trust, these settlements involved diversion and distribution of river water by a single agency rather than by individual farmers. Most of these settlements were eventually successfully established as permanent communities and industries either through being incorporated into irrigation schemes established by the commonwealth and state governments from 1908 to the 1950s, or operating as private collectives of irrigation farmers formally organised as private trusts.

Simultaneously with the development of group irrigation settlements there was development in the form of private water diversion. Private diversion involves individual landowners undertaking both diversion of water from the river and distribution to their own land. Some private diversion of water from the River Murray commenced in the late nineteenth century, although it was not until after 1920 that there was a significant extent of private diversion. This occurred mainly in the Lower Murray where water was diverted by gravity channels to reclaimed swamplands within the river valley. It was not until after 1950 that substantial private diversion occurred in the Riverland, bought about by improvements in pumping technology for lifting water from the river valley.

Irrigation development in both schemes and private diversion has occurred predominantly aʿ ribbon development within the river valley and in the highlands immediately adjacent to the valley. The principal reason for this pattern of development is the inability to divert water cheaply long distances from the valley. This constraint on development is a result of the incised valley formation that requires diversion to occur by pumping rather than by gravity-fed canal systems (Menzies and Gray, 1983 p. 66).

Currently a total of about 35 000 ha of land are irrigated by about 4100 farm businesses in the Riverland and Lower Murray regions. Predominant land uses are orchards and vines in the Riverland region and pasture and fodder in the Lower Murray region. The latter is predominantly for dairying. Vegetable crops, particularly large areas of potatoes and onions, are cultivated in both regions.

Water distribution and irrigation technologies
As most irrigation occurs on river terraces or highland areas outside of the River Murray valley, water diversion typically requires the raising of water in excess of 20 m above the mean level of the river in summer months, commonly closer to 40 m for some of the highland areas. Pumping is thus a prerequisite to irrigation settlement. The only use of diversion by gravity channels is in the irrigation of land within reclaimed swamplands within the river valley in the Lower Murray region.

Diversion of water from the river was initially undertaken using steam-driven centrifugal pumps (Menzies and Gray, 1983 p. 66). These were replaced by diesel-powered pumps after World War I, and by electric pumps in the mid-1940s (Menzies and Gray, 1983 p. 109).

The group irrigation schemes of the Riverland region initially used unlined or concrete-lined channels for water distribution. Pressurised-pipe distribution was used in a few districts after about 1920, but not on a large scale until after World War II (Menzies and Gray, 1983 p. 77). Replacement of channels with pressurised pipes in government irrigation areas and the Renmark Irrigation Trust has occurred since the 1980s and particularly during the 1990s with the 'rehabilitation' of distribution infrastructure in the government areas. Piped distribution is now predominant and all channels in the government areas are destined to be replaced by pipes by the year 2000.

In horticultural and orchard developments, water application was initially almost entirely by furrow irrigation (Menzies and Gray, 1983 p. 79). Large-scale use of overhead sprinkler systems was initiated in schemes developed after World War II and on private irrigation farms. Low-level sprinklers have been increasingly used since the 1960s, mainly in response to growing salinity problems and advantages in uniform water allocation, particularly on highland soils. Drip and micro-sprinkler systems have been in use since the mid- to late 1970s (Menzies and Gray, 1983 pp. 115–17), although overhead and low-level sprinklers remain the predominant method of water application. Centre-pivot sprinklers are the predominant method of water application for annual horticultural crops.

Flood irrigation is commonly used for pasture production in the swamplands of the Lower Murray region.

The Riverina and Murrumbidgee Regions of New South Wales

Geography
The Riverina and Murrumbidgee regions of New South Wales are located in the south-central part of the state. There are three principal regions of off-stream irrigation development which constitute the bulk of irrigation development: the Murrumbidgee irrigation areas and districts located in the Murrumbidgee valley to the north of the Murrumbidgee River; the Coleambally irrigation area located in the Murrumbidgee valley to the south of the Murrumbidgee River; and the Murray irrigation areas and districts located on the northern side of the River Murray. In addition to these off-stream developments, there is substantial irrigation occurring on properties located close to the major river channels.

Both the Murray and Murrumbidgee Rivers arise in the Great Dividing Range and Snowy Mountains of eastern New South Wales and Northern Victoria. The eastern parts of the river catchments comprise hilly and mountainous regions. To the west the landscape becomes more subdued, ultimately giving way to a broad and generally flat alluvial floodplain, on which most of the irrigation development has occurred (Department of Water Resources New South Wales, c. 1993 pp. 3–5). Catchment boundaries between the two river systems are poorly defined in the western parts of the river valleys due to the virtually flat landscape.

Soils of the irrigation regions are typically heavy clays, clay loams or loams, together occupying about 90 per cent of the area. The remainder comprises generally sandier soils of sand hills and old stream channels (Department of Water Resources New South Wales, c. 1993 p. 12; Coleambally Land and Water Management Plan Committee, 1996 p. 7; Cadell Land and Water Management Plan Working Group, 1995 p. 14).

The irrigation regions occur within a low-rainfall to semi-arid area. Average annual rainfall varies from about 400 mm in the south-east to 300 mm in the north-west. The entire area has a predominantly winter and spring rainfall incidence and is characterised by high annual variability in rainfall, particularly in the west. Warm to hot temperatures are experienced over the area during summers and cool to mild temperatures in winter (Department of Water Resources New South Wales, c. 1993 pp. 5–6).

Water resources
Virtually the entire water resource of the Murrumbidgee River arises from runoff in the eastern margins of the catchment and diverted flows from another river system, the Snowy River, via the Snowy Mountains Hydro-Electric Scheme. River flows are regulated by two dams built specifically for irrigation purposes (Burrinjuck Dam and Blowering Dam), several dams of the hydro-electric scheme, and a small amount of excess capacity in dams servicing the water-supply needs of the Australian Capital Territory. There are also seven major weirs and one re-regulating storage on the river near the irrigation areas (Department of Water Resources New South Wales, c. 1993 p. 21).

There is a large region in the approximate centre of the Murrumbidgee Valley, including much of the irrigation areas and districts, for which alluvial groundwater aquifers yield large quantities of low-salinity water (<500 mg/L dissolved salts). There are also several smaller zones of high-yield and low-salinity groundwater in other areas close to the river channel and associated with paleochannel aquifers (Department of Water Resources New South Wales, c. 1993 pp. 17–19).

Flows of the River Murray are derived mostly from runoff in the Snowy Mountains and Victorian Alps. Flows are regulated by two major reservoirs (the Hume and Dartmouth Reservoirs) and by weirs diverting water to two major delivery channels to irrigation areas. There are no large aquifer systems in this section of the Murray valley that yield groundwater supplies of sufficient quantity and volume for large-scale irrigation.

As a result of climatic variability and consequent fluctuations in river flows, the volumes of water available for irrigation vary from year to year, less so for the Murrumbidgee River than the River Murray. In view of the variability in water supply, the volume of water made available for irrigation also varies from year to year and typically ranges between 85 per cent and 150 per cent of a nominal volumetric entitlement for the majority of irrigators that have 'variable' entitlements. Allocations are announced by a state regulatory agency (the Department of Land and Water Conservation) at the commencement of each irrigation season according to the amount of water available in storages. The allocations are typically increased through the irrigation season as inflows occur to storages. In addition to the announced allocations, irrigators also have access to 'off-allocation' water: water that can be used without debit to their announced allocation. The off-allocation water generally arises as a result of accretions to river flow below the major storages, or spills from the storages. While not debited against an irrigator's allocation, off-allocation water is included as a normal delivery for the purposes of pricing. Access to off-allocation water is administered by designating periods during the irrigation season for which off-allocation supplies can be procured.

History of irrigated agriculture

Large-scale irrigation development commenced in the Murrumbidgee valley in 1908 with the construction of Burrinjuck Dam, diversion weirs and canals by the New South Wales state government. Development continued through to the late 1960s (Department of Water Resources New South Wales, c. 1993 pp. 10–11). Development of large-scale irrigation in the Murray valley commenced in the late 1930s and continued until the 1960s.

Irrigation development occurred as group schemes of government irrigation areas, government irrigation districts, irrigation trusts and joint water-supply schemes; and by individuals undertaking private diversion. By far the majority of irrigation development was as the government irrigation districts and areas. These types of organisation for irrigation are briefly described below.

Irrigation areas were the original model of irrigation development in the Murrumbidgee valley and were fully organised by the New South Wales state government under statutory provisions of the Irrigation Act 1912. Four irrigation areas were developed in the Murrumbidgee valley and one in the Murray valley (Bureau of Agricultural Economics, 1987 p. 34). These were established with the primary intent of creating farms with an emphasis on irrigation activities. As such, the state government assumed responsibility for full organisation including resumption, subdivision, leasing and selling of land, and construction and operation of water-distribution infrastructure (Department of Water Resources New South Wales, c. 1993 p. 11). The government maintained control over irrigation and farming practices by retaining rights to control the size and ownership of farms with irrigation areas, the crops grown on particular farms and the volume of water available to each farm (Bureau of Agricultural Economics, 1987 p. 34). Two major classes of farm were established in irrigation areas: 'horticultural farms' being smaller blocks considered suitable for intensive production of fruit trees and vines; and 'large area' or 'mixed' farms being larger blocks of land considered suitable for cropping and pasture production.

Irrigation districts comprised a second model of government-initiated irrigation development and were established under provisions of the Water Act 1912. Four irrigation districts were established in the Murrumbidgee valley between 1935 and 1946, and virtually all the government-initiated irrigation development in the Murray valley occurred in development of a further four irrigation districts from the late 1930s to the 1950s. With irrigation districts, the government assumed responsibility only for the provision of a water supply and there was no direct government control over land ownership. Drainage also remained largely the responsibility of the landholder (Bureau of Agricultural Economics, 1987 p. 35). Water was initially supplied to the irrigation districts for stock and domestic supplies and the original title of the developments – Domestic and Stock Water Supply Districts – reflected this intention. However, with development of water-storage infrastructure on the river systems and consequent improved security of water supplies, irrigation developed as the predominant water use (Department of Water Resources New South Wales, c. 1993 p. 11). Nevertheless, farms in the irrigation districts tend to be larger, have lower water allocations per unit of land area, and have greater areas devoted to dryland farming activities.

Until the 1980s, the irrigation areas and districts were managed and administered by the state government's Department of Water Resources. Through the 1980s, decision-making power was progressively devolved to management boards comprising irrigators and government representatives. In the Murray valley, the process of devolution continued to full privatisation of the irrigation areas and districts to form a private corporation owned by irrigation farmers: Murray Irrigation Limited. The company owns all infrastructure of water distribution. In the Murrumbidgee valley, as of 1997, the irrigation areas and districts were managed by two autonomous state-government agencies: Murrumbidgee Irrigation and Coleambally Irrigation. Each has a management board comprising irrigation farmers, industry representatives and directors with specialist skills in engineering and finance. As of 1997, both these agencies were destined to become state-owned corporations.

There are currently about 3000 irrigation-farm businesses in irrigation areas and districts of the Murrumbidgee valley and about 1800 in irrigation areas and districts of the Murray valley.

Private irrigation development took place where the construction of water diversion and distribution infrastructure was undertaken entirely by private landholders. This occurred as development by individual landholders, usually owning land in close proximity to one of the river channels, and development by group schemes organised as trusts or private authorities. The area of land irrigated by individual private irrigators and in private schemes totals about a quarter to a third of the areas in the irrigation areas and districts.

The activities of irrigated agriculture are highly varied. Pasture and fodder irrigation is an important activity in all areas, being used predominantly for production of beef cattle and for dairying, the latter particularly in the eastern irrigation districts of the Murray valley. Rice production is a major activity in the irrigation areas and districts, utilising about 25 per cent of the land area irrigated from surface-water sources, but utilising about half of the total supply of irrigation water. Rice production has historically not been undertaken outside of the irrigation areas and districts due to state-government regulations that restricted rice production to the irrigation areas and districts (Bureau of Agricultural Economics, 1987 pp. 40–41). Other major irrigation activities are grain crops other than rice, including irrigated cereal crops, and, for the Murrumbidgee region, fruit orchards and vineyards.

Water distribution and irrigation technologies
For the irrigation areas and districts, water diversion from the river systems is predominantly by means of weirs diverting water into off-stream channels. Water distribution in the areas and districts is almost entirely by open channels.

For private water diversion by trusts, authorities and individuals, water diversion is predominantly by pumping. Water distribution is again almost entirely by means of open channels.

Water application is by flood irrigation of grain crops and pastures, and furrow or sprinkler irrigation of tree crops, vegetables and vineyards.

CURRENT INSTITUTIONS FOR USE OF WATER RESOURCES

Institutional Hierarchies

The interpreted institutional hierarchies for the regulation of use of surface-water resources in the two case-study areas are similar and are summarised in Figure 3.2.

The institutional hierarchies for the two case-study regions share a common sequence of property-right regimes: a top level of common property amongst the state and commonwealth governments; a second level of state property where each state controls a share of the total resource; a third level of common property amongst groups of irrigators sharing infrastructure for water supply; and a fourth level of private water entitlements of individual irrigators. These property-right regimes and the institutions of entitlement systems, initial allocation and re-allocation that link the levels of the hierarchy are described below.

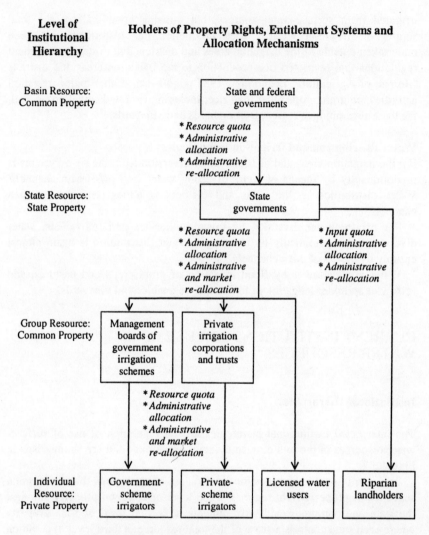

Figure 3.2: Institutional Hierarchy for Regulation of Surface-Water Use in the Lower Murray and Riverland Regions of South Australia and the Riverina and Murrumbidgee Regions of New South Wales

Common Property Between the State and Federal Governments

The property-right regime at the first level of the institutional hierarchy is that of common property between the state governments of Queensland, New

South Wales, Victoria and South Australia, and the commonwealth government. Voluntary agreements between these governments have established rules for joint regulation and use of the resource to avoid a situation of open access whereby each state would promote use of the resource without consideration of effects on other states.

The principal agreement between state governments is the Murray–Darling Basin Agreement of 1992 between the Commonwealth, New South Wales, Victorian and South Australian governments and relating to the use of water, land and other natural resources of the Murray–Darling Basin. There are three other interstate agreements relating to the allocation of surface-water resources of the Murray–Darling Basin.

i.   The New South Wales–Queensland Border Rivers Agreement 1946 that establishes rules for sharing surface-water resources of tributary streams of the Darling River that cross the border between the two states (Department of Water Resources New South Wales, 1995 p. 11; Crabb, 1988 p. 12).
ii. The Snowy Mountains Agreement 1957 between the Commonwealth, New South Wales and Victoria that establishes rules for sharing of water diverted from the Snowy River and its tributaries to the River Murray and its tributaries (Crabb, 1988 p. 12).
iii. The Seat of Government Severance and Acceptance Acts 1909 that establish rules for the sharing of water resources between the Australian Capital Territory and New South Wales (Crabb, 1988 p. 12).

The Murray–Darling Basin Agreement establishes a governing council comprising ministers of each participating government and an administrative agency, the Murray–Darling Basin Commission. The principal component of the agreement is the rules for sharing of water resources between the three states and the means of accounting for those shares. Entitlements to use of the water resource are all from the category of resource quotas, directly specifying an entitlement to the water resource in terms of either a volumetric entitlement or a proportional share of the available resource. The principal features of entitlement systems established by the agreement and classifications as types of quota are as follows.

•   South Australia has monthly volumetric entitlements to water flow in the River Murray varying between 32 000 and 159 000 ML, plus an additional entitlement of 58 000 ML per month to provide for dilution of the salt load in the river and for losses by evaporation and seepage: a resource quota defined as a quantified volumetric entitlement.
•   In time periods of 'special accounting' (i.e. drought) declared by the Murray–Darling Basin Commission, South Australia has an entitlement to

a one-third share of the water available for use by the three states: a resource quota defined as a quantified proportional share.

- New South Wales and Victoria are each entitled to all of the water in tributaries to the River Murray, other than the Darling River, arising in each respective state, prior to the water entering the River Murray: resource quotas defined by geographical areas.

- New South Wales and Victoria are each entitled to half shares in the water of the Darling River except when flows fall below a threshold volume, in which case New South Wales has preferential rights of use: resource quotas defined as quantified proportional shares.

The initial allocation of water entitlements between states was decided by the administrative mechanism of negotiations between the participating governments leading up to the first River Murray Waters Agreement in 1914. The allocations have since been altered by similar processes of negotiation and administrative decision.

In addition to the allocation of the water resource, other major components of the agreement include division of funding responsibilities for the Murray–Darling Basin Commission, defining responsibilities of the commission with respect to construction, operation and maintenance of river infrastructure; the roles of the commission with respect to the monitoring and investigation of water quality and establishment of water-quality objectives; and the powers and roles of the commission in making representations and recommendations to the contracting governments.

State Property

All the states of Australia have enacted legislation empowering the respective governments to administer schemes of water allocation. The legislation is similar between states and has the principal feature of crown ownership of all water resources, both surface water and groundwater, and the state governments having rights to the use, flow and control of the resources (Bartlett, 1995).

New South Wales and South Australia each hold entitlements to use of water from the River Murray, specified by the Murray–Darling Basin Agreement as described above. The states allocate water entitlements to the common-property entities of group irrigation schemes and the private-property entities of individual irrigators and riparian landholders. The entitlement systems are from the categories of both resource and input quotas, and are described as follows.

In South Australia, water entitlements are allocated by means of the licences to group irrigation schemes and individual irrigators are specified in terms of quantified volumetric entitlements. Licensees may also in some years be assigned an entitlement to take additional ('surplus') water from the river in periods of high flow, usually specified as a proportion of the licensed volumetric entitlement. This corresponds to a proportional-share entitlement, where shares in surplus river flows are related to the nominal volumetric entitlements of each licence.

In New South Wales there are two types of irrigation licence, both establishing resource quotas on access to the water resource. 'High-security' licences are issued for irrigation of 'permanent' crops (vines and orchards) and provide entitlements to water that do not vary between years and that are specified in terms of volumes. These correspond to quantified volumetric entitlements. 'Low-security' licences are issued for irrigation of annual crops and have a nominal volumetric entitlement but actual entitlements vary from year to year according to the available supply of water and are specified as a per centage of the nominal entitlement. The entitlements of low-security licences correspond to proportional-share entitlements, with the nominal volumetric entitlement of the licence corresponding to a share in the available resource rather than an absolute annual entitlement.

In both South Australia and New South Wales, the water entitlements pertaining to riparian rights are defined by statutory restrictions on the uses to which water can be put, including a limitation on areas able to be irrigated. The entitlement system is thus one of an input quota, defining entitlements to water indirectly through restrictions on the activities for which water can be used.

The initial allocation of water entitlements by the states was undertaken by administrative decision. For the water entitlements of riparian landowners the allocation decisions involved a principle of providing entitlements on the basis of the historical common-law rights to water associated with ownership of riparian land. For water licences issued to individual irrigators and group schemes, there was a combination of two allocation principles. Firstly, water entitlements were allocated on the basis of a 'first come first served' principle whereby water entitlements were provided in turn to each new group irrigation development and each applicant for individual licences until the water resource was considered to be 'fully utilised'. The South Australian Government ceased issuing new licences for the Riverland and Lower Murray regions in 1968, and the New South Wales Government ceased issuing new licences for the Murrumbidgee and Riverina regions in the late 1970s. The second principle of allocation developed with the application of volumetric entitlements to licences in the 1970s. This was a principle of 'reasonable requirement' whereby quantified water entitlements applied to licences were determined on the basis of the areas and types of crops irrigated or planned to be irrigated, soil characteristics and annual rainfall.

The allocations of water entitlements to riparian landholders and licence holders can be altered by either administrative mechanisms or by market mechanisms.

There are two general forms of administrative mechanisms for the re-allocation of water entitlements. First, the property rights to water held by the states include powers to alter, under certain circumstances, the entitlements issued to parties in subordinate levels of the institutional hierarchies. Second, there are administrative rules in place to re-allocate entitlements in response to variations in the total water supply to all holders of entitlements.

The powers of state governments to alter water entitlements are either implicit in powers of governments to alter legislation and regulations, or are conferred by existing legislation and regulations. An example of the former is the power of state governments to alter the entitlements to water of riparian landowners. Both the South Australian and New South Wales state governments have enacted legislation that replaced common-law entitlements with circumscribed statutory rights. Similarly, the governments have powers to amend water-resources legislation to bring about other re-allocations. Powers conferred on state governments by water-resources legislation in relation to re-allocation include powers to cancel licences, alter the volumetric water entitlements pertaining to licences, or to alter the conditions under which water is to be utilised. In practice, the power of the governments to alter licences has not been used to re-allocate water entitlements between specific licensees, although the powers have been exercised to alter licence conditions uniformly for large groups of licensees to achieve policy objectives of governments with respect to the management of water resources. Examples include the application of volumetric entitlements to all licences in both South Australia and New South Wales in the 1970s, and reducing access of New South Wales licensees to 'off-allocation' water in the late 1980s and 1990s.

The second general type of administrative mechanism for re-allocation of entitlements is that of administrative rules whereby a re-allocation occurs in response to certain changes in the natural or economic environment of water use. For both the government licensing schemes and the allocation schemes of irrigation groups there are regulatory provisions for altering individual water entitlements in periods of low water supply. In South Australia, where the water supply is of high security, the nature of adjustments to entitlements is not specified, but instead powers are conferred on the relevant government minister to alter water entitlements according to criteria of 'fairness'. These criteria would include consideration of types of crops being grown and potential economic injury to different groups of water users. The adjustments to entitlements would probably not be uniform across all water users and would thus represent a proportional re-allocation of entitlement. In New South Wales, the water supply is far less secure, and rules for adjusting entitlements in circumstances of low water supply have been incorporated into entitlement systems through use of high-security and low-security entitlements.   Under circumstances of low water supply, the high-security entitlements are satisfied prior to the supply of water to meet low-security entitlements.   This effectively represents a proportional re-allocation to holders of high-security entitlements that occurs automatically in years of low water supply.

Water entitlements pertaining to licences issued by the state governments can be re-allocated by a market.   Both individual irrigators and group organisations can transfer entitlements on either a temporary or permanent basis by privately negotiated trades.   In practice, the freedom to trade water entitlements is high amongst individual licence holders, but strongly attenuated for the group licence holders.   The group organisations generally have rules restricting the possible transfer of entitlements away from the groups, with the objective of maintaining intensities of irrigation within the group areas and thus the viability of operating the infrastructure for water distribution.

Common Property in Group Irrigation Schemes

Two of the types of organisations receiving licences for water diversion and use are group entities, comprising collectives of individual water users.

i.   Quasi-autonomous government irrigation agencies servicing irrigation farmers within irrigation schemes for which distribution infrastructure is owned by the state government.   These include the two agencies (Murrumbidgee Irrigation and Coleambally Irrigation) administering irrigation areas and districts of the Murrumbidgee Valley in New South Wales. Decision-making power over water use within the areas served by these organisations lies predominantly with management boards made up of irrigation farmers, although the government still holds some executive powers.

ii. Private agencies distributing water to individual irrigation farmers where the distribution infrastructure is collectively owned and managed by the irrigation farmers. The formal mechanisms of group association include trusts, corporations, and various other associations provided for under water-resources legislation. Decision-making power over water use within the areas served by these organisations lies with management boards or trusts made up of irrigation farmers.

The primary functions of the group organisations are the allocation and distribution of water to individual properties and coordination and/or management of drainage works. The organisations also typically have some powers to regulate water-use practices by individual water users. The entities holding the licences for water entitlements may be either the collective management agencies of the groups, or the individual water users within the groups. Although in the latter case the rights to water strictly reside with individual farmers, the group organisations can still be interpreted as having a mix of *de jure* and *de facto* common property rights over the water entitlements. These rights arise from control over the infrastructure of water distribution, and some powers to alter water supplies to individual irrigators in certain circumstances.

The initial allocation of water entitlements within group irrigation schemes was made typically by administrative decision, with water entitlements accompanying the allocation of land. Allocation principles were the same two principles as described above for allocation of licences by state governments: allocation of entitlements on a 'first come first served' basis, and later quantification of the entitlements according to a principle of a reasonable requirement. With some irrigation schemes, land and water were allocated simultaneously under a policy of providing individual irrigators with sufficient allocations of land and water to produce a level of income judged by policy makers to be sufficient for the support of family-farm enterprises. The principle of a reasonable requirement was thus extended to include consideration of the amounts of land and water that would enable irrigation farmers to generate a certain level of income.

There was perhaps an element of market allocation of water entitlements in irrigation schemes where land allotments and associated water entitlements were sold by government or private developers. It can be expected that with the developers hoping to maximise the prices obtained for the land sales and leases, any economic value of water entitlements would have been factored into land prices. However, at least for the government schemes, reliance on markets for resource allocation was limited and allocation in most irrigation areas was made by administrative allocation to applicants. Settlement of the government irrigation areas typically involved government subsidy of settlers rather than sale of the entitlements to land and water, particularly with soldier settlement schemes after the World Wars I and II (Menzies and Gray, 1983 p. 194; Williams, 1974 pp. 227–62).

Re-allocation of water entitlements amongst individual irrigators in group schemes can occur by similar administrative or market mechanisms as already described for water licences. Administrative re-allocation occurs through powers of the management authorities to alter entitlements issued to individual irrigators within these groups. These powers are conferred either by the state legislation governing the activity of the group irrigation schemes or by contractual agreements between irrigators participating in private group schemes. Administrative re-allocations have generally not been used to re-allocate water entitlements between specific irrigators, but rather have been applied to the entitlements of particular subgroups of irrigators to achieve management objectives for the entire group irrigation schemes. An example occurs in the rehabilitation of the previously government irrigation areas in South Australia (now organised as a private trust), where the water entitlements of some irrigators were suspended due to the land associated with the licences being deemed by the managing government agency to be unsuitable (for environmental reasons) for supply with water from the distribution schemes or unsuitable for irrigation activities. In another mechanism of administrative allocation, in group irrigation schemes of New South Wales the water entitlements of individual irrigators may be issued as high-security or low-security entitlements, as with the issue of licences by the state. A proportional re-allocation of water to high-security licences occurs automatically in times of water shortages.

Individual water entitlements in the group irrigation schemes can in principle be re-allocated by private trading, including transfer via the common-property organisation, to irrigators in other schemes and to private holders of water licences. There are, however, generally substantial constraints on transfers imposed for the purposes of maintaining intensities of irrigation within the group schemes and thus protecting the economic viability of the groups' infrastructure for water distribution.

Private Property of Individual Water Users

Virtually all use of water in irrigated agriculture ultimately occurs on private farms with an individual entitlement to water that can be regarded as private property. The individual entitlements are established and enforced by one of three generic mechanisms: allocation of entitlements to riparian landholders by state legislation; allocation of entitlements directly to individual irrigators by the state regulatory agencies through licensing schemes; and allocation of entitlements by group organisations to individual irrigators within group irrigation schemes.

The characteristics of the individual entitlements vary according to the mechanism by which they were created. Differences occur in the degree and type of attenuation of the authority of entitlement holders to make decisions with respect to disposition of both the entitlement and the water received at their property. Differences in the attributes of property rights associated with individual water entitlements are summarised semi-quantitatively in Figure 3.3 using the conceptual model of Scott (1989a, 1989b), as described in Chapter 2. This model compares the property rights of riparian entitlements, group-irrigator entitlements, and individual-licence entitlements in terms of attributes of flexibility, exclusivity, quality of title, transferability, divisibility and duration. There is no consistent metric used in the comparison, but points closer to the ends of each axis indicate a less attenuated property right in terms of each attribute.

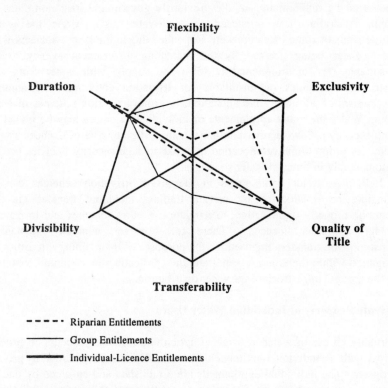

*Figure 3.3: Comparison of Property-Right Attributes in Water
Entitlements of Individual Irrigators*

In terms of the six attributes of property rights used in Figure 3.3, riparian rights rank high in comparison with the other types of individual entitlement in terms of the duration of the right and the quality of title. The riparian rights are defined in legislation, are not reliant on periodic renewal of licences, and have well-specified rights and obligations of the riparian landholder. The riparian rights rate less well in terms of exclusivity, the water entitlement associated with the right being a correlative entitlement and dependent upon the extent to which the same rights are exercised by other riparian landholders. The riparian rights are also strongly attenuated in terms of flexibility of water use, being limited essentially to non-commercial uses by the legislation, and in terms of divisibility and transferability, being transferable only with transfer of ownership of the riparian land and being divisible only with subdivision of the riparian land.

The property rights associated with individual entitlements derived from group irrigation organisations rank lower in terms of duration than the riparian rights, being subject to periodic renewal of group water licences, but rank as high or higher for other attributes. Quality of title is high, with the rights and obligations of individual irrigators being specified by legislation, group-licence conditions, entitlement documents, trust agreements, etc. Exclusivity is enhanced by the entitlement being defined in terms of quantified annual allocations, and not being dependent upon the actions of other entitlement holders. There is high flexibility in use of water with individual irrigators having authority over crop types, irrigation methods and the like, although in most instances the management agencies of the group can and do exert influence over many aspects of water use including areas of land irrigated, method of irrigation, crop types, drainage, and disposal of saline drainage water. The entitlements are generally divisible and transferable to other landholders, although in most cases rules established by the groups limit the extent of transfers to maintain financial viability in operation of the infrastructure.

The least attenuated individual property rights to water are those associated with water licences issued to individual irrigators that are not part of group irrigation organisations. Whilst being similar to the rights of group irrigators in terms of duration, exclusivity and quality of title, the property rights of individual licence holders do not have the same constraints imposed by the group organisations on divisibility, transferability and flexibility of use.

CONCLUSIONS: IMPLICATIONS FOR POLICY ANALYSIS

The description of institutions of water use for irrigation using the model of an institutional hierarchy illustrates an important aspect of interpreting institutions discussed in Chapter 2. That is, it generally makes little sense to describe a resource in terms of a single property-right regime. By doing so, many features of the institutions regulating the use of the resource would be unavoidably ignored or unnoticed. With the institutions of water use for irrigation in South Australia and New South Wales, for example, all water use is ultimately undertaken within regimes of 'private property'. Yet 'private property' is an incomplete description of institutions of water allocation for two principal reasons.

Firstly, the major types of private property (water entitlements of group-scheme irrigators, entitlements of private licensees; entitlements of riparian landholders) differ substantially in the powers of decision making associated with the property rights.

Secondly, only a subset of the allocation decisions for the water resources are made under private property, i.e. by holders of individual entitlements to water. This subset of decisions includes allocation of water between individual holders of water entitlements (through provisions for private trading of entitlements) and allocation to agricultural activities within farm businesses. Other decisions of allocation are made under regimes of common property by groups of framers within allocation schemes, regimes of state property, and a regime of common property between the states.

The institutional system for water use is far more complex than can be described in simple terms as 'private property', 'state property' or 'common property'. Rather, several property-right regimes exist simultaneously relating to different areas of decision making in regard to resource allocation.

Implications for policy analysis relating to institutions of water use are profound. Rather than focusing on alternative and supposedly mutually exclusive property-right regimes, policy analysis should address firstly the distribution of property rights with a hierarchy of rights for the range of decisions that need to be made for allocation of a resource, and secondly the most appropriate institutions of allocation that provide for these decisions to be implemented (entitlement systems and mechanisms of allocation and re-allocation).

As described in Chapter 2, transaction-cost analysis may be used to analyse and compare alternative institutional structures. Different assignments of property rights and different allocative institutions for water in the Murray–Darling Basin could be compared by determining the transaction costs associated with making allocation decisions under different institutional arrangements. This framework for policy and institutional analysis has not been used in the past. In Chapter 4, the importance of transaction costs in making allocation decisions will be examined by investigating the transaction costs associated with one part of the institutional hierarchy for regulation of water use in the Murray–Darling Basin. The particular subset of institutions examined is the market system for re-allocation of water entitlements between private water users in South Australia. Analyses such as this form the basis for comparative-static analyses of alternative institutional arrangements, but address one aspect of a transaction-cost approach to institutional choice. Subsequent chapters give attention to the dynamic aspects of institutional change and the manner in which transaction costs of institutional change will affect institutional choice.

4.   Static Transaction Costs in Allocation of Water Resources

INTRODUCTION

In Chapter 3 the institutions of water use for irrigation in two states of the Murray–Darling Basin were described in terms of an institutional hierarchy. The previous discussion of institutional theory in Chapter 2 suggested that the institutional structure evident in this hierarchical model would have developed as a result of two transaction-cost considerations: (i) the development of institutions to minimise static transaction costs in allocation of water resources, and (ii) constraints on institutional development arising from the dynamic transaction costs of institutional change. The objective of Chapter 4 is to describe an assessment of the importance of static transaction costs in the study of institutions. This will be drawn upon in Chapter 5 when a historical study of the institutional arrangements is made to determine the impact of both static and dynamic transaction costs in the development of institutions for water use.

For this chapter, the importance of static transaction costs in shaping allocation decisions occurring under a given institutional structure was determined by investigating the transaction costs associated with one part of the institutional hierarchy for water use in the Murray–Darling Basin. The subset of institutions examined is the market system for re-allocation of water entitlements between private water users in South Australia. There were two reasons for selection of this subset of institutions. Firstly, the focus of recent institutional reform has been on the definition of private property rights in the water resources and the establishment of market institutions for the re-allocation of these rights. This reform has largely been undertaken on the basis of analyses that promised benefits from market trading of water rights but ignored transaction costs in trading. Hence determining the influence of transaction costs on outcomes from private rights and market trading should make an important contribution to contemporary policy analysis. Secondly, a large amount of literature in the area of resource economics, including several textbooks, has accepted the existence of transaction costs in the administrative allocation of resources, particularly allocation by government decision making, while ignoring transaction costs associated with markets. Consequently an investigation of transaction costs in private decisions within a market will provide a more convincing illustration of the importance of transaction costs in comparative institutional analysis than an analysis of the transaction costs associated with decision making by government or common-property agencies.

The investigation of transaction costs in private trading of water rights examined the market for permanent trades of water entitlement in the South Australian section of the Murray–Darling Basin. In this chapter, a description of institutions for water allocation and trading in South Australia is followed by a discussion of features of the market for water entitlements that may give rise to transaction costs. A review is given of relevant theory and past empirical studies relating to the examination of price dispersion as an indicator of imperfect information and associated transaction costs. This is followed by a description of a conceptual model for the pricing of water entitlements that accounts for transaction costs, and quantification of this model using historical data on water trades and prices. From this model, conclusions are drawn in relation to the static transaction costs in market trading of water entitlements, how these may affect the efficacy of market mechanisms in efficiently allocating the resource, and implications for policy analysis relating to institutional choice.

INSTITUTIONS FOR MARKET TRADING OF WATER ENTITLEMENTS

As already described in Chapter 3, there is an extensive irrigated-agriculture industry in South Australia using water from the Murray River. This occurs in two government statistical and administrative regions: the Riverland region comprising the northern portion and the Lower Murray region making up the southern portion (previously indicated in Figure 3.2).

The two regions differ with respect to principal irrigation activities. The Riverland region is dominated by vineyards and citrus orchards, each occupying about 45 per cent of the total irrigated area. The remainder is used mainly for stone fruit and other orchards, vegetable crops, and pasture and fodder. The Lower Murray region is the principal dairying region of South Australia and approximately 85 per cent of the irrigated land area is used for pasture and fodder. The remainder is used mainly for vineyards, orchards and vegetable crops.

Under South Australian legislation the Murray River is a proclaimed watercourse and water can only be diverted from the river if permitted by a diversion licence issued by the state's Department of Environment and Natural Resources. Features of diversion licences issued for irrigation purposes are as follows.

- For the purposes of licensing, there is no distinction made between different types of irrigation organisations of which there are three general types: private diverters, irrigation trusts and private irrigation boards. For the trusts and private irrigation boards, single diversion licences are held by the collective organisations that undertake the water diversion and distribution to individual irrigators. Private diversion licences include both diversion licences for individual farms and licences held by local governments, sporting clubs and the like where these organisations divert water from the river for irrigation purposes.

- Licences are issued for a period of one year and, by convention, are renewed automatically at the end of each licence period subject to payment of a licence fee of approximately $250 per annum.

- All licences specify water entitlements as 'resource quota': a quantitative limit on the amount of water that may be diverted from the river. These volumetric entitlements are virtually 100 per cent secure and there has never been a need to reduce entitlements in response to a water shortage. The security arises from an interstate agreement that in almost all years guarantees South Australia a minimum flow of water in the Murray River, and also from the state government's conservative allocation of water within the limits of this minimum quantity. Diversion of 'surplus water' in excess of the licence entitlement may be permitted during periods of high river flows. Surplus water allocations of up to 20 per cent of licence entitlements have been permitted in several years since the quantification of water entitlements in the 1970s.

- There is no system of priority rights to water. In the case of inadequate supply of water to meet all licence entitlements, the responsible state-government minister has the power under the relevant legislation to restrict water diversion, and to implement systems of preferential allocation to certain water uses or users. These powers have never had to be exercised.

- Licences are associated with specified parcels of land. Ownership or occupancy of irrigable land (or control of the land in the case of a group irrigation district) is a prerequisite to holding a diversion licence and water diverted from the river can only be applied to the parcel or parcels of land specified in the licence. Licences may, however, be 'amalgamated' such that water taken from the river under two or more licences can be applied on any or all parcels of land pertaining to these licences, subject to the constraint that the total abstraction of water does not exceed the sum total of the entitlements of the individual licences.

- Water entitlement associated with licences can be traded between individuals or the relevant irrigation organisations subject to certain conditions. The trading of licences is further discussed below.
- For the collective organisations of trusts, private irrigation boards and government irrigation areas, a second level of water allocation exists below the level of water licences that specifies individual quantitative entitlements for each water user.

Since 1968 it has been a policy position of the South Australian government not to allow any increase in the sum total of licensed water entitlements from the Murray River for irrigation purposes. There is no issuing of new licences or increases in the volumetric entitlements of existing licences except as allowed for by transfers of water entitlement.

There is a two-tiered system of regulations for the transfer of water entitlement pertaining to the licences. Firstly, there is a system for transfer between holders of licences issued by the state regulatory agency with responsibility for water resources: the Department of Environment and Natural Resources. This includes the licences issued to group organisations: the trusts and irrigation boards. Secondly, the group organisations have their own internal regulations for the transfer of water entitlement by their member irrigators. Both of these levels of regulation are described below.

There are three mechanisms by which water entitlement can be transferred. These are transfer with land ownership, amalgamation of licences, and permanent trading. Each of these is described below.

Transfer with land ownership. When land that is the subject of a water licence changes ownership, the existing water licence automatically lapses. If the new landowner makes application for a water licence for the same purposes, a licence will automatically be issued under the same conditions, including the water entitlement, as the previous licence. Thus water licences are transferable with ownership of land.

Licence amalgamations. An owner of two or more parcels of land with separate water licences for the same purpose relating to each parcel, or two or more different landowners with separate water licences for the same purpose, may obtain an amalgamation of these licences. An amalgamation of water licences allows the diversion of water to any of the parcels of land relating to the licences, subject to the total diversion being less than the total entitlement of the water licences. Amalgamations apply for a predetermined period of time of up to several years, at the end of which they automatically lapse.

Where two or more landowners are involved in an amalgamation, the amalgamation effectively represents an arrangement for the temporary transfer of water entitlement between licensees. The role of the Department of Environment and Natural Resources in administering amalgamations is limited to assessing applications for amalgamations, monitoring the total water diversion, and ensuring that the licences revert to original conditions when the amalgamations lapse. The department does not typically become involved in the terms of amalgamation agreements between participating licensees, or the partitioning of water charges between the licensees. All licensees involved in an amalgamation are jointly and severally liable for total water use and the related charges. In some instances the department may, for reasons of environmental protection or constraints on drainage, place limits on the maximum quantities of water that may be applied to particular parcels of land.

Permanent trades. A permanent transfer of water entitlement involves the transfer of part or all of the water entitlement pertaining to a licence to another landowner. Such transfers have been permitted in South Australia since 1982. Although licences are only issued for one-year periods, they are by convention renewed automatically at the end of each licence period and hence the trading of water entitlement between licences is, for all practical purposes, perpetual.

Permanent transfers of water entitlement are initiated by application to the Department of Environment and Natural Resources either by the parties to the transfer, or by a real-estate agent who is usually acting on behalf of the vendor of entitlement and who is paid a commission from the sale. The department undertakes an assessment of the application that includes the following.

- Providing advice to any mortgagor of the property from which water entitlement is to be transferred that the application has been received.[1]
- Assessing whether the transfer may have any detrimental impact on other lands, or on water quality within the Murray River, particularly in regard to land or water salinisation.
- Assessing the technical adequacy of a mandatory irrigation and drainage management plan for the property to which the water entitlement is being transferred. A transfer may be approved in advance of a plan being approved, whereupon an embargo is placed upon use of the water until approval has been obtained. The irrigation and drainage management plans must demonstrate that the land is suitable for irrigation, that the additional water to be transferred is actually required for irrigation, and that irrigation techniques will be such that there will not be unacceptable external impacts on the environment or neighbouring land.

Assessment and approval of transfer applications made to the Department of Environment and Natural Resources typically takes two to three months, although this has extended to up to eight months in some cases, usually due to inadequate or insufficient information being provided by the applicants. Rejections of transfer applications are rare.

Applications for permanent transfers attract a fee payable to the Department of Environment and Natural Resources. In 1995/96, this fee was $12.00 per megalitre of annual water entitlement transferred.

Within group irrigation areas, rules of transfer of water entitlements vary from virtual prohibitions on transfer to similar arrangements to those that apply for transfers between holders of diversion licences. For the purposes of this current investigation, attention was restricted to transfers of water entitlement between irrigators within the ex-government irrigation areas that were privatised in 1997 to form the Central Irrigation Trust. Transfers of water entitlement between irrigators within the irrigation areas under the control of the Trust have been permitted since 1983 under similar arrangements of permanent transfers and amalgamations to those existing for the system of diversion licences administered by the Department of Environment and Natural Resources. Since 1994, transfers have also been permitted between irrigators in different areas, and between irrigators in the group areas and private diverters.

For transfers between two irrigators located within a single irrigation area, applications may be made for transfer of the whole or part of an entitlement and are assessed on the basis of similar criteria to those described above for the transfer of diversion licences. An additional criterion is that any transfers must not cause the capacity of the water-distribution system to be exceeded, although this has not been a practical constraint to transfers. Assessment and approval typically take up to three months, similar to the transfer of diversion licences.

Transfers between irrigators of different irrigation areas are also administered by the Central Irrigation Trust. Other 'external' transfers that involve transfer either to or from a private diverter or to or from an irrigator in another irrigation area are administered jointly by the Trust and the Department of Environment and Natural Resources. Transfers out of the Trust irrigation areas are subject to restrictions on the size of the transfer. The maximum portion of water that can be transferred from an individual entitlement within a government area is 25 per cent, except where the land in question is being developed for a higher use (municipal or industrial) or is certified unsuitable for irrigation. Further, the net reduction to the total entitlement of the government has in the past not been allowed to exceed 1 per cent of the total entitlement pertaining to the water licence for the area. Again, transfer applications are assessed on the basis of similar criteria to those described above for the transfer of diversion licences, including the provision of irrigation and drainage management plans.

All applications for permanent transfers of water entitlement that are assessed by the Trust incur a fee at the same level ($12.00/ML in 1995/96) as that for transfer applications made to the Department of Environment and Natural Resources.

TRANSACTION COSTS IN MARKET TRADING OF WATER ENTITLEMENTS

Previous studies of transaction costs in water markets in the western states of the USA have considered administrative and legal costs to be the most important cause of transaction costs of trading in water rights. This is not considered to be the case in South Australia due to significant differences from the USA in the nature of water rights and in the administrative process of trading. In the USA, trading of water rights often requires extensive administrative and judicial work to define the rights being traded and to identify and resolve any third-party effects of proposed trades, the costs of which constitute substantial transaction costs (Boggs, 1989; Colby, 1990, 1995). This is not the case in South Australia where potential third-party and environmental impacts of water transfers are assessed by the relevant regulatory agency, and the administrative processes associated with trading and the transfer of water rights are simple and inexpensive to the parties engaging in trading. Anecdotal evidence has suggested that a more important cause of transaction costs in the market for water entitlement in South Australia has been imperfect information amongst market participants in relation to the value of water entitlement and the identities of potential trading partners.

Imperfect information gives rise to a requirement for a seller or purchaser of water entitlement to expend resources in estimating the value of water entitlement, locating trading partners and negotiating contracts. This has two results. Firstly, market participants may bear direct costs in obtaining information. Secondly, it would be reasonable to assume an increasing marginal cost of information and to conclude that a potential market participant would not expend sufficient resources to obtain perfect information. The result is the conduct of trade under imperfect information which, as will be described later, may result in price dispersion within the market.

There are thus three measures of potential transaction costs arising in the market for water entitlement in South Australia: (i) administrative and regulatory fees and charges associated with a transfer of property rights in water entitlement; (ii) the costs incurred by a market participant in obtaining information; and (iii) price dispersion within the market that is due to residual imperfect information amongst market participants.

Some of the direct costs incurred by traders in water entitlement have already been mentioned in the previous section. These included the administrative fee of $12.00 per ML levied by the regulatory agencies for water entitlements, and a commission that may be paid by a vendor of entitlement to a real-estate agent acting as a broker or sales agent. These costs will be considered again later in this chapter. The following section examines transaction costs arising from residual imperfect information, and the investigation of price dispersion as a measure of these costs.

IMPERFECT INFORMATION AND PRICE DISPERSION

Economic Theory

Markets, even competitive markets, do not generally produce unique clearing prices for the products to which they relate. Instead, prices tend to follow non-degenerate distributions. Apart from the consideration that markets may not at any given moment be in equilibrium, there are two contributing factors to price dispersion: product heterogeneity and imperfect information.

Product heterogeneity refers to either perceived differences in a product, such as in the qualitative characteristics of different brands, or variation in the provision through a market place, such as in the location of sale or nature of distribution outlets. The heterogeneous products are close, but not perfect, substitutes and face different consumer-demand schedules. Conventional consumption and market-equilibrium theories can be used to show differences in market prices that arise according to the extent of product heterogeneity and differences in demand.

The influence of imperfect information on market prices is a more complex issue that first received formal attention in George Stigler's seminal article 'The economics of information' (Stigler, 1961). Imperfect information in this context refers to incomplete or uncertain knowledge on the part of the vendors and/or purchasers of a product in regard to market characteristics, that is, imperfect knowledge of supply schedules, demand schedules, and prices asked and offered across the market.

During the 1970s several economists gave attention to the existence and persistence of price dispersion in competitive markets (for example Rothschild, 1973; Salop and Stiglitz, 1977; Salop, 1977; Reinganum, 1979). Market equilibria with price dispersion were demonstrated to be possible under conditions of imperfect information and asymmetry in information holdings, that is, where (i) purchasers of a product hold incomplete information on prices being offered by various vendors in a market and face positive search costs for the vendor with the lowest price; and (ii) vendors of the product realise that purchasers hold incomplete information and strategically set prices to exploit this.

The strategies adopted by the vendors in setting prices vary according to the nature of the supply schedules of the vendors and the demand schedules of the purchasers. In a situation where (i) the demand schedules of purchasers are identical (although elastic), (ii) the purchasers vary in their costs of search, and (iii) the vendors differ in their supply schedules and marginal costs, a Nash equilibrium with price dispersion may occur in the market due to the vendors facing different trade-off functions between numbers of purchasers and marginal profit (Reinganum, 1979). Where demand schedules differ between purchasers, and vendors have knowledge of these schedules, price dispersion may also result from limited 'monopoly' powers of the vendors to engage in price discrimination (Salop, 1977; Salop and Stiglitz, 1977). In both cases typical pricing strategies involve either discounting prices to induce purchasers to search for their outlet, or raising prices in the knowledge that when faced with positive search costs some purchasers will randomly select a vendor and risk paying a higher price rather than engaging in costly searches for lower prices.

Although past studies have tended to focus on the potential existence of price equilibria rather than the extent of price dispersion, some conclusions can be drawn in regard to the latter.

- For homogeneous goods, the range of price dispersion will be bounded by the perfectly competitive price and the monopoly price (Salop and Stiglitz, 1977).
- The extent of price dispersion depends upon the magnitude of information (search) costs and differences in these costs between purchasers. The lower the costs of information, the less the degree of dispersion and the closer the general level of market prices to the perfectly competitive price (Salop and Stiglitz, 1977).
- Price dispersion is increased by variation in cost structures between vendors (Reinganum, 1979).
- Price dispersion can increase where purchasers differ in their demand functions (Salop, 1977; Salop and Stiglitz, 1977). Where vendors are aware of differences in demand schedules between purchasers, the costs of information search and differences in demand may allow vendors to engage in price discrimination (Salop, 1977).

Empirical Studies

Since development of 'the economics of information' and theories of price dispersion there have been several empirical studies of imperfect information and price behaviour. Many studies have examined labour markets in terms of imperfect information, job searching and wage differentials (for example McCall, 1970; Lippman and McCall, 1976; Hofler and Murphy, 1992). Numerous other studies have investigated markets for a wide range of goods and services. These include studies of markets for medical services (Gaynor and Polachek, 1994), legal services (Cox *et al.*, 1982), insurance policies (Dahlby and West, 1986), gasoline (Marvel, 1976) and airline tariffs (Borenstein and Rose, 1994). Most of these studies discovered substantial price dispersion within the markets being studied, much of which was attributable to imperfect information.

Fewer studies have been undertaken of price behaviour in markets for natural resources, and these have generally been less detailed and less rigorous than the investigations of markets for other products. The low number of empirical studies of markets for natural resources may be a reflection of a historical reliance on non-market allocation mechanisms that has only recently altered over the last few decades with innovative programmes such as tradable fishery quotas, tradable water entitlements and tradable pollution permits.

There have been a few studies of the operation of markets for water entitlement in the western states of the USA, where attention has been focused on the allocation of water resources by demand for re-allocation of water from irrigated agriculture to municipal uses. The first such study of water prices was probably that of Gardner and Miller (1983), who examined time trends in prices of shares in the Colorado–Big Thompson water scheme. There was, however, no discussion of price dispersion or assessment of how well the market was meeting the price-setting function. Bonnie Colby and colleagues at the University of Arizona have investigated the behaviour of water-right prices in several of the western states both in terms of whether market prices reflect the economic values of water resources and in terms of price trends and price dispersion (Colby Saliba *et al.*, 1987; Colby *et al.*, 1993). While it is difficult to make general conclusions about these water markets from only a few studies, it appears that the water markets in the western states of the USA have been characterised by substantial price dispersion both as a result of high degrees of heterogeneity in the characteristics of water entitlements and imperfect information in the market.[2] No attention appears to have been specifically directed towards determining the implications of imperfect market pricing for resource allocation and social welfare.

Water trading and prices of water entitlement in South Australia have previously been studied by Bjornlund and McKay (1996a, 1996b) who used a hedonic-pricing method to estimate the implicit prices paid for water entitlement in sales of irrigation farms, and also collected data on prices paid for water entitlement separately from land. They related these implicit prices to characteristics of the sellers and purchasers. Cursory econometric analyses indicated that there may be some systematic price dispersion related to these characteristics. Little attention was given to the features of the market that enable price dispersion to persist.

An analysis of the operation of markets for tradable quotas in New Zealand fish stocks has indicated substantial dispersion in quota prices and a general failure of arbitrage processes in the quota market to deliver unique market-clearing prices that reflect the economic value of the associated access to the fisheries (Lindner, 1990). No detailed analysis of price determination was undertaken in the study, but it was speculated that the price dispersion was likely to be at least partly due to imperfect market information and to wide divergence in the value of quotas across fishing enterprises due to differences in levels of sunk investment in capital equipment.

A CONCEPTUAL MODEL OF PRICE DISPERSION

There are two possible approaches to the empirical analysis of prices paid for water entitlement and price dispersion. Firstly, an analysis of price dispersion may be carried out by examining measures of variance in prices over discrete periods of time or for particular categories of products, and relating the variance to features of the market that reflect product heterogeneity, the costs and quality of available market information, and the costs and benefits of collecting information. This approach has previously been used in the analyses of price dispersion in markets for legal services (Cox *et al.*, 1982) and airline travel (Borenstein and Rose, 1994). The problem with this approach is that a large data set is required to enable extraction of data subsets that are large enough to provide a statistically valid measure of variance for each time interval and yet still have enough time intervals and data points for further analysis. There were insufficient data available on water trading in South Australia to take this approach.

Secondly, an analysis can be made of disaggregated price data, relating the price paid in individual transactions to the characteristics of the product purchased and the extent of information search undertaken by purchasers. This approach has been adopted in studies of wage rates (Hofler and Murphy, 1992), prices of automobile insurance (Dahlby and West, 1986) and prices of medical services (Gaynor and Polachek, 1994), and is the approach taken in this study.

The above discussion of price dispersion suggests that the contract price of a transaction will be a stochastic function of product heterogeneity, the information advantage that vendors hold over purchasers, and the costs and benefits to purchasers of searching for information. The potential influences of product heterogeneity and imperfect information on price dispersion in trades of water entitlement in South Australia are described below.

Product Heterogeneity

At first glance there appears to be little product heterogeneity in the South Australian water market. Any unit of water entitlement from the Murray River has identical characteristics of conditions of use, potential locations of use and priority of access to the water. This is different to systems of water rights that are used in other places such as the western states of the USA where systems of water rights typically incorporate a scale of priorities for access to the water resources based upon when the water right was first granted.

On closer examination there are differences in parcels of water offered for trade that constitute systematic product heterogeneity. These relate to differences in transaction costs that would accrue to the purchaser through administrative costs imposed by regulatory agencies; whether an agent was involved in offering the water entitlement to the market on behalf of a vendor; and variability in the quality of irrigation water depending upon the location of water use. These three causes of product heterogeneity are discussed in turn below.

All transfers of water entitlement have been subject to payment of the administrative fee for the transfer of $12.00 per ML. Some sales of water entitlement from irrigators in the ex-government irrigation areas of the Central Irrigation Trust have attracted an additional levy that was paid by the purchaser. The origin of this levy lies in a government programme for upgrading the water distribution infrastructure within the government irrigation areas. This programme was progressively implemented since 1993 and was partially financed by a levy on the irrigation farmers. The levy was calculated in proportion to the water entitlement of each farmer and payment was spread over a period of five years. The value of the levy was approximately $7.50 per ML per annum. When water entitlement was sold outside a government area, the purchaser of the water was required to pay the residual of the levy for the amount of time remaining of the five-year period. Thus water sold at the commencement of the rehabilitation period would have attracted a levy payment by the water purchaser of approximately $7.50 × 5 years = $37.50 per ML. Water sold three years into the rehabilitation period would attract a levy of approximately $15.00 per ML

($7.50 × 2 years). The only exception to payment of this levy by a water purchaser was where the purchased water entitlement originated from land that during the process of infrastructure improvement had been excluded from future water delivery for reasons of environmental problems of irrigation, unsuitability of land for commercial irrigation activities or logistical problems in water delivery. Sale of the water entitlement pertaining to this land did not attract the levy. There is thus a difference in parcels of water offered to the market in terms of whether this levy is payable or not. The price for a parcel of water entitlement that attracts the levy would be expected to be less than that for the same parcel of water purchased elsewhere, the expected difference being equal to the value of the levy payment.

The second cause of product heterogeneity is the involvement of an agent in offering parcels of water entitlement to the market on behalf of vendors. The involvement of an agent would reduce the transaction costs of a prospective purchaser of water entitlement through reducing costs of search for a trading partner. This is further discussed below in relation to imperfect market information.

The third cause of product heterogeneity is differences in the quality of water according to the location of water use. The section of the Murray River in South Australia has essentially no new water accretions from runoff. Evaporation and discharges of saline drainage waters from irrigation areas lead to increasing salinity along the length of the river, with significantly higher water salinity in the Lower Murray region than in the Riverland region. Thus the willingness to pay for irrigation water may be lower in the Lower Murray region than in the Riverland region. If vendors of water are able to price discriminate between water purchasers in the two regions, the differences in demand may contribute to price dispersion. This is also further discussed below in relation to imperfect information.

Imperfect Information

There are two aspects of imperfect information that are considered to contribute to price dispersion in the market for water entitlements. The first is differences in the 'package' of information associated with parcels of water entitlement offered on the market. This actually contributes to product heterogeneity whereby parcels of water entitlement differ in terms of the transaction costs incurred by the purchaser in terms of locating a vendor and undertaking the commercial transaction. If the identity of a vendor is cheaper to ascertain and/or the commercial transaction is cheaper or less risky to undertake, then the parcel of entitlement would assume a greater value and the purchaser would be willing to pay a higher price. Such differences between parcels of water entitlement would occur according to whether an agent or broker presents the parcel of water to the market (Pendse, 1986). The purchaser does not pay any direct charges to the agent and, as a result of the reduced costs of searching for a water vendor and handling by the agent of many aspects of the commercial transaction, the value of the parcel of water is correspondingly greater and the purchaser should be willing to pay a higher price.

Secondly, imperfect information would contribute to price dispersion through the costs that would necessarily be incurred by a purchaser in collecting information. This is the component of price dispersion that is of interest as an indicator of the magnitude of transaction costs associated with acquiring information. According to the established theory of market information and price dispersion, a prospective purchaser of water entitlement would be faced with a perceived distribution of prices. The purchaser could either select a vendor at random and pay the respective price or engage in a costly information search with the intent of identifying a vendor with a low price. There is a stochastic relationship between the extent of search and the contract price. Searching increases the probability of the purchaser securing a low price but does not guarantee this. As searching is costly, information asymmetries alter the relative negotiating positions of parties to a contract and the relative abilities of each party to capture the economic surplus of the transaction. Prices will tend to be higher where the purchaser has incomplete information on market prices *and* there is information asymmetry favouring the vendors. Conversely, a greater amount of market information held by purchasers reduces the ability of vendors to exploit the imperfect price information of the purchasers and leads to lower and less variable market prices.

In the South Australian market for water entitlement, both buyers and sellers typically make few repeat transactions and both would therefore hold relatively little information about the market without engaging in an information search. However, sellers are often represented by agents who, due to their frequent involvement in the market, would accumulate information on the willingness and capacity of different purchasers or classes of purchasers to pay, and thereby create an information asymmetry between vendors and purchasers. Prices may vary if the agent is able to discriminate between purchasers on the basis of their demand schedules. For example, if demand schedules vary according to the crop types for which the water is used, then prices may vary according to these crop types. Differences in demand schedules may also result from location: use of water in the Riverland implies use of water that is of substantially lower salinity than in the Lower Murray and hence is of greater value in irrigation.

Collection of information by purchasers will act to reduce price dispersion by reducing the extent of information asymmetry between vendors and purchasers. The collection of information will depend upon the costs and benefits of searching to the individual purchaser. The costs and benefits are discussed as follows.

The cost of obtaining an additional unit of information depends upon the direct costs of search and opportunity costs. The former relates to resources used in searching, such as communication costs. The latter relates mainly to the time taken to search that would otherwise be used in other activities. Measuring these costs either directly or using proxy variables is difficult. The level of education has been used as a proxy measure of direct costs and the efficiency of search (Marvel, 1976) but is at best a very crude measure and requires detailed information on each purchaser. The opportunity cost of search is still more difficult to measure. Income has been used as a proxy measure under the assumption that high income corresponds to a high marginal value of time and consequently a high opportunity cost in devoting time to an information search (Marvel, 1976; Gaynor and Polachek, 1994). This, however, seems a remarkably crude measure that is likely to incorporate wealth effects on the elasticity of demand as well as opportunity costs of information search. No suitable proxy measure of either direct or indirect search costs has been identified for this study. It is possible to surmise, however, that the costs of search may be reduced by learning behaviour if a purchaser repeatedly participates in the market and gains improved knowledge of sources of market information. The extent of search would therefore tend to increase and the price for water entitlement decrease when the purchaser makes repeat transactions.

The benefits of search relate to the reductions in the expected price to be paid by the purchaser when a greater amount of information is held. Thus the gross benefits from an additional unit of information are the expected reduction in the unit price of the product being purchased multiplied by the number of units to be purchased. The gross benefits of an additional unit of information are thus greater when a large purchase is being made or where repeat purchases are made within a period of time during which the collected information is expected to remain valid (Marvel, 1976).

ECONOMETRIC ANALYSIS

Conceptual Model

Table 4.1 describes an *a priori* regression model for the price of water entitlement under a hypothesis of imperfect information. The model relates the price for an individual entitlement trade to heterogeneity in parcels of water entitlement, asymmetry of information between the vendors and purchasers, the gross benefits of information search, and the proposed irrigation activity of the purchaser.

Table 4.1: Conceptual Regression Model of Water-Entitlement Prices, Entitlement Heterogeneity and Information Search

Economic Parameter	Measured Parameter	Effect on Price of Water Entitlement	Expected Coeff. Sign
Dependent Variable			
Water entitlement prices	Recorded prices of entitlement trades	–	–
Regressors			
Differences in transaction costs of purchaser	Rehabilitation levy payable	Levy is generally paid by the purchaser, reducing the value of the water entitlement	Negative
	Transaction mediated by an agent	An agent reduces the transaction costs of the purchaser and hence increases the value of the water entitlement	Positive
Information asymmetry	Transaction mediated by an agent	Information advantages of vendors represented by agents allows price discrimination, hence the prices for trades mediated by agents would tend to be higher than in the absence of agents	Positive
	Proposed location of water use in the Riverland region	Water in the Riverland is of better quality and greater value	Positive
	Irrigation activities	Vendors with information advantages may price-discriminate according to the irrigation activity of the purchaser and their demand schedules for water	Positive or negative
Benefits of information search	Volume of purchase	Higher volumes increase the potential benefits of search and hence promote search and lower trade prices	Negative
	Repeat water purchases	Repeat purchases increase benefits of market search and hence promote search and lower trade prices	Negative
Costs of information search	Repeat water purchases	Repeated market participation reduces cost of information search, promotes search and leads to lower trade prices	Negative

Data Sources and Collection

A listing of 485 permanent transfers of water entitlement over the period June 1988 to June 1996 was compiled using data from two sources: records of the South Australian Department of Environment and Natural Resources for transfers relating to water licences; and records of the South Australian Water Corporation for transfers relating to the ex-government irrigation areas (now the Central Irrigation Trust). In view of a range of data compilations being used to compile this list and the consequent ability to cross-check much of the data, this list was regarded as a close to complete record of permanent trades over this period. Information on transfers prior to 1988 was not readily available.

The information compiled for each permanent transfer was as follows.

• The identities of vendor and purchaser. (For approximately 25 per cent of the listed transfers, the identity of the vendor could not be ascertained from available records.)
• The quantity of water transferred.
• The date when the transfer was approved by either the Department of Environment and Natural Resources or the South Australian Water Corporation as applicable.

The prices of water entitlement are not routinely recorded by the regulatory agencies. Price data were therefore collected by undertaking a survey of the purchasers of water entitlement and of several real-estate agents in the region that also act as agents for the trading of water entitlement. Data on prices were thus collected for 172 of the 485 listed transfers (35 per cent). The survey of irrigation farmers and real-estate agents also provided information on a limited number of trades occurring prior to June 1988 and in July 1996. This brought the total number of transfers with known prices to 188.

The survey was also used to collect information on the following characteristics of the vendors, the purchasers and the transactions.

• Locations of the water vendor and purchaser (Riverland or Lower Murray).
• Whether the vendors and purchasers were private diverters or government irrigators.
• Whether the transfer of water involved payment of a rehabilitation levy to a government irrigation area.
• Whether the trade was undertaken through an agent.
• The intended use of the purchased water.

Information on the prices of major output commodities of irrigated agriculture (wine grapes and citrus) were collected for possible use in explaining gross trends in the price of water entitlement.   Sources of commodity price data were unpublished records of the South Australian Department of Primary Industries and commodity statistics compiled by the Australian Bureau of Agricultural and Resource Economics (1995).

As a result of the nature of trade records held by the state regulating agencies and of the use of a survey for collection of much of the price data, there are three potential measurement errors and biases within the data set.

Firstly, the recorded date of a transaction would ideally be the date of agreement on a trade price. This information could not be collected since accurate records were not available either from the regulatory agencies or the parties to the trade. Instead, the date of approval of the transfer by either the Department of Environment and Natural Resources or the South Australia Water Corporation was used.   This would post-date the date of price determination by about three months and occasionally up to six months. Due to different times taken for processing of transfer approvals, the data set would contain errors in the 'order' of the transactions.

Secondly, minor inaccuracies may occur in some of the price data that were gleaned from surveys of water purchasers, many of which depended on the recollection of individuals rather than documented records. These errors are, however, expected to be small.   Some cross-checking of data was possible where price data for the same transactions were obtained independently from both the water purchasers and real-estate agents.   This cross-checking indicated that the data obtained from the survey are accurate.

Thirdly, a large proportion of the data for the period from 1995 onwards was obtained from a single agent. For the price data collected over the period May 1995 to June 1996, 85 of 101 observations (84 per cent) were from this source. During the same period this agent mediated 85 of 208 recorded water trades (41 per cent), and was by far the dominant agent in the market. Consequently the results of any analysis of the price data, particularly for the period from mid-1995 onwards, need to be qualified by the possibility that the observed prices for this period may be generally higher than for the market as a whole.   Higher prices may be due to the ability of this agent to price-discriminate amongst vendors and achieve price premiums by virtue of transaction-cost savings to purchasers.

Overview of the Water Trading and Price Data

The distribution of trades over time during the period 1988 to 1996 is shown in Figure 4.1 and indicates 15 to 40 permanent trades per annum up to 1992/93 and then a rapidly increasing number up to a maximum of 163 trades in

1995/96. The increase in the number of trades from 1993 onwards is considered to be a result firstly of the implementation of regulations enabling irrigators in government districts to transfer water entitlement externally, and secondly of the programmes of infrastructure rehabilitation in government areas that forced many transfers.

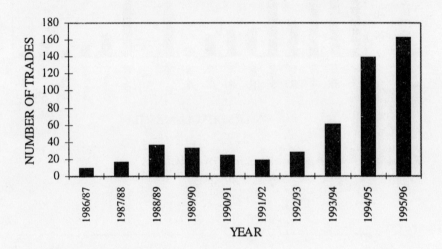

Figure 4.1: Annual Numbers of Permanent Water Transfers

A frequency distribution of trade volumes over the period 1986/87 to 1995/96 is shown in Figure 4.2 and indicates a predominance of trades with annual entitlement volumes of less than 50 ML and 100 to 200 ML. Closer examination of the data indicates that the size of individual trades tends to decrease after 1992/93. This is probably a consequence of relatively small volumes of water being traded by irrigators in government irrigation areas after this time.

Prices for trades of water entitlement are shown in Figure 4.3 for nominal prices and Figure 4.4 for deflated prices (1989/90 dollars, calculated using quarterly or annual consumer price indices published by the Australian Bureau of Statistics). These data relate only to the 180 trades of water entitlement for which prices were obtained.

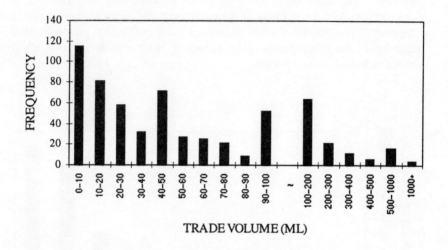

Figure 4.2: Frequency Distribution of Trade Volumes

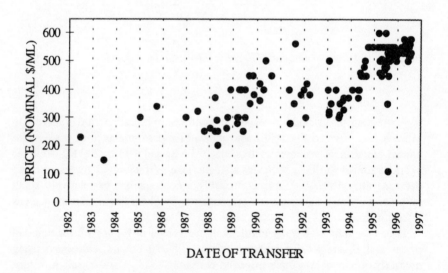

Figure 4.3: Nominal Prices Paid for Water Entitlement

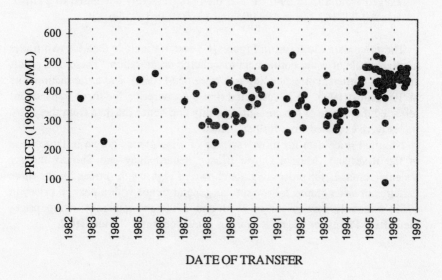

Figure 4.4: Deflated Prices Paid for Water Entitlement

Visual analysis of Figures 4.3 and 4.4 indicates the following characteristics of water prices.

- There is a positive trend in nominal water prices over the period 1982 to 1996, with prices rising from approximately $200/ML in 1982/83 to $580/ML in 1996. While there are only a few data points prior to 1987 upon which to draw firm conclusions in this regard, this trend is consistent with the anecdotal history of the market provided by an agent involved with the market for much of its history.
- Water prices corrected for inflation do not show the same positive trend. With the exception of a short period of relatively high water prices in 1989 and 1990, deflated prices appear to have remained reasonably constant over the period 1982 to 1994. In 1994 deflated prices increased by about $150/ML.
- Over the period from 1987/88 to 1995/96, prices were dispersed, with a difference between the minimum and maximum nominal prices in any year of $150 to $260/ML. The variance in prices appears to decrease from 1993 onwards and there is a marked reduction in price dispersion after mid-1995. Standard deviations of prices in the years 1987/88 to 1992/93

ranged from $52 to $94/ML and then progressively decreased to $47/ML
in 1993/94, $42/ML in 1994/95 and $31/ML in 1995/96.

The price data displayed in Figures 4.3 and 4.4 include data for two trades
involving sale of water entitlement to a church organisation. These data points
appear as outliers, corresponding to a price of $110/ML and a transaction date
of 19 August 1995. It is suspected that the low price for these transactions
reflected the nature of the purchasing entity and hence the data from these two
trades were excluded from further analysis.

Nominal price data for three varieties of wine grapes grown in large areas
of the Riverland (Muscat Gordo Blanco, Chardonnay and Shiraz) and for
Valencia oranges for processing are shown in Figure 4.5. Prices for the three
varieties of wine grapes follow similar general trends with a peak in prices in
1989, relatively low prices in 1991 and 1992 and generally rising prices
thereafter. Prices for Valencia oranges show peaks in 1989 and 1992.

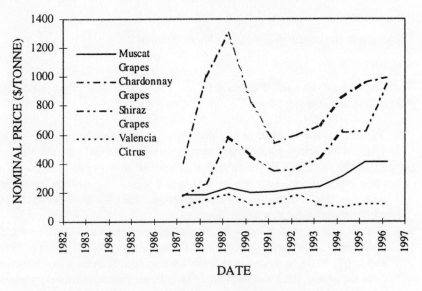

Figure 4.5: Nominal Prices of Four Major Output Commodities of
Irrigated Agriculture in the Riverland Region

Major features of the data set of water trades and prices used to estimate the
model are summarised below.

- There was a non-uniform distribution of data points over the time period of analysis. Sixty data points related to the period 1987 to June 1994, and 118 data points related to the period July 1994 to July 1997.
- Agents mediated 151 of the 178 trades in the data set. Of the 151 trades mediated by an agent, 87 were mediated by the dominant agent in the market.
- One hundred and seventeen of the 178 trades in the data set involved a purchaser making more than one trade of water entitlement within a twelve-month period.
- One hundred and thirty one of the 178 trades involved a purchaser located in the Riverland region.
- Thirty seven of the 178 trades attracted payment of a rehabilitation levy by the purchaser.
- Nearly half (82) of the water purchases were intended at least partly for irrigation of vineyards. Other substantial uses cited by purchasers were: vegetables – 33; citrus or other orchards – 51; pasture, lucerne or other fodder – 15; and municipal and industrial – 12.

Econometric Analysis

The data set of 178 observations on trade prices and transaction characteristics for the period 1987 to 1996 was used to specify and quantify the regression model. Parameters are described in Table 4.2 and represent measures of the variables described in Table 4.1 as well as the prices of major output commodities. For the purposes of analysis, all price data for water entitlement and output commodities were converted to 1989/90 dollar values.

Ordinary least squares was used to estimate coefficient values for the model. Statistical analysis was undertaken using the Microfit 4.01 software (Pesaran and Pesaran, 1995). Diagnostic tests for serial correlation (Durbin–Watson statistic and Lagrangian multiplier test), omitted variables (Ramsey's reset test) and heteroscedasticity (a test based on a regression of squared residuals on squared fitted values) were used to determine an appropriate model specification in terms of functional form and appropriate methods for estimating coefficients and standard errors. A further criterion used to select the model form was that elasticities inferred from the estimated relationship between water prices and commodity prices could not be negative; that is, a rise in deflated prices of output commodities must cause a non-negative change in the deflated price of water entitlement.

Table 4.2: Regression Parameters

Parameter	Abbreviation	Units
Price paid for water entitlement	WTRRLP	1989/90 dollars per megalitre
Output commodity prices:		
Muscat wine grapes	GDRLP	1989/90 dollars per tonne
Chardonnay wine grapes	CHRLP	1989/90 dollars per tonne
Shiraz wine grapes	SHRLP	1989/90 dollars per tonne
Valencia oranges	CIRLP	1989/90 dollars per tonne
Volumetric entitlement traded	VOL	Megalitres
Mediation of the trade by an agent	AGNT	Dummy variable equal to one if an agent mediated the trade
Multiple transactions by a purchaser	RPT	Dummy variable equal to one if a purchaser made two or more trades in a one-year period
Compulsory rehabilitation levy payable by the entitlement purchaser	RLEVY	Dummy variable taking the value of one if the levy was payable
Geographic location of the entitlement purchaser	BUYLOC	Dummy variable taking the value of one if the purchaser was located in the Riverland region
Intended water use by the purchaser other than for vineyards:		
Citrus or other orchards	CITORC	Dummy variable taking the value of one if the predominant intended use of water was citrus or other orchards
Pasture	PL	Dummy variable taking the value of one if the predominant intended use of water was pasture, lucerne or other fodder crops
Vegetables	VEG	Dummy variable taking the value of one if the predominant intended use of water was vegetable crops
Municipal and industrial	MI	Dummy variable taking the value of one if the predominant intended use of water was municipal or industrial.

The selected functional form was a linear regression of the price of water entitlement against the following independent variables.

- Commodity prices as described in Table 4.2 and the squares of these prices. The squares of commodity prices were added to the model in response to serial correlation in the residuals of the model when estimated with the un-squared prices only, and indications from plots of these residuals that the model was poorly estimating water prices at times of high and low commodity prices. Inclusion of the squared prices implies a quadratic relationship between commodity prices and the price of water entitlement.
- The natural logarithm of the entitlement volume. The logarithmic transformation was used to account for a pre-supposed non-linear relationship between the entitlement volume and the trade price. The reasoning behind this was that higher trade volumes would induce greater search by the purchaser for lower prices but that the marginal benefit of search, in terms of securing a lower price, decreases with the extent of search.
- The dummy variables described in Table 4.2 and representing various characteristics of the transaction and intended water uses.
- An additional dummy variable introduced for a subset of eight consecutive trades in the latter part of 1989 and the first half of 1990. These trades attracted relatively high prices that could not be adequately explained by any of the explanatory variables. Justification for this dummy variable is provided by the passing of new water-resources legislation in South Australia in mid-1990. There may have been an increase in the demand for water entitlement in the period leading up to this legislation due to uncertainty in regard to policies for water allocation.

Estimates for the model are shown in Table 4.3. The estimated model had an R^2 value of 64 per cent and satisfied tests for serial correlation, but appeared to suffer from heteroscedasticity in the residuals, meaning that the estimated standard errors and t-statistics are potentially biased (Maddala, 1992 pp. 209–11). Examination of plots of residuals suggested that the variance of the error term decreased over time. An explanation for this that is consistent with both the data and the economics of price dispersion is that the variance in price decreases as the frequency of transactions increases. Examination of plots of residuals against numbers of trades in six- and twelve-month periods preceding each transaction indicated a negative relationship between residuals and the number of trades in the preceding twelve months, and an approximately linear negative relationship between the residuals and the square root of the number of trades in the preceding twelve months.

Given this possible explanation of heteroscedasticity, the procedure recommended by Maddala (1992 pp. 215–17) was used to correct the data for heteroscedasticity and enable statistical inference for coefficient estimates. All variables were inflated by multiplying by the square root of the number of trades in the twelve months preceding each observation. The regression model was re-estimated using the transformed data to derive t-statistics and to test the statistical significance of the coefficient estimates in the model as originally estimated. The significance levels for the t-statistics of the transformed data are also shown in Table 4.3, and it is these levels that should be used to judge whether the coefficient estimates are significantly different from zero.

Table 4.3: Ordinary Least Squares Regression for the Price of Water Entitlement*

Regressor Variable	Coefficient Estimate	Standard Error	t-Statistic. Probability	t-Statistic. Probability (transformed data)**
INPT	−346	253	0.173	0.006
D1990	82.7	26.0	0.002	0.020
GDRLP	1.44	1.55	0.356	0.128
$GDRLP^2$	-1.51×10^{-3}	-2.63×10^{-3}	0.568	0.168
CHRLP	0.402	0.161	0.014	0.174
$CHRLP^2$	-2.89×10^{-4}	-8.70×10^{-5}	0.001	0.045
SHRLP	0.307	0.201	0.129	0.729
$SHRLP^2$	-1.64×10^{-4}	-1.56×10^{-4}	0.300	0.836
CIRLP	2.93	1.60	0.070	0.016
$CIRLP^2$	-7.29×10^{-3}	-5.60×10^{-3}	0.194	0.070
ln(VOL)	−5.14	3.05	0.094	0.929
AGNT	20.2	9.07	0.027	0.006
RPT	8.15	7.09	0.252	0.905
RLEVY	−18.0	8.52	0.036	0.001
BUYLOC	−32.8	8.94	<0.001	0.012
ORC	24.2	7.73	0.002	0.002
PL	−2.34	12.5	0.851	0.819
VEG	15.1	9.42	0.110	0.050
MI	19.87	14.5	0.173	0.949

* Refer to notes at the end of the chapter for diagnostic statistics on the regression.

** Regression with variables, including dummy variables and the intercept term, multiplied by the square root of the number of water trades in the twelve months preceding each observation.

The principal inferences from the regression are as follows.

- Gross trends in the time series of deflated prices for water entitlement appear to be related to movements in the deflated prices of at least some of the major output commodities of irrigated agriculture: wine grapes and citrus for processing. Coefficient estimates for the prices and squared prices of Muscat and Chardonnay grapes and Valencia oranges had t-ratio probabilities of less than 0.2. The relationships between water-entitlement price and commodity prices appeared to be similar for all four commodity types, with positive coefficients on the prices and negative coefficients on the squares of prices, indicating a positive but less than linear response of water prices to commodity prices. The inferred elasticities between entitlement prices and commodity prices ranged between zero and 1.7 when estimated for entitlement prices and commodity prices in the ranges evident in this study.
- The estimated coefficient for the logarithm of the volumetric entitlement traded was not significantly different from zero, indicating that there was no systematic variation in price with the volume of water entitlement traded.
- The estimated coefficient for the dummy variable representing mediation of the transaction by an agent was of the expected sign (positive) and statistically significant. The estimated value indicates that, on average, the involvement of an agent increased the price of the water entitlement by about $20/ML (1989/90 dollars), corresponding to about 5 per cent of an approximate average entitlement price of $425/ML.
- The estimated coefficient for the dummy variable representing repeat trades by entitlement purchasers was not significantly different from zero, indicating that there was no systematic variation in price according to whether or not the purchaser was making more than one transaction.
- The estimated coefficient for the dummy variable representing payment of the rehabilitation levy by entitlement purchasers was of the expected sign (negative) and statistically significant. The estimated value indicates that, on average, the imposition of the levy on the purchaser reduces the entitlement price by about $17/ML (1989/90 dollars), or about 4.5 per cent of the approximate average entitlement price.
- The estimated coefficient for the dummy variable representing location of the purchaser in the Riverland region was statistically significant but of the opposite sign to that expected. As discussed above, the substantially lower salinity of water in the Riverland was expected to result in a higher price for water trades where the purchaser was located in this region. The negative estimate of the coefficient indicates to the contrary; that is, water buyers in the Riverland paid generally lower prices for water entitlement

by about $30/ML (1989/90 dollars), corresponding to 7.5 per cent of the approximate average entitlement price.

• The estimated coefficients for the dummy variables representing the intended water use by the purchaser indicate that small but statistically significant premiums were paid for water entitlement when the intended use is for orchards or vegetables. The magnitudes of the premiums for each water use were similar at $24/ML and $15/ML (1989/90 dollars) respectively, corresponding to 6 per cent and 4 per cent of the approximate average entitlement price.

The above inferences were not altered to any material extent by deletion from the model of the parameters for which estimates of coefficients were not significantly different from zero.

The model was also estimated using data only from trades mediated by agents. Price dispersion in the form of premiums paid for particular water uses would be expected to be greater for this data subset, due to greater asymmetry in information holdings between vendors (the agents) and water purchasers. Results did not differ substantially from those presented above, with the exception that the coefficient estimate for the dummy variable representing an intended municipal and industrial use of water was statistically significant at the 10 per cent level, indicating that purchases of water entitlement for municipal and industrial purposes may also have added a premium to the water price, in this case of about $27/ML, about 7 per cent of the approximate average entitlement price. This indicates a greater extent of price discrimination by vendors when they are represented by agents, consistent with expectations derived from theory.

CONCLUSIONS: STATIC TRANSACTION COSTS IN MARKET ALLOCATION OF WATER ENTITLEMENTS

Disregarding price dispersion for the moment, the results of the analysis indicate that the market for water entitlement was functioning well in terms of setting price levels that reflect the economic value of the water. There are two items of evidence for this. Firstly, gross trends in water prices can be explained by movements in prices of major output commodities. It can be inferred from this that prices for water entitlement are positively related to the profitability of irrigation activities. Secondly, the cost of the rehabilitation levy for water purchased from government districts seems to be reasonably well factored into entitlement prices in trades where the levy applies, although this would be expected since the levy is a readily observable 'out-of-pocket' expense.

Contrary to this evidence for effective arbitrage processes in the water market are observations relating to transaction costs and price dispersion.

Two principal types of transaction cost were identified as occurring in the market trading of water entitlement in South Australia. The first of these comprises a range of fees and charges imposed on trading parties by the regulatory agencies that administer the transfers. These comprised an administrative charge for processing the transfer ($12/ML transferred in 1995/96) and a 'rehabilitation levy' of up to about $38/ML payable for some transfers from irrigators in the ex-government irrigation areas. In total, the transaction costs arising from administrative charges have therefore comprised about $12 to $50/ML, equivalent to 3 per cent to 12 per cent of an approximate average price for water entitlement of $425/ML.

The second principal type of transaction cost comprises costs arising from imperfect information in the market. The study described in this chapter examined price dispersion in historical water trades as an indicator of the magnitude of imperfect information in the market and of the associated transaction costs.

The analysis indicates substantial dispersion of prices in the market, particularly prior to 1995 when prices tended to be dispersed within a range of $150 to $200/ML. The occurrence of heteroscedasticity in the residuals of the estimated model is symptomatic of the greater extent of price dispersion prior to 1995.

Some of this price dispersion can be explained by heterogeneity in characteristics of parcels of traded entitlement. The heterogeneity arose from application of the rehabilitation levy to some trades and to the involvement of a mediating agent in some trades. The cost of the rehabilitation levy appears to have been reasonably well factored into the price paid for the water entitlement, or perhaps just slightly under-accounted for. Coefficient estimates for the dummy variable representing payment of the levy suggest an average reduction in price of $15 to $17/ML. This is at the lower end of the range of actual levy payments: $13 to $34/ML in 1989/90 values. The premium of about $20/ML paid for mediation of trades by agents may include a component of price discrimination by the agent as well as product heterogeneity (transaction-cost savings to the purchaser), but indicates that this source of product heterogeneity makes at most a small contribution to price dispersion. The total contribution of product heterogeneity to price dispersion may be up to $30 to $40/ML.

Price dispersion that cannot be accounted for by product heterogeneity can be attributed to imperfect information amongst market participants and asymmetry in information holdings. The above analysis provides four items of evidence for conditions of imperfect information in the water market of South Australia.

Firstly, there was substantial variability in prices that could not explained by any of the explanatory variables of price included in the model. The R^2 value was only 64 per cent and model residuals were commonly in the order of ± \$75/ML in the period prior to 1995 and ± \$35/ML in 1995 and 1996. The result is consistent with there being a distribution of prices in the market created by imperfect price information held by vendors and purchasers.

Secondly, both vendors and purchasers of water entitlement have been willing to make payments to agents and brokers to mediate transactions. Purchasers have paid a price premium for water entitlement purchased via an agent equal to approximately \$20/ML. This premium could be due to a combination of product differentiation and information effects, as previously discussed, but there is at least a possibility that agents may have had an information advantage over purchasers which provided opportunity for price discrimination. Many vendors utilise the services of an agent at a cost of approximately 4 per cent of the transaction value, also equal to about \$20/ML. The implication of these expenditures by vendors and purchasers is that transaction costs of obtaining the information through avenues other than utilising the services of an agent would be in excess of these amounts.

Thirdly, there is evidence of price discrimination amongst purchasers on the basis of the intended water use, with premiums being paid for entitlement when the intended water use is citrus, other orchards, vegetables, and possibly municipal and industrial uses. The premiums are, however, relatively small: \$8 to \$14/ML, constituting only about 3 per cent of the water price. This indicates an information asymmetry between vendors and purchasers, possibly resulting from the representation of vendors by agents with an information advantage over purchasers.

Fourthly, there is some evidence of differences in prices between the Riverland and Lower Murray regions. On the basis of differences in water quality it would be expected, all other things being equal, that water prices would be greater in the Riverland than the Lower Murray due to lower water salinity. The analysis of prices indicates the reverse. Thus there is possibly an imperfect transmission of price information between the two regions. It is worth noting here that the agents operating in the market for water entitlement tend to restrict their activities to one or other of the regions and thus may not provide a means of information transmission through the entire market.

The lack of relationships between price and both the volume of trades and repeat purchases indicates that an increasing value of purchases does not induce greater price search. This is contrary to theory and may reflect high costs of information search that have not been explicitly included in the model and which preclude information search even when multiple transactions are being made. Experience in collection of the price data used in this analysis suggests that collection of price information by a prospective purchaser would be very costly due to the geographic dispersion of the market and lack of centralised collection and publication of trade prices.

A summary of estimates of transaction costs is provided in Table 4.4.

Table 4.4: Summary of Transaction Costs for Trading of Water Entitlement

Transaction-Cost Parameter	Known or Estimated Value ($/ML)	Proportion of Approximate Average Trade Price ($425/ML)
Administrative Fees and Charges		
Transfer fee	12	3
Rehabilitation levy	0 – 38	0 – 9
Costs of Obtaining Information		
Commissions paid to agents	20	5
Costs from Residual Imperfect Information		
Lower bound of costs for forgone information	0 – 75 (pre-1995) 0 – 35 (post-1995)	0 – 18 0 – 8
INDICATIVE TOTAL*	12 – 125	3 – 29

* The total transaction costs would be less than the sum of figures in the table as all costs would not be incurred in all trades and some costs would be mutually exclusive, as for example with commissions paid to agents and costs of forgone information.

The direct 'out-of-pocket' transaction costs associated with water trade may comprise up to $60 to $70/ML in administrative fees and charges and fees paid to agents providing a brokerage service for the trades. In addition to these are indirect or implicit costs associated with imperfect information and the costs of information search by market participants. The level of price dispersion may be used as an indicator of the costs of information. In the absence of any costs of information, market participants would undertake information searches that would result in arbitrage processes removing any price variability other than that reflecting product heterogeneity. The study of prices has indicated that such information search does not occur and there has been resultant price dispersion within the ranges of ± $75/ML in the period prior to 1995 and ± $35/ML in 1995 and 1996. If it is accepted that the costs associated with imperfect information are the cause of the price dispersion beyond that which can be explained by heterogeneity of water entitlements, then imperfect information has given rise to additional transaction costs of up to $75/ML prior to 1995 and up to $35/ML after 1995. Transaction costs of obtaining market information must have been in excess of these amounts or such price dispersion would have been eliminated. Total transaction costs incurred by participants in a transfer of water entitlement may therefore have ranged from a minimum of $12/ML in the administrative fee for transfer of entitlement, to greater than $125/ML for transactions characterised by imperfect information. This range corresponds to a range of 3 per cent to 29 per cent of the approximate average price for water entitlement of $425/ML.

The analysis suggests that the extent of price dispersion and the transaction costs associated with imperfect information decreased between 1994 and 1995 in association with an increase in the frequency of transactions. Arbitrage processes appear to have been relatively ineffective in pricing water prior to 1993/94 due to the 'thinness' of the market. That is, prior to 1993/94 the efficacy of the market system in pricing water was limited by a low frequency of trades that was insufficient for generation and transmittal of price information to market participants. For the water market in the South Australian Murray region, it appears that a 'thin' market constitutes less than about 50 to 100 trades per annum.

There are two major implications of this analysis for the study of institutions for market trading as a mechanism for re-allocation of water entitlements. The first is that there are substantial transaction costs associated with trading of water entitlements, particularly when the market is thin. It is not possible to extrapolate the relationship between trade frequency and price dispersion to water markets in other regions of the Murray–Darling Basin since the relationship could be affected by factors specific to particular circumstances such as the geographic dispersal of market participants, the activities of agents, and the regulatory institutions for water trading. Nevertheless, the results are broadly applicable. In all irrigation regions of the Murray–Darling Basin, there are likely to be similar transaction costs arising from administration charges and imperfect information. Markets for all regions tend to be relatively thin with permanent trades numbered in the tens rather than hundreds (Murray–Darling Basin Ministerial Council, 1995). Transaction costs may therefore be of similar magnitudes to those of the South Australian market. In view of the impact of imperfect information on transaction costs and water prices, there may be a greater role for government regulatory agencies to play in providing market information if there is to be a continued reliance on market processes for efficient resource allocation. In particular, these agencies should consider the collection and publication of trade prices. This is an accepted role of regulatory agencies in other markets such as those for land, housing, and industrial stocks where compiling and distributing market information is generally considered to improve the efficiency of the market as an institution of allocation. Similar conclusions to these were drawn in a study of trading in pollution permits where transaction costs resulting from poor market information were deemed to reduce market participation (Gangadharan, 1997).

The second implication of the findings of this study is that many of the *ex ante* policy studies of market institutions have been deficient in so much as they have relied upon simplistic spatial-equilibrium models of market allocation that do not recognise the imperfections of thin markets (for example Flinn and Guise, 1970; Wong and Eheart, 1983; Vaux and Howitt, 1984; Hall *et al.*, 1994; Jones and Fagan, 1996; Scoccimarro, *et al.*, 1996; Branson and Eigenraam, 1996; Eigenraam *et al.*, 1996; Lo and Horbulyk, 1996). An implicit assumption in the use of spatial-equilibrium models is that an equilibrium market price is established prior to any trades taking place. This can be interpreted as there being zero transaction costs associated with imperfect information, or that there is a sufficiently large number of trades so that any trades undertaken prior to an equilibrium market price being established (and this price becoming universally known) are insignificant relative to the total amount of trading. With thin markets this is an unrealistic and misleading assumption that would undoubtedly have resulted in the potential efficiency gains of market reforms being overestimated. Market institutions may be the best of a range of possible institutional structures for re-allocation of water entitlements. However, there is a strong implication that market reforms have been made more on the basis of faith in the efficiency of allocations arising under market institutions rather than rigorous analysis of potential gains from trade in the presence of transaction costs.

This chapter has thus demonstrated the importance of transaction costs in affecting outcomes arising under a particular institutional structure for utilising a resource. In Chapter 5, the static transaction costs of decision making for resource allocation will be shown to be a major factor, together with dynamic transaction costs, influencing the development of institutions for resource allocation. Later in Chapter 7, consideration of static transaction costs will be incorporated into a generic policy problem for institutional choice.

NOTES

1. As the water licence is attached to a particular parcel of land, a mortgager has an interest in ensuring that the water entitlement pertaining to the mortgaged land parcel is not diminished.
2. In some water markets of the western USA, practices have been implemented to collect and distribute information on water prices, including computerised trading information. This would

be expected to reduce transaction costs and price dispersion. To the knowledge of the author there have been no studies examining such effects.

Notes on the Regression (Table 4.3)

Summary Statistics and Diagnostic Tests (Regression of Untransformed Data)

$R^2 = 0.64$
F-Statistic: $F_{18,159} = 15.57$ (p = <0.001)
Durbin–Watson Statistic = 1.89
Lagrange Multiplier Test of Serial Correlation: $F_{1,158} = 0.522$ (p = 0.471)
Ramsey's Reset Test of Functional Form: $F_{1,158} = 6.12$ (p = 0.014)
Heteroscedasticity Test (based on regression of squared residuals on squared fitted values):
$F_{1,176} = 4.98$ (p = 0.027)

Summary Statistics and Diagnostic Tests (Regression of Transformed Data*)

Durbin–Watson Statistic = 1.90
Lagrange Multiplier Test of Serial Correlation: $F_{1,158} = 0.429$ (p = 0.514)
Ramsey's Reset Test of Functional Form: $F_{1,158} = 0.392$ (p = 0.532)
Heteroscedasticity Test (based on regression of squared residuals on squared fitted values):
$F_{1,176} = 0.344$ (p = 0.558)

5.   Transaction Costs and Institutional Change

INTRODUCTION

In Chapter 3, contemporary institutions of water allocation for two case-study areas in the Murray–Darling Basin were described using a static model of institutional hierarchies. This examination demonstrated that multiple regimes of property rights and associated institutions may exist simultaneously. As a consequence, assessing the performance of institutions may need to consider more than just single choices between alternative property-right regimes and allocation mechanisms. Assessment should consider the allocation of decision-making powers across levels of an institutional hierarchy. In Chapter 4, it was demonstrated that static transaction costs have a significant impact on the functioning of allocative mechanisms arising within a particular level of an institutional hierarchy, in this case the market institutions for allocation of water between private water users at the lowest level of an institutional hierarchy for use of water in irrigation. It is reasonable to extrapolate from this analysis of transaction costs in water markets to conclude that static transaction costs are an important consideration in determining the allocation of property rights across levels of institutional hierarchies and selecting institutions for resource allocation and re-allocation.

The objective of this chapter is to extend the examination of institutions to include an intertemporal dimension and assess the importance of dynamic transaction costs in decisions for institutional change. Dynamic transaction costs were previously defined as the costs arising in the transition from one institutional structure to another. In this chapter, these costs will be generally referred to as transition costs.

To assess the importance of transition costs in institutional change, the dynamic model of institutional change developed in Chapter 2 is used to examine historical changes in the formal institutions of water allocation for irrigated agriculture in the Murray–Darling Basin of eastern Australia. This examination traces the development of institutions from origins in English common law to the structure that existed as of 1997. The major changes in institutions are considered in terms of the demands for institutional change, reflecting desires to reduce static transaction costs, and the supply of new institutions that is constrained by transition costs.

The chapter is organised as follows. Firstly, the conceptual model of institutional change developed in Chapter 2 is revisited and described in the context of water use in the Murray–Darling Basin. Secondly, the model is used to analyse the dynamics of the major changes in institutions of water use from nineteenth-century origins in English common law to 1997. Particular emphasis is placed on the influences of static and dynamic transaction costs in the demand for, and supply of, institutional change. Finally, general observations and conclusions are made as to the incremental nature of institutional change, the path-dependency of change, and implications for assessing the merits of alternative institutional structures.

REVISITING THE CONCEPTUAL MODEL OF INSTITUTIONAL CHANGE

The model of institutional change described in Chapter 2 was based on the work of North (1990) and presented institutional change as arising from the individual behaviour of 'private entrepreneurs' and 'political entrepreneurs'. These agents of institutional change endeavour to increase their rewards by altering an institutional structure at the margin. A slightly respecified model that is better suited to the analysis of institutions of water regulation is presented in Figure 5.1 and described below.

The model describes institutional change as a process of interaction between two entities: economic entrepreneurs and political entrepreneurs. The original model developed in Chapter 2 also included private and political collectives in the process of institutional change. For the sake of simplicity these collectives have been dropped from the model, but can be considered as being included in the 'black boxes' of economic and political entrepreneurs. The contribution of collectives is undoubtedly important in institutional change (Campos, 1989) but their inclusion in the model does not contribute greatly to the general understanding of institutional change that can be gained by consideration of static and dynamic transaction costs as two broad classes of costs.

The economic and political entrepreneurs are defined in a very broad sense as classes of persons or collective groups at different levels in an institutional hierarchy. Generally speaking, agents that hold property rights at one level of a hierarchy have decision-making power over the institutions that regulate behaviour of the agents at the immediately subordinate level of the hierarchy. For the purposes of this model, the agents with the decision-making power over institutional change are the 'political entrepreneurs' and the agents subject to the institutional change are the 'economic entrepreneurs'.

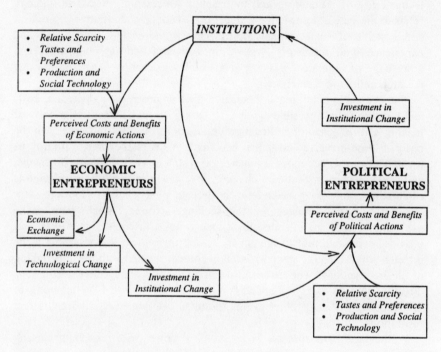

Figure 5.1: Conceptual Model of Institutional Change

By these definitions, the classification of agents at a particular level of an institutional hierarchy as economic or political entrepreneurs will vary according to the particular subset of institutions being examined. For example, in considering the institutions affecting water use by private water users within a group irrigation scheme, the private water users are the economic entrepreneurs and members of the management board of the group (that may comprise a collective of all individual water users or their elected representatives) are the political entrepreneurs. However, when considering the institutions affecting water use by group irrigation schemes, the members of the management board of the group are the economic entrepreneurs and members of the state government are the political entrepreneurs.

The environment faced by the economic entrepreneurs comprises existing institutions, the entrepreneurs' tastes and preferences, and the states of production technology and social technology. Existing institutions would include laws and regulations of water use including property rights, entitlement systems, allocation mechanisms, and the 'constitutional' rules that define the processes for changing institutions. Production technology refers to the available means of water storage, diversion and use, as well as technologies of monitoring and information processing. Social technology refers to the state of knowledge with respect to possible alternative institutions and systems of social organisation. This would include knowledge and experience with regulatory systems in Australia and internationally, and knowledge of regulatory systems and social organisation generated through research in the social sciences.

The economic entrepreneurs perceive their environment as potential costs and benefits for all possible actions, including the static transaction costs of making and implementing allocation decisions for a water resource. On the basis of these perceived costs and benefits they undertake actions from three broad categories: economic exchange; investment in technological change; and investment in institutional change. Investment in institutional change is essentially rent-seeking behaviour, as defined by Nicholson (1995 p. 846): 'economic agents engage in rent-seeking activities when they make expenditures that are intended to influence political choices in a way that provides economic rent to the agent'. Such investment is considered to be directed at reducing the static transaction costs associated with the undertaking of desired actions. The economic entrepreneurs cannot alter institutions directly, but can exert a demand for institutional change by attempting to influence behaviour of other agents (political entrepreneurs) who can affect institutions.

Political entrepreneurs are in positions of power with respect to altering institutions. This power arises from their participation in the governing collectives that determine and administer institutions. In the context of regulation of water resources for irrigated agriculture in the Murray–Darling Basin, these collectives may comprise the Murray–Darling Basin Commission, state governments, and the management boards or trusts of collective irrigation schemes. Again, the designation of a political entrepreneur very much depends on the particular institution or institutional change being considered. The political entrepreneurs maximise some form of objective function by investing effort in the relevant political collective to achieve or prevent institutional change.

The environment faced by political entrepreneurs comprises existing institutions that define permissible political actions, tastes and preferences, states of production technology and social technology, and the investment by economic entrepreneurs in institutional change. As with the economic entrepreneurs, the environment is perceived as a set of costs and benefits of all possible actions. Costs arise through transition costs incurred in assessment of alternatives, processes of decision making, and political costs. Benefits arise through the political benefits of meeting the demands for institutional change of the economic entrepreneurs or through satisfying the political entrepreneurs' own preferences in regard to institutional structures and resource allocations. On the basis of these costs and benefits the political entrepreneurs make choices with respect to investing effort in institutional change.

In terms of a demand and supply model of institutional change, demand for institutional change can arise from either economic or political entrepreneurs when either of these agents perceive a potential for net benefits from investment in institutional change. In the event that demand arises from the economic entrepreneurs, the demand would be expressed as investment of resources in activities to alter the perceived costs and benefits of political entrepreneurs through voting processes or forms of lobbying.

Demand for institutional change implies the existence of benefits to the political entrepreneurs in supplying change. However, whether a demand for change actually results in a corresponding supply depends also upon the transition costs of institutional change. Transition costs are the costs incurred by political entrepreneurs as a result of their participation in a governing collective, and the effect on processes of decision making of factors such as the unequal distribution of costs and benefits of institutional change, public-goods problems, and collective-action dilemmas in institutional supply.

The following section uses this model of institutional change to examine major developments in institutions for regulation of water use in the New South Wales and South Australian sections of the Murray–Darling Basin.

INSTITUTIONAL DEVELOPMENT FOR ALLOCATION OF WATER RESOURCES IN THE MURRAY–DARLING BASIN

Principal Developments in Institutions

With British settlement of Australia in the eighteenth and nineteenth centuries, English law provided an initial structure of formal institutions for social organisation. This included laws for the allocation of natural resources. In the case of water resources, the imported English law comprised common law for the allocation of groundwater and surface water, incorporating principles of 'non-regulation' for groundwater resources, and of riparian rights for surface-water resources (Bartlett, 1995). With Australia being a much drier land mass than Britain and there being correspondingly greater relative scarcity of water resources, these principles became manifestly inadequate in the nineteenth century and governments (colonial and later state and commonwealth) reacted by replacing common law with legislation.

The development of regulatory institutions for water resources of the Murray–Darling Basin commenced under colonial governments in the latter half of the nineteenth century with the enactment of specific water-resources legislation. In the initial stages of institutional development the primary issue of concern was allocating water amongst private users rather than allocation to each of the colonies. The problem of the latter was to arise in the late nineteenth and early twentieth centuries as increasing diversion of water resources threatened river navigability and water supplies in the downstream state of South Australia. A demand consequently arose for institutions to allocate water resources between states and coordinate management of the resources. Also in the early twentieth century, development of large-scale off-stream irrigation schemes commenced and new institutional structures became necessary for management of these schemes. The latter half of the twentieth century witnessed increased resource scarcity and competition for resource access. This, together with emerging environmental constraints on irrigated agriculture, particularly salinity problems, resulted in demands for institutional innovation to promote efficiency in resource use.

The principal stages in development of institutions to meet the above demands and requirements were as follows, listed in approximate chronological order.

- Eighteenth and nineteenth centuries: importation of English common law.
- Late nineteenth and early twentieth centuries: development of water-resources legislation by the colonies and correspondingly of state property rights and private property rights over these resources.
- Late nineteenth and early twentieth centuries: development of institutions for organisation of group irrigation schemes.
- Early twentieth century: development of institutions of common property over water resources amongst governments of the three states of New South Wales, Victoria and South Australia, and the Commonwealth.
- 1970s and 1980s: changes in the definition of water entitlements from input quota, usually specified in terms of land areas able to be irrigated, to volumetric resource quota.
- 1980s and 1990s: introduction of market institutions for the re-allocation of water entitlements.
- 1990s: transfer of property rights in group irrigation schemes from state governments to common-property organisations of irrigation farmers.

Each of these changes is examined in detail below using the conceptual models of institutional hierarchies and institutional change described earlier.

Common-Law Rights to Water

The importation of English common law was concomitant with European settlement of the Australian continent. There were two aspects of the common law that affected the property-right structure for water resources. The first was recognition under common law of private ownership in land, reflecting customs of land use in Britain at the time of settlement. Since land was therefore typically under private ownership and control, there was a demand for accompanying private rights to the use of water resources. This demand was reflected in the second important aspect of common law, that of the riparian doctrine whereby the common law assigned and protected rights to water of riparian landowners (Dragun and Gleeson, 1989; Bartlett, 1995).

The first post-colonisation institutional structure for the use of water resources of the Murray–Darling Basin can thus be represented by the institutional hierarchy shown in Figure 5.2. In this structure the physical resource was exploited within a regime of open access. The only recognised property rights in water were usufructory rights of riparian landholders for whom a private-property entitlement was defined in terms of ownership or occupancy of riparian land. Thus water entitlements were essentially defined as an input quota, with the input being land. Initial allocation of entitlements occurred by an administrative process whereby the entitlements were automatically allocated with ownership of land. Similarly, re-allocation of water entitlements was also by an administrative process whereby entitlements were transferred with changes in ownership or occupancy of the land.[1] Colonial governments had no formal powers over water allocation, although some state property rights existed in terms of the power of colonial governments to enforce the underlying riparian rights and the power, as later evident, to override the allocative principles of common law with legislation. In Figure 5.2, the ill-defined or weak property rights of the colonial governments are represented by a broken border to the box representing a state-property entity.

Water-Resources Legislation, State Property and Private Property

Historical context and demand for institutions
With increasing densities of land settlement in the Murray–Darling Basin in the nineteenth century, the riparian doctrine of common law became inadequate, or at least foreseeably inadequate, as an institutional structure for allocation of water resources. In particular, the riparian doctrine only allowed

for 'ordinary' use of water, meaning use for domestic and livestock purposes, and did not allow any riparian landowner to use water to the extent of 'sensibly diminishing' the natural flow of the surface-water stream (Dragun and Gleeson, 1989; Bartlett, 1995). Common law did not provide for allocation of water to parties remote from surface-water streams, and for allocating water for projects of wider public interest such as municipal use or irrigation (Bartlett, 1995).

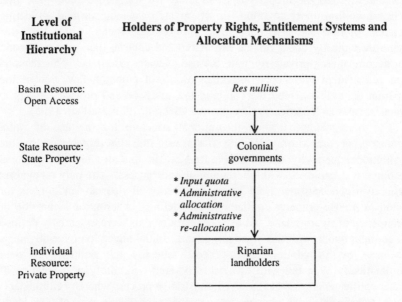

Figure 5.2: Institutional Hierarchy for Surface-Water Use in New South Wales and South Australia from Settlement to the 1880s

The history of water allocation in the western states of the USA indicates that institutions for water allocation to supplement the common law may develop regardless of whether or not governments take regulatory initiatives. In the USA, institutions for water allocation arose from riparian rights of English common law and from customs developed amongst resource users. The resulting institutions were later ratified by court decisions and legislation and included doctrines of prior appropriation, pueblo rights and acquisitive rights (Wilkinson, 1985; Attwater and Markle, 1988). These systems of rights have in common an underlying principle of 'first in time – first in right'. Such institutional developments can easily be accommodated within the conceptual model of institutional change. The owners and occupiers of land remote from surface-water streams (economic agents) demanded changes in the rules of water allocation that would enable them to gain rights of use. The judiciary recognised these demands as being consistent with concepts of social 'fairness', and the demands motivated political agents in state legislatures to react to perceived political benefits and supply these changes in water-resources law.

This path of institutional development did not occur in Australia. Instead of legislative recognition of several doctrines of private claims to property rights in water as in the USA, colonial governments in Australia replaced the common-law institutions with institutions of state property of water resources and institutions of allocation based on administrative decision by government agencies.

In the Australian situation, the process of institutional change from the origins in common law appears to have been driven mainly by political agents and their demand for institutional change, rather than demand for change by economic agents or water users. Clark (1982) attributes implementation of a system of state property rights to the initiatives of a politician of the Victorian colonial government, Alfred Deakin, and the Royal Commission on Water Supply which he chaired in Victoria in 1884 and 1885. As part of the Royal Commission, Deakin made a visit to the western states of the USA to investigate irrigation practices and the associated institutions of water allocation. He was unimpressed by the prior appropriation doctrine of allocation that had developed from customs of water users and in the absence of an interested state polity. Deakin considered the legal and administrative complexities of this system of judicial apportionment to cause unnecessarily high costs in settlement of disputes between claimants to water resources (Clark, 1982). In economic terms, this corresponds to an assessment that the system of water allocation in the USA involved excessively high static transaction costs in defining, adjudicating and altering property rights over water. For this reason and the envisaged impediments to government initiatives in development of irrigation industries, Deakin recommended that in Victoria the Crown should assume ownership and control of water resources and that the common-law riparian rights to water be abolished or greatly circumscribed by legislation (Deakin, 1884 pp. 71–2).

Supply of institutions

It ensued that the Victorian colonial government supplied institutions that met most of the recommendations of Deakin's Royal Commission. The Victorian Irrigation Act 1886 vested ownership of all water resources in the Crown, restricted rights pertaining to riparian landholders, and established the legislative foundations for administrative allocation of water to users. This legislative precedent added to the social technology of water-resources regulation and provided a model for development of similar legislation by other colonial and subsequently state governments in the late nineteenth and early twentieth centuries.

In developing institutions for the administrative allocation of water resources by the state, the Victorian government was essentially providing a public good to the other colonial governments that used the Victorian legislation as models for their own. That the 'public-good problem' of institutional supply did not arise in this circumstance indicates that the envisaged benefits of institutional development to Victoria exceeded the expected transition costs. Envisaged benefits were reductions in static transaction costs of water allocation and reduced costs of future government activity in developing irrigation schemes and settlement of rural areas. Transition costs in development of water-resources legislation would have been both the explicit costs of research and development of legislation and the implicit political transaction costs of developing and implementing the requisite legislation. Since there had been relatively little resource development prior to development of this regulatory system, political costs of implementation were low with respect to repercussions from confiscation of existing water rights of individuals that existed through common law or custom. This contrasts with the situation in the western states of the USA where a large amount of water-resource diversion and development of customs to allocate water had occurred prior to government involvement in regulation. Nevertheless, there were some potential political transaction costs in Victoria as evidenced by the new water laws not totally abolishing riparian rights, as recommended by Deakin; these rights were instead redefined and circumscribed in legislation.

The institutional changes occurring in New South Wales and South Australia followed the lead of Victoria. The introduction of colonial/state legislation for water resources resulted in augmentation of state property rights as well as changes to the private property rights existing for water, the systems of water entitlements and the institutions of resource allocation. These changes are summarised in a new institutional hierarchy shown in Figure 5.3 and described below.

Property rights
The enactment of water-resources legislation in the colonies and states augmented the state-property level in the institutional hierarchy. The colonial/state governments obtained greater decision-making power with respect to the disposition of water resources within their jurisdiction. Nevertheless, the state property rights over water resources in the Murray– Darling Basin still remained poorly defined since a regime of open access still existed for the entire resource. Consequently the state property rights are still denoted by a broken border in Figure 5.3.

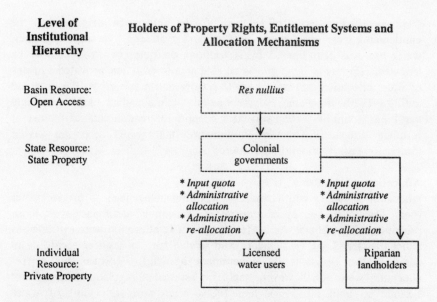

| Level of Institutional Hierarchy | Holders of Property Rights, Entitlement Systems and Allocation Mechanisms |

Basin Resource: Open Access — *Res nullius*

State Resource: State Property — Colonial governments

* Input quota
* Administrative allocation
* Administrative re-allocation

* Input quota
* Administrative allocation
* Administrative re-allocation

Individual Resource: Private Property — Licensed water users / Riparian landholders

Figure 5.3: Institutional Hierarchy for Surface-Water Use in New South Wales and South Australia after Introduction of Water-Resources Legislation

Water-resources legislation created a new form of private property right. The legislation was developed within an institutional context of private ownership of land and it is a likely consequence that there would have been demands from economic agents for private rights in water. Further, there appears also to have been a demand by political agents for private rights in water. In the first progress report to the Victorian Royal Commission on Water Supply, Deakin strongly recommended that ownership of water be associated with ownership of land to foster beneficial use of water resources and to avoid farmers being at the mercy of 'capitalist' owners and suppliers of irrigation water (Deakin, 1884 pp. 61–2). As a consequence of these demands, the administrative systems of water allocation recognised a second category of private rights in the form of licences to use water, issued by the regulatory agencies of the colonial/state governments. Private rights in the form of riparian rights continued to exist although now more rigorously defined and circumscribed in terms of the allowable uses of water.

Entitlements

Rights to the use of water were allocated by the government agencies in the form of an input quota. That is, the rights to water use for irrigation farmers were specified in terms of an area of land able to be irrigated and the entitlements were attached to specific parcels of land. In some instances, water use was also limited by restrictions on types of crops able to be irrigated. The use of input quotas on land area or crop type provided a means of water allocation that was cheap to specify and monitor. At the time and until the 1970s, the water resource was relatively abundant and it is unlikely that there would have been sufficient benefits to create a demand for use of resource quotas (volumetric entitlements) that would result in higher transaction costs in monitoring resource use.

Allocation mechanisms

Allocation of water entitlements by government agencies to private water users was undertaken by administrative decision in accordance with loose principles of 'beneficial use'. Mechanisms of re-allocation were restricted to either transfer of the entitlements with sale of land, or transfer according to administrative decisions by government agencies. Mechanisms of re-allocation were not, however, important aspects of regulation and did not become so until the 1970s and 1980s when new allocations of water effectively ceased. Recommendations for administrative mechanisms of allocation by Deakin's Royal Commission suggest that demand for administrative mechanisms of allocation was from political agents and was derived from desires for government control and coordination of the development of irrigated agriculture. Allocation of water entitlements has generally been a secondary consideration in government initiatives of resource development and social policy. In South Australia, the development of irrigation was primarily a tool of government policy for development of agricultural industries, settlement of unemployed persons during periods of economic depression, and post-war repatriation of ex-servicemen (Menzies and Gray, 1983 pp. 1–3). In the Murrumbidgee and Riverina regions of New South Wales, development of water resources occurred for similar reasons of industry development, closer settlement and drought protection (Bureau of Agricultural Economics, 1987 pp. 34–6).

Institutions of Organisation in Group Irrigation Schemes

Historical context and demand for institutions

There were two principal types of development of group irrigation organisations in the late nineteenth century and throughout the twentieth century: government-initiated schemes and privately initiated schemes.

The government schemes were established in accordance with government policies for agricultural development, closer settlement of inland areas, and soldier settlement after the two world wars. In South Australia, the schemes comprised government irrigation areas in both the Riverland and Lower Murray regions, developed from 1908 to the 1950s (Menzies and Gray, 1983 pp. 138, 162). Management boards with a majority of private water users were established, although the schemes remained administered and operated by government agencies, and executive powers were retained by the responsible government ministers. In New South Wales, the schemes comprised the irrigation areas and districts of the Murrumbidgee and Riverina regions. These schemes were totally managed and administered by government agencies until the 1980s when a process of institutional change commenced in both states with the objective of transferring ownership and/or control of the infrastructure for water distribution to irrigators. This institutional change is described in detail later in this chapter.

Private irrigation schemes were established by private organisations and investment, although in many cases their establishment was prompted by government initiative and substantial government sponsorship. In South Australia, a private irrigation scheme, the Renmark Irrigation Trust, comprised the first substantial irrigation development in the late 1880s and 1890s. Further private schemes developed concurrently with the government schemes. In New South Wales, private schemes developed concurrently with the government irrigation areas and districts from the 1920s to the 1960s.

For a short period during the 1890s there was a third form of group irrigation organisation: the 'village settlement schemes' in the South Australian Riverland region. These schemes were a colonial government initiative involving establishment of communal irrigation areas for the purposes of promoting settlement and relieving unemployment arising from the 1890s economic depression (Menzies and Gray, 1983 p. 180). Both land and water were communally organised and management was by an elected board (ibid.). The schemes were unsuccessful and by the early 1900s had been either incorporated into government irrigation areas or converted to irrigation trusts with private land and water entitlements (ibid. p.183).

The motivations for establishment of group irrigation schemes were government policies of inland settlement and the capture of economies of scale in the water-diversion and distribution infrastructure. In the Riverland region, the deeply incised nature of the river channel necessitated diversion of water from the river by pumping, initially by steam-powered and later by diesel- and electricity-powered pumps. The economies of scale captured in diversion of water to irrigation districts were necessary to enable provision of water at sufficiently low cost for use in irrigation, even though most irrigation development still occurred within close proximity to the river. Indeed, in the Riverland region the costs of diversion effectively prevented irrigation development other than by group schemes until the 1940s and 1950s, when the costs of lifting water from the river channel were reduced by advances in pump technology. In the Lower Murray region of South Australia, water diversion to group irrigation schemes involved government-funded drainage of swamplands and construction of gravity-fed channels. Government development provided finance and coordination of infrastructure development for drainage and water delivery. In New South Wales, the economic incentive for irrigation development in group schemes was also one of capturing economies of scale. For the government irrigation areas and districts the economies were in the provision of weirs for the diversion of water into gravity channels and in the provision of channels for the distribution of water to areas remote from the river channels. The smaller, private schemes were established to capture economies of scale in diversion of water by pumping and distribution to non-riparian land.

With the development of the group irrigation schemes there was an associated demand for institutions for management of group infrastructure. There is no clear information in the literature as to the demands for institutions. Nevertheless, two important factors in demand for institutions can be surmised. Firstly, for the government irrigation schemes there was probably a demand amongst the political entrepreneurs of state governments to maintain decision-making power over publicly owned assets of irrigation infrastructure. This corresponds to a demand for institutions that minimise the static transaction costs of government decision making with respect to the use of this infrastructure. Secondly, for the private irrigation schemes there would have been a demand for management institutions that minimised the transaction costs of collective investment in infrastructure and subsequent management.

Supply of institutions
For the group irrigation schemes, developers and management boards or agencies would have to contend with the potentially high transaction costs associated with problems of collective action. The establishment and maintenance of group irrigation organisations require development of institutional rules including those for general management, securing an exclusive water supply; allocation of water to individual users; development, management and maintenance of infrastructure; administration and provision of services of water supply; monitoring and enforcement to ensure compliance with group rules; and sharing of costs for these activities. As previously described in Chapter 2, the development of institutions for collective action poses a second-order dilemma with a lack of incentive for individuals to invest in the development of institutions that have characteristics of a public good amongst the participants within an irrigation scheme. Ostrom (1990) provided several empirical examples of institutional innovation by groups sharing a

water resource which demonstrate that the development of institutions can involve high costs that may discourage voluntary supply.

In establishing the group irrigation schemes of South Australia and New South Wales, there were two factors that enabled the problem of potentially high transition costs in institutional supply to be overcome. Firstly, institutional supply was undertaken by colonial or state governments, either entirely in the case of government irrigation areas and districts, or at least in large part for privately organised groups. For the government irrigation areas institutional supply occurred though legislation. The unilateral decision-making powers of governments would have made the transition costs of such institutional change relatively inexpensive. For privately organised groups, institutions for the administrative functioning of the groups were established by public investment through legislation enabling creation of irrigation trusts and private irrigation authorities. Secondly, in almost all cases, institutions of group operation were developed and implemented prior to development of irrigation and water-distribution schemes. Thus the development and implementation of new institutions was not impeded by opposition arising from vested interests in a *status quo* institutional structure.

From a perspective of a transaction-cost analysis of institution supply, the supply of institutions for group schemes by the state governments represents a subsidy to the groups that reduces the transition costs incurred by these groups in developing and enforcing institutions for collective action. Other case studies of institution supply for group cooperation in use of water resources have suggested that transition costs can be a significant barrier to development of institutions for collective action. Reliance on private investment for supply can greatly slow the rate of innovation in institutions as well as limit chances of success in group cooperation (Ostrom, 1990).

The institutional innovations associated with the development of irrigation schemes were common property in water entitlements and irrigation infrastructure and a new form of private property in water: the entitlements held by individual irrigators within the schemes. These new property rights were associated with new institutions of entitlements, allocation and re-allocation. These changes are summarised in the new institutional hierarchy shown in Figure 5.4 and described below.

Property rights

There were three general types of property-right structures created for the operation of group irrigation schemes: (i) private trusts and private water authorities as with the Renmark Irrigation Trust and private developments in both South Australia and New South Wales; (ii) common property in the government irrigation areas of South Australia; and (iii) state property in the irrigation areas and districts of New South Wales. The common-property or state agencies held property rights in the water entitlement of the group, these rights being either *de jure* or *de facto*. *De jure* rights existed with some private trusts and private authorities where the management agency of the group held a water entitlement issued by the state government. *De facto* rights existed where the management agency held decision-making power over the water through control of distribution infrastructure and rights to withhold supply to individual irrigators under certain circumstances such as inadequate water supply, failure to pay rates and charges, or failure to meet drainage requirements in water use.

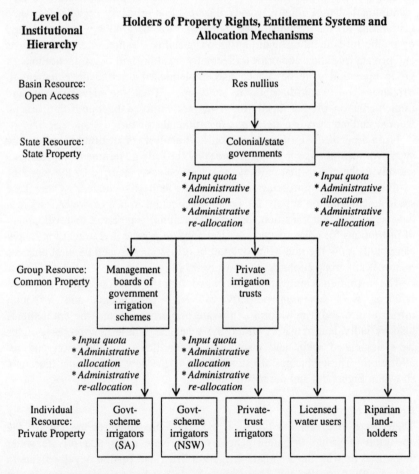

Figure 5.4: Institutional Hierarchy for Surface-Water Use in New South Wales and South Australia after Development of Private and Common-Property Irrigation Schemes

Development of group irrigation schemes also resulted in creation of new types of private property for the irrigation farmers within these schemes. These rights provided an entitlement to water use, although this was highly attenuated compared with the property rights of irrigators outside the group schemes. Regulations at the level of group management constrained activities for which water could be used; the conditions of water use, such as drainage requirements; and the transfer of water entitlements between farmers or plots of farmland.

The importance of transaction costs in institutional choice can be seen in two aspects of the institutional innovations associated with group irrigation schemes.

Firstly, with the primary incentive for formation of group organisations being that of economies of scale in provision of infrastructure for water diversion and distribution, the question can be asked why in many cases was there was a demand for institutions granting group organisations property rights over water entitlements as well as the distribution infrastructure. A possible answer can be drawn from Dahlman's (1980) study of common property in the feudal system of land tenure in Europe. Dahlman suggested that common property over grazing land was necessary to prevent individual graziers removing their 'share' of the land from the system of common usage and thus imposing costs on other graziers. The same rationale may provide motivation for group ownership of a water entitlement, that is, an ability to use the powers pertaining to the common property right to control behaviour of individual irrigators within an irrigation system, and prevent individuals imposing costs on remaining irrigators. This corresponds to a minimisation of static transaction costs in making and implementing collective decisions that are not always Pareto-efficient and may at times impose costs on individuals within the groups.

Secondly, why were there three different types of property-right regimes for group irrigation schemes: common property, a mix of common and state property, and state property? Possible answers can be provided by the circumstances in which each developed and the institutional choices made to minimise static transaction costs and transition costs.

The first irrigation schemes of significant scale were developed by private interests with the ultimate intent of developing into common-property organisations. These schemes were those occurring at Renmark in South Australia, later the Renmark Irrigation Trust, and a similar scheme developed at Mildura in Victoria. This form of development has been interpreted by Menzies and Gray (1983 p. 61) to be a response to a lack of production and social technology in Australia for large-scale irrigation developments. The lack of technology was explicitly recognised by the Victorian Royal

Commission on Water Supply and prompted the Chairman of the Royal Commission, Alfred Deakin, to undertake a tour of the western states of the USA to examine large-scale irrigation developments (Deakin, 1884 p. 5).

From the study of irrigation developments in the USA, Deakin proposed private development of irrigation schemes with institutional support provided by the state (Deakin, 1884 p. 63). Deakin encouraged two developers of irrigation settlements in southern California to come to Victoria for the purpose of establishing similar group schemes. George and William Chaffey brought with them the social technology of group irrigation settlements as well as pumping and agricultural technology. The Chaffey brothers developed the irrigation settlements at Renmark in South Australia and Mildura in Victoria, both at the encouragement of the relevant colonial governments. The governments provided land concessions and a legislative basis for development, and the developers provided financial investment in land subdivision, infrastructure and initial operation. Farms were sold to private farmers, with the intent of passing of control of the settlement to the irrigators after sale of all farms. For the Renmark Irrigation Trust, development of the common-property organisation developed after financial failure of the original private enterprise of the Chaffey brothers, and development in this form was an outcome of joint decision making by the colonial government and the farmers of the scheme (Menzies and Gray, 1983 p. 178).

The processes for establishment of the Renmark and Mildura irrigation schemes contributed in two ways to minimising transition costs in development of institutions for collective management. Firstly, social technology imported from the USA provided precedents for new institutional structures. The existence of institutional precedents has been demonstrated in other studies to be highly important in reducing costs of institutional development and change (Ostrom, 1990). Secondly, the establishment of the irrigation schemes by a private corporation with later transfer of property rights to a collective of irrigators allowed the institutions of collective action to be established by unilateral decisions of the corporation. As a consequence, the transition costs of institutional development would have been far lower than they may have been if the development had been undertaken by a collective of the irrigation farmers involved in the schemes.

Later development of irrigation schemes within organisation structures of common property occurred under similar principles of governments providing institutional support for private investment. The institutional support provided powers to developers for developing infrastructure, such as powers to obtain easements for water conveyance over private lands, and also the institutions for organisation of ownership and management. As already mentioned above, government support in this manner constitutes a subsidisation of the transition costs of institutional development.

Despite the potential for the private irrigation schemes to minimise transaction costs associated with institutional innovation, the development of irrigation schemes in South Australia that were organised as a mix of common property and state property occurred as a result of perceived inadequacies of purely private investment for group schemes. The perceived inadequacies related principally to inadequate investment in infrastructure. The government resolved this problem by developing infrastructure through public investment. The government then retained an interest and executive powers in subsequent ownership and management, although irrigator management boards were established for involvement of irrigators in management decisions for the schemes. This process of development would have had similar advantages to a private-investment model for irrigation schemes in so far as transition costs for development of the necessary institutions were minimised. In the case of the government schemes, the requirements for new institutions were small as the schemes remained predominantly within the existing regime of state property rights.

The development of purely state-controlled irrigation schemes in New South Wales is more difficult to interpret, but may be due simply to a lack of demand for, and supply of, institutions of common property arising from either a lack of perceived advantages of collective management, or high transition costs of changing institutions from state property to private property. The irrigation schemes were developed by public investment in response to political objectives of inland development. Strong government control over land tenure was initiated and maintained in response to these objectives (Bureau of Agricultural Economics, 1987 p. 36). Maintenance of state control over infrastructure could be associated with the pursuit of these political objectives rather than economic objects of efficiency (low static transaction costs) in management of irrigation infrastructure. Also, the development of large-scale irrigation schemes in New South Wales lacked precedents of irrigator ownership and control of infrastructure that had been available and were promoted in Victoria and South Australia. Transition costs in development of common-property institutions may therefore have appeared higher. Common property rights were, however, developed for these in the 1980s and 1990s. These institutional changes are examined later in this chapter.

Entitlements and allocation mechanisms
The institutions of entitlements, allocation and re-allocation established for the group irrigation schemes and for the individual water users within the schemes were similar to the institutions for providing water rights to individual water users, already described above. That is, entitlements in the form of input quotas defined in terms of land area; allocation based on administrative

decision in association with allocation of land; and provisions for administrative re-allocation of entitlements under certain circumstances. Demands for these forms of institutions would have had the same origins as for the institutions for individual water users: ease of defining entitlements in terms of irrigable land areas, and the primary goal of allocation being political objectives of settlement and agricultural development.

Interstate Common Property

Historical context and demand for institutions

With the growth of actual and planned diversion of water resources from the River Murray in the late nineteenth century, demand came from South Australia and to a lesser extent from Victoria for an agreement between the three colonies of New South Wales, South Australia and Victoria in regard to sharing of the water resources. The environment within which Victoria and South Australia were pressing for institutions of interstate water allocation had the following characteristics.

- Historical and immutable establishment of colonial boundaries which caused the River Murray Basin to occur within multiple jurisdictions.
- Existing vesting of property in water resources in the colonies prior to federation in 1901, strengthened by colonial water-resources legislation vesting water resources in the Crown under control of the colonial governments.

Given this environment, there were three options for property-right regimes over the water resource of the River Murray: the *status quo* of open access of each colony/state to the resource; management as common property between the states; or legislative intervention by the emerging Commonwealth government to override the property interests of the states. The regime that emerged was one of common property between the three states and the Commonwealth through the first River Murray Waters Agreement of 1914.

The positions of each state in respect of institutions for sharing of water resources were as follows (Clark, 1971a).

- A claim by South Australia to maintain navigability in the River Murray itself and major tributaries in New South Wales, and to that end to prevent diversion by Victoria of water from non-navigable tributaries.
- A claim from Victoria, as the first colony to realise and exploit the advantages of irrigation, to a right to divert water from the upper Murray and all tributaries within its state boundaries.

- A claim by New South Wales, based on territorial rights declared by the British Imperial Parliament, to the exclusive use of waters in the River Murray above the South Australian border and in its territorial tributaries, with no regard to the claims of Victoria and South Australia.

The demands for institutions of water allocation and regulation changed over time. In the early part of the twentieth century South Australia's claims to water shifted to a focus on irrigation as a result of the demise of river transport associated with the expansion of railways.

The starting-point for the development of institutions was the absence of any principles for sharing of water resources between political jurisdictions, and uncertainty of existing law, particularly on the following two issues (Clark, 1983).

- An imperial law of 1855 established the New South Wales–Victoria border on the Victorian side of the River Murray. This created a *prima facie* case for New South Wales having jurisdiction over the water resources of the River Murray. In practice, however, the border and hence rights over water were imperfectly defined. Uncertainty existed over whether the bank of the River Murray on the Victorian side was part of New South Wales or Victoria, and over the location of the boundary where the river did not flow within defined banks.
- Legal uncertainty existed over applicability of common-law riparian rights to colonial/state governments.

Supply of institutions
A historical characteristic of the River Murray Waters Agreement and subsequently the Murray–Darling Basin Agreement has been the extreme slowness in development of agreements and institutions that address the concerns of the states, particularly the downstream state of South Australia. Principal efforts to secure supply of institutions were as follows.

- Intercolonial conferences were held in 1857, 1863 and 1865 but no agreements on rights to water and regulation of the watercourses were reached (Clark, 1971a).
- An 1885 agreement between New South Wales and Victoria that entitled each of the two colonies to make full use of waters of tributaries in each respective colony and to entitle each state to a half-share in the waters of the Murray. South Australia was excluded from the agreement (Clark, 1971a).
- Convention debates for federation in the 1890s, and consideration of a prospective role for the Commonwealth (Clark, 1983).

- Development of a negotiated agreement between the three states in the early twentieth century.

Access to water of the River Murray by the three states of New South Wales, Victoria and South Australia was one of the principal intercolonial issues that gave impetus to the federation movement in the late eighteenth century and federation was seen, particularly by the downstream state of South Australia, as a means of resolving the issue (Clark, 1983). The commonwealth government did not, however, gain legislative powers over the river and the allocation of water. To the contrary, a clause of the Australian constitution (Section 100) limited the right of the Commonwealth to enact legislation which removed power for water regulation from the states: 'The Commonwealth shall not, by any law or regulation of trade or commerce, abridge the right of a State or of the residents therein to the reasonable use of the waters of rivers for conservation or irrigation'. The absence of commonwealth intervention has been interpreted as being a result of an already established Australian political paradigm of state parochialism and jealous guarding of sovereignty by New South Wales and Victoria (Crabb, 1988 p. 2).

In the absence of overriding commonwealth legislation, the options for property rights to the water resources of the Murray–Darling Basin were either a regime of common property brought about by voluntary agreement, or a condition of open access. In 1902 some movement was made towards developing an agreement, when the three states participated in a joint Royal Commission investigating the legal basis of claim to water (Clark, 1971a). Interstate negotiations continued after this, but it was not until 1914 that the River Murray Waters Agreement was created. Development of the agreement after 1914 to address concerns over water quality and other issues continued to be slow and it was not until the 1980s that amendments to the agreement directly addressed issues of water quality and environment quality (Crabb, 1988 p. 3).

The slow rate of institutional development suggests a problem of institutional supply arising from a lack of incentives for the negotiating states to invest in and commit to institutional change. There are three general factors that may have contributed to this situation through creating high transition costs of institutional change.

i. The absence of any overlying institutions to state property in the water, such as commonwealth water law, that could compel or impose an agreement and consequently the need for any agreement to be created by voluntary and unanimous decision of the three state governments. As a result, development of institutions for collective action between the states was hampered by collective-action dilemmas and commitment problems.

ii. A lack of institutional precedents for agreements over interjurisdictional rights to water resources. Successive versions of the River Murray Waters Agreement and the subsequent Murray–Darling Basin Agreement have generally been abreast with, or more advanced than, similar interstate agreements elsewhere in the world, such as in Canada and the USA (Crabb, 1988 p. 21). As a consequence, institutions have generally had to be designed from scratch and initial negotiating positions of the states may have been more divergent than would have been the case if precedents had been available.

iii. The benefits and costs of implementing new institutions were unevenly distributed between the three states. Whilst the development of institutions for management of the Murray–Darling Basin may have improved the welfare of the three states in total, the benefits have accrued disproportionately to the downstream state of South Australia and opportunity costs disproportionately to upstream states of New South Wales and Victoria.

The three factors of a lack of supporting institutions, a lack of institutional precedents and uneven distribution of costs and benefits have been highlighted as impediments to institutional change in many other situations of common property (Ostrom, 1990).

Given these impediments to development of institutions, the history of development of the Murray–Darling Basin Agreement can be seen as a process constrained by existing institutions of state sovereignty, and where advances in institutional development occurred in response to 'threats' to the upstream states that altered the envisaged costs and benefits of institutional change and provided a basis for negotiation. After the upstream states of New South Wales and Victoria held out against formalising property rights to water of the River Murray until the early 1900s, there were two possible factors that provided impetus for a political agreement. First, in 1904 the Prime Minister suggested that the Commonwealth might act when the states were asked whether they would hand over control of the Murray to the commonwealth government (Clark, 1983). Second, South Australia commenced preparations for litigation against New South Wales and Victoria with regard to maintaining the navigability of the river (ibid.). The result was negotiations for a political solution that led to proposals for water sharing in 1906 and eventually to the first River Murray Waters Agreement in 1914 and the associated rules for water allocation between the three states (Clark, 1971b, 1983). Further threats of litigation by South Australia in the 1950s and 1970s provided the impetus for 1959 and 1981 amendments to the agreement that provided South Australia with a greater share of water and introduced powers for the interstate management agency (then the River Murray Commission and subsequently the Murray–Darling Basin Commission) to manage water quality in the South Australian section of the river (Clark, 1983).

The need for coercion of some parties to enable an agreement to be reached that improves the welfare of the group in total is consistent with theoretical studies of the economics of group behaviour. Mancur Olson in his seminal study *The Logic of Collective Action* (1971) demonstrated a proposition that 'unless the number of individuals is quite small, or unless there is coercion or some other special device to make people act in their common interest, rational, self interested individuals will not act to achieve their common or group interests' (Olson, 1971 p. 2). In the typical circumstances of common-pool resources, all individuals will benefit by appropriate collective action, but if a limited number of individuals free-ride on the collective action of all others, then these individuals will benefit more by so doing at the expense of the others. 'Coercion or some other special device' is needed to negate the incentive for free-riding. The problem of interstate allocation of water resources is somewhat different from this in so far as collective action and maximising the welfare of all states typically involves a redistribution of benefits away from upstream states and towards downstream states. A mechanism is required to force or induce the upstream states to make these sacrifices, such as a capacity of the potential losers under open access to impose penalties on other parties if a common-property regime is not implemented. In this case, threats of litigation from South Australia introduced the possibility of high costs being imposed on New South Wales and Victoria. The inability of South Australia to make similar and credible threats against Queensland may at least partially explain why Queensland has never been party to the Murray–Darling Basin Agreement.

Further amendments to the interstate agreement were made in 1982, 1987, 1990 and 1992. The amendments broadened the scope of the agreement to include the New South Wales section of the Darling River Basin and to widen the charter of the interstate managing agency with respect to water quality and management of land and environmental resources. Unlike the 1959 and 1981 amendments, however, it appears that the later amendments were made at least partly in response to emerging 'moral standards' in management of river basins (Crabb, 1988 pp. 1–2). In terms of the model of institutional change, this can be considered as a change in tastes and preferences of economic and political agents that drives institutional change. Crabb (1988 pp. 1–2) refers to the following changes in the moral standards underlying institutional change: principles of the river basin being the basic hydrological unit of management; of no state having claim to exclusive access to waters of an interstate river basin; of individual states being entitled to reasonable and equitable participation in control and apportionment of the resource; of protection and non-abuse of the resource; and acknowledging interrelationships of the water resource and other natural resources (Crabb, 1988 pp. 1–2).

The factors contributing to the development and continuance of the Murray–Darling Basin Agreement can thus be summarised and interpreted in terms of transaction costs as follows.

- The development of institutions of interstate water allocation was hampered by high transition costs arising from collective-action dilemmas and the absence of institutional precedents.
- Institutions of common property between the three states and the Commonwealth were only developed once the threats of litigation by South Australia and intervention by the Commonwealth made institutional change inevitable. The path of institutional change ultimately selected (interstate common property) was that commonly perceived by all the three states to have the lowest transition costs both in terms of forming an agreement and minimising uncertainty over the institutional outcome.
- Despite development of the common-property institutions, the static transaction costs incurred in making resource allocation decisions between the states, and the transition costs in modifying the common-property institutions, have remained high and resulted in very slow processes of decision making and institutional reform.

The institutional changes bought about by development of the River Murray Waters Agreement are indicated in Figure 5.5 and summarised below.

Property rights

The principal change to property rights resulting from development of the River Murray Waters Agreement was the instigation of common property at the first level of the institutional hierarchy. The initial agreement assigned decision-making power over water resources of the River Murray jointly to the commonwealth government and the state governments of New South Wales, Victoria and South Australia. Subsequent developments of the agreement have extended the joint decision-making power to issues of land management within the Murray–Darling Basin.

The organisation through which the joint decision-making power is exercised is the Murray–Darling Basin Ministerial Council consisting of up to three ministers 'who have primary responsibility for matters relating to water, land and environment' from each of the participating state governments and from the commonwealth government (Murray–Darling Basin Agreement 1992, Clause 3). Resolutions of the Council require unanimous agreement of participating ministers (Clause 12(3)). Unanimity rules may contribute to high static transaction costs in group decision making (Buchanan and Tullock, 1962), but such a rule may have been necessary to reduce the transition costs associated with developing the common-property institutions.

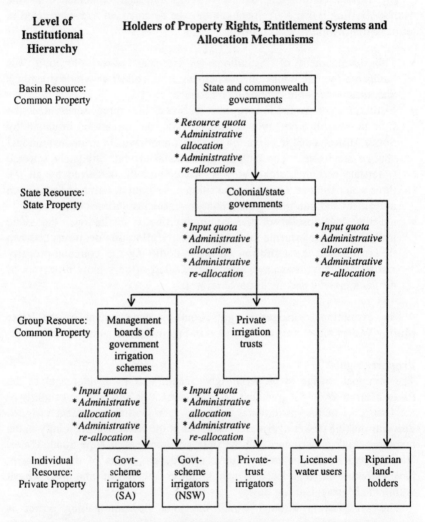

| Level of Institutional Hierarchy | Holders of Property Rights, Entitlement Systems and Allocation Mechanisms |

Figure 5.5: Institutional Hierarchy for Surface-Water Use in New South Wales and South Australia after Development of the River Murray Waters Agreement

A secondary change in property rights arising from the interstate agreement was strengthening of property rights held by the states, particularly of Victoria and South Australia. The agreement defined shares in the resource for each state and thus increased the powers of the states to make decisions of water allocation without the exercise of these decisions being subject to the actions of the other states.

Entitlement system
At the top level of both the institutional hierarchies, the River Murray Waters Agreement and subsequently the Murray–Darling Basin Agreement and other interstate agreements specified entitlements to water for each of the states of Queensland, New South Wales, Victoria and South Australia. The principal features of entitlement systems established by the Murray–Darling Basin Agreement have already been described in Chapter 3. The entitlements are all resource quotas, directly specifying an entitlement to the water resource in terms of either annual volumes of water or proportional shares in the available resource based on rights to water flows from particular areas of the basin. The use of resource quotas is envisaged to minimise the static transaction costs of specifying entitlements and monitoring compliance due to the relative ease of specifying shares in the resource within the context of low requirements for accuracy in measurement, and a consistent calculus for measuring and comparing resource use. Monitoring shares of the states initially required only coarse estimates of use in various regions of the basin and estimates of river flows at a few locations in major river channels. This monitoring has become progressively more refined as computer technology has allowed detailed modelling of water flows within the basin and as entitlements to consumptive water use became specified as resource quota.

Allocation mechanisms
The initial distribution of water entitlements between states was determined by negotiations between the state governments of Victoria, South Australia and New South Wales and the commonwealth government leading up to the first River Murray Waters Agreement. Subsequent re-allocations also occurred by negotiated decision, particularly with respect to increasing South Australia's entitlement in the 1950s. This constitutes a process of administrative allocation, with the principal factor influencing the decision being the negotiating power of each state.

Introduction of Volumetric Water Entitlements

Historical context and demand for institutions
At the state-property level of the institutional hierarchy, the entitlement systems for water allocation have remained unchanged since establishment through the River Murray Waters Agreement, that is, resource quotas in the

form of proportional shares or quantified volumetric entitlements. The entitlement systems below the level of state property have undergone substantial change. Up until the 1970s, entitlement systems were almost entirely based on input quotas in the form of limits on areas of land and types of crops that could be irrigated, either by entire irrigation groups, or by individual irrigators. In the 1970s and early 1980s, systems of resource quotas were implemented for water entitlements of both groups and individuals, other than holders of riparian rights. The resource quotas comprised quantified volumetric or proportional-share entitlements.

The choice of entitlement systems can be analysed in terms of minimising static transaction costs, where these costs comprise the costs of determining and adjusting quotas, and the costs incurred in monitoring and enforcement. The use of input quotas through most of the history of irrigation in the case-study areas can be interpreted as a response to the initial aims of allocation and the transaction costs of enforcement. A principal aim of initial allocation was establishing a fair division of water entitlements, where 'fair' related to providing sufficient water to individual irrigators to generate a level of income that could support a farming family. Since income was related to the irrigated area of a farm rather than water use *per se*, it was easier (lower transaction cost) to establish a quota on irrigated land area rather than the volume of water. The cost-efficiency of input quotas was also contributed to by relatively rigid production functions of irrigated crops with respect to water use, with farmers tending to apply water at fixed time intervals and/or fixed per-area rates. Input quotas on essentially only two inputs (area and crop type) could limit water use to the required degree of precision. Furthermore, areas of land irrigated can often be easier to monitor than volumes of water use, particularly when the land use is for perennial crops such as orchards or vineyards. As the water resources were relatively abundant at the time, the higher static transaction costs associated with monitoring of resource quotas could not have been justified.

Demand for quantification of water entitlements occurred in response to increasing scarcity of water relative to the demands of irrigation development, and environmental problems arising from irrigation. There was a felt need amongst resource managers to restrict quantities of water used and to improve irrigation technologies. Also, in New South Wales the security of water supplies was diminishing and there was a need for an entitlement system that could be readily altered on a year-to-year basis according to available water supplies. There were thus changes in management objectives for the water resources to increase the efficiency of water use and providing for variable entitlements. The entitlement system was changed to a resource quota to allow these policy objectives to be pursued. This would have increased the transaction costs of water allocation, with costs now being incurred for the monitoring of water use on individual properties and enforcement of limits. However, given the new policy objectives, the transaction costs associated with resource quotas would have been lower than those incurred with relatively inflexible and imprecise input quotas used for the same purposes.

Supply of institutions
Supply of institutions for entitlement systems was predominantly undertaken by the state governments through changes in legislation and regulations, amendment of licence schemes and amendment of entitlements in government irrigation areas. The ability of government to make unilateral decisions for institutional change would have contributed to low transition costs.

The institutional changes arising from the change in entitlement systems are indicated in Figure 5.6. With the exception of riparian water entitlements which remained defined by an input quota on land, all water entitlements were now defined as resource quotas.

Market Institutions for Re-allocation of Water Entitlements

Historical context and demand for institutions
In the 1970s and 1980s, the institutions governing re-allocation of water amongst water users and group irrigation schemes were altered to allow transferability of water entitlements between irrigation farms and farmers on the basis of privately negotiated transactions. Provisions for the transfer of water entitlements were progressively introduced from 1979 in South Australia and from 1983 in New South Wales. Transferability was introduced first for temporary transfers in individual-licence entitlements, and later for permanent transfers and for transfers of individual water entitlements within group irrigation schemes.

There are three aspects of the institutions of water allocation that warrant explanation in terms of demand and supply of institutions: the introduction of commercial trading as a mechanism for re-allocation of water entitlements; the different degrees of attenuation of property rights with respect to capacity to trade; and continued reliance on administrative mechanisms for re-allocation of entitlements in some circumstances.

There appear to have been several sources of demand for the introduction of trading as a mechanism for re-allocation of water entitlements. The most important was probably a demand from holders of water entitlements for the right to trade. Less important were demands from political agents in state governments arising from a primary policy objective of allocative efficiency, and a demand from both water users and political agents for trading to provide a means of compensating water users affected by administrative re-allocation of water entitlements. Each of these is discussed in more detail below.

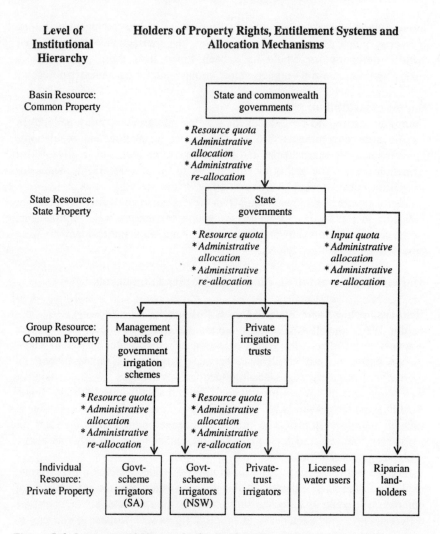

Level of Institutional Hierarchy

Holders of Property Rights, Entitlement Systems and Allocation Mechanisms

Basin Resource: Common Property — State and commonwealth governments

* Resource quota
* Administrative allocation
* Administrative re-allocation

State Resource: State Property — State governments

* Resource quota
* Administrative allocation
* Administrative re-allocation

* Input quota
* Administrative allocation
* Administrative re-allocation

Group Resource: Common Property — Management boards of government irrigation schemes | Private irrigation trusts

* Resource quota
* Administrative allocation
* Administrative re-allocation

* Resource quota
* Administrative allocation
* Administrative re-allocation

Individual Resource: Private Property — Govt-scheme irrigators (SA) | Govt-scheme irrigators (NSW) | Private-trust irrigators | Licensed water users | Riparian land-holders

Figure 5.6: Institutional Hierarchy for Surface-Water Use in New South Wales and South Australia after Introduction of Volumetric Water Entitlements

The demand by water users for transferability of water entitlements arose in the 1970s after embargoes were placed on the issue of new licences and volumetric limits were placed on existing licences. After introduction of the embargoes, access to water by an entrant to the irrigation industry could only be obtained by purchase of land with an associated water entitlement. This situation created an unsatisfied demand for entitlements to water by landholders with irrigable land but either no water entitlement and/or insufficient entitlement to undertake a desired level of irrigation. This demand was satisfied to some extent by exploiting a loophole in regulation that in some circumstances permitted water entitlements to be transferred between allotments of land under common ownership. An individual wanting to increase his or her water entitlement could thus purchase an allotment of land with a water entitlement, transfer the water entitlement to an allotment of land already owned, and then re-sell the purchased land back to the original vendor without the water entitlement (Sturgess and Wright, 1993 p. 12). This procedure was, however, associated with high transaction costs as a result of the legal complexities of the land transactions and the time necessary to undertake the transactions. There was thus demand by both prospective purchasers and sellers of water entitlement for state governments to alter regulations of water allocation to allow the transfer of water entitlement independently of land, and thereby reduce the static transaction costs associated with re-allocation of water entitlements.

Further demands for the transferability of water arose in response to the application of volumetric limits to water entitlements. This was particularly the case in New South Wales where the capacity to transfer water entitlement temporarily (annually) has become an important tool for irrigation farmers to respond to annual variation in water supplies. Demand by farmers in New South Wales to allow temporary transfers of water during the drought year of 1982/83 was a major impetus for institutional change in New South Wales (Simmons *et al.*, 1991 p. 14).

Demands arose in the 1980s and 1990s from resource-management agencies and governments for efficiency in water allocation and for the use of markets as a mechanism of allocation. Many economists had been promoting an increased use of markets in allocation of rights to utilise natural resources since early studies relating to fisheries and pollution in the 1950s and 1960s (Gordon, 1954; Dales, 1968) and later water resources (Randall, 1981). These developments may have influenced political ideologies of Australian governments with respect to property rights and transferability of water entitlements resulting in the 1994 policy position of the Council of Australian Governments (COAG) with respect to regulation of water resources. The Council made resolutions for reform of water-resource institutions that included specification of resource entitlements and property rights, and allowing and facilitating exchange or trading of water entitlements to allow water to be used in higher-value uses (Working Group on Water Resource Policy, 1995; Scoccimarro and Collins, 1995). However, many of the institutional innovations relating to the trading and transferability of water entitlements preceded the COAG agenda by a decade or more, particularly in relation to the rules governing the trade of water entitlement between holders of individual licences for water diversion. As such, the *laissez-faire* ideologies implicit in the agenda are likely to have been less important as a motivating factor for institutional change than direct demand for change by the holders of water entitlements.

Government microeconomic policies may, however, have had more of an impact on tradability of water entitlements for irrigators within group irrigation schemes. In both South Australia and the Murrumbidgee and Riverina regions of New South Wales, irrigators of government irrigation areas were not able to trade water entitlements with parties outside of the irrigation areas until the 1990s, due to restrictions imposed by management boards of the areas for the purposes of maintaining intensities of irrigation. Anecdotal evidence suggests that the partial relaxation of these restrictions was due more to government pressure than preferences of the management boards.

The third source of demand for institutional reform in the transferability of water entitlements arose from the capacity for trading to provide a means by which entitlement holders may be compensated for implementation of compulsory controls on water use within group irrigation schemes. This motivation for institutional change has only occurred to a limited extent in South Australia. As already mentioned in Chapter 3, the government irrigation districts in the Riverland region of South Australia underwent a process of rehabilitation of infrastructure in the 1990s. This involved the compulsory suspension of water entitlements of some landholders. As a means of compensating these landholders for the loss of water entitlements, exemption was provided from the usual restrictions applying to trade of entitlement from government irrigation areas, and the water entitlements could be sold or otherwise transferred to irrigators or land within or outside of the government irrigation area. The related institutional reforms were a mechanism to reduce the transaction costs to government in making the compulsory re-allocations of water entitlements, both through providing compensation payments without direct cost to government and reducing opposition to the management decisions.

Having thus indicated the origins of demand for institutions allowing trading of water entitlements, the second aspect of institutional development that warrants examination is the attenuation of property rights with respect to the transfer and trade of water entitlements: why are there substantial restrictions on trading of water entitlements, particularly for group irrigators? The principal restrictions include the necessity of having water entitlements attached to irrigable land, limits on transfer of water entitlements out of group irrigation schemes, and trades of entitlements being subject to assessments of the environmental impacts of the change of location in water use. In part, these restrictions have resulted from political concessions made to the concerns of irrigation farmers to prevent water entitlements being transferred out of the irrigation industry and to ensure that ownership of water entitlements is maintained with irrigation farmers rather than 'absentee landlords'. Nevertheless, there are potentially valid transaction-cost explanations for some restrictions, particularly those that address potential externalities arising from transfers of water entitlements. Restrictions on transfers of water entitlements out of irrigation areas are directed in part at preventing an individual farmer in a group scheme from ceasing irrigation activities and requiring that other farmers pay an increased share of the fixed costs of operating group-owned infrastructure. Requirements for environmental impact assessments of water transfers have been implemented to prevent changes in the locations of water use from causing drainage or salinity problems and imposing external costs on other users of the land and water resources. Both sets of restrictions involve administrative decisions for the re-allocation of water entitlements. However, due to large numbers of parties often having an interest in these decision and information uncertainties, the administrative processes may be cheaper in terms of transaction costs than market mechanisms for producing the same allocation outcomes.

Administrative mechanisms of re-allocation have also been retained for other forms of allocation decisions. Two examples are (i) the re-allocation of water entitlements that is implicit in the high-security–low-security licence system of New South Wales (an automatic re-allocation of water occurs in drought years to growers of perennial crops); and (ii) the compulsory re-allocation of entitlements accompanying rehabilitation of government irrigation areas in South Australia. Reasons based on transaction costs can be offered to explain why these allocation decisions are or have been made by administrative decisions rather than by market trading. The re-allocations implicit in the system of high- and low-security licences are made on the premise that if deprived of water in a drought year, growers of perennial crops would suffer yield losses in both the current year and future years due to drought damage of the perennial plants. In drought years, the value of water would be correspondingly greater for these farmers than for growers of annual crops that bear the costs only of yield losses in the current year. An administrative system that automatically re-allocates water to the growers of perennial crops in drought years may be a means of achieving efficient re-allocations without incurring the transaction costs of market trading. Similarly, the partial use of administrative processes for re-allocation of water entitlements accompanying the rehabilitation of government irrigation districts in South Australia may have the advantage of lower transaction costs rather than relying on market trading to achieve the same re-allocation outcomes. The rehabilitation programmes required a coordinated re-allocation of water away from many small-scale irrigation farmers. An administrative process would probably be able to achieve this coordination with lower transaction costs than reliance on voluntary trade. In this situation, the decisions to re-allocate water entitlements away from certain users were made by a centralised administrative process, whilst the recipients of the entitlement were determined through market trading.

Supply of institutions
The supply of institutions for the market re-allocation of water was predominantly undertaken by the state governments either in their capacities as the administrators of licence schemes or as the owners and managers of group irrigation schemes. Substantial transition costs were incurred in designing and implementing the institutional arrangements for trading. This has been the case particularly in New South Wales, where rules for inter-regional trade have had to take into account such factors as constraints imposed on the delivery and movement of water by capacities of channels and storage structures, and differences in 'losses' through evaporation and seepage as entitlements are transferred to different areas of use. On local scales where these constraints are of lesser importance, institutions for trading of water entitlements have been relatively easily and cheaply designed and implemented. Transition costs have also been incurred in some political opposition to market institutions. Generally, the enhancement of private property rights implicit in the introduction of market institutions (rights of transfer and rights to the asset value of water entitlements) has seen irrigation farmers support the institutional changes. However, political opposition has arisen to interregion and interstate transfers of water entitlements where irrigation farmers have perceived the freedoms to trade entitlements as threatening the future intensity of irrigation in particular industries or regions. Remaining constraints on interregional trade, and particularly interstate trade, may in some instances be the result either of barriers to institutional changes arising from transition costs to political decision makers, or concessions to irrigation farmers to reduce transition costs associated with implementing the institutional reforms.

The institutional changes bought about by introduction of market mechanisms for re-allocation of water entitlements are indicated in Figure 5.7. The changes highlighted in this figure are the mechanisms of re-allocation of entitlements associated with water licences issued by the government, be these held by individuals or groups, and entitlements held by individual irrigators within group schemes.

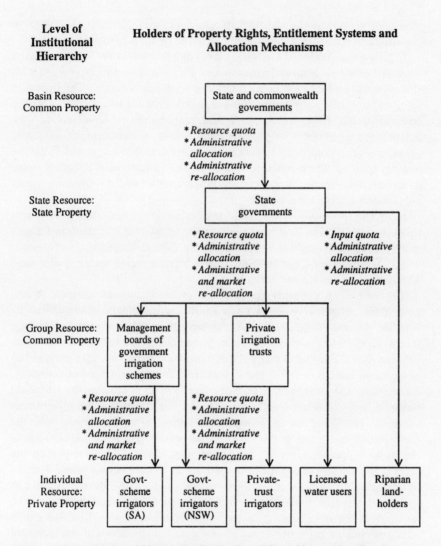

Level of
Institutional
Hierarchy

Holders of Property Rights, Entitlement Systems and
Allocation Mechanisms

Basin Resource:
Common Property

State and commonwealth
governments

* Resource quota
* Administrative
allocation
* Administrative
re-allocation

State Resource:
State Property

State
governments

* Resource quota
* Administrative
allocation
* Administrative
and market
re-allocation

* Input quota
* Administrative
allocation
* Administrative
re-allocation

Group Resource:
Common Property

Management
boards of
government
irrigation
schemes

Private
irrigation
trusts

* Resource quota
* Administrative
allocation
* Administrative
and market
re-allocation

* Resource quota
* Administrative
allocation
* Administrative
and market
re-allocation

Individual
Resource:
Private Property

Govt-
scheme
irrigators
(SA)

Govt-
scheme
irrigators
(NSW)

Private-
trust
irrigators

Licensed
water users

Riparian
land-
holders

Figure 5.7: Institutional Hierarchy for Surface-Water Use in New South
Wales and South Australia with Tradability of Water Entitlements

Privatisation and Corporatisation of Government Irrigation Schemes

Historical context and demand for institutions
In the 1990s, the state governments of New South Wales and South Australia
commenced a process of 'privatising' the government irrigation schemes in
each state. This involved the passing of property rights (ownership and/or

management rights) in the infrastructure of the schemes to collective organisations comprising the irrigators serviced by the schemes.

In New South Wales, the irrigation areas and districts in the Riverina region were privatised as Murray Irrigation Limited, a non-profit corporation with shares owned by irrigation farmers serviced by the corporation. The irrigation areas and districts in the Murrumbidgee region were not transferred to private ownership, but have had management responsibilities devolved to two autonomous agencies with management boards independent of the state government and comprised largely of irrigation farmers. As of mid-1997, the two agencies of Murrumbidgee Irrigation and Coleambally Irrigation were destined to become state-owned corporations whilst retaining their independent management boards.

In South Australia, ownership and control of the state-government irrigation areas in the Riverland region were transferred to irrigation farmers in July 1997 as a single business entity, the Central Irrigation Trust. As of mid-1997, irrigation schemes in the Lower Murray region remain under state government ownership and control.

The origin of demands for transfer of ownership or control of the government irrigation schemes to irrigators are difficult to discern; that is, whether demand originated with the irrigation farmers serviced by the schemes, or from within the state governments. Anecdotal information suggests that the initial demand for institutional change was associated with government initiatives to increase charges for water to meet costs of operating, maintaining and refurbishing infrastructure, and thus ceasing the historical public subsidy of water supply to irrigation farmers within the government schemes. The 1980s and 1990s were characterised by political preferences for the privatisation of public instrumentalities providing private goods, such as the water-supply services of the irrigation schemes. However, once the process of change was commenced, there seems to have been a strong demand by irrigation farmers for the institutional changes. This demand appears to have been associated with the perception amongst irrigation farmers that the administrative costs of managing the irrigation schemes would be lower with management by a collective group of irrigation farmers than with management by government agencies. This is consistent with the premise of demand for institutional change arising from perceptions of potential reductions in transaction costs.

Supply of institutions

Institutions for both the transfer of the ownership or control of the schemes, and for the organisation of the agencies assuming the ownership or control, were supplied by the state governments through legislation. The South Australian Irrigation Act 1994 provided for the conversion of government irrigation schemes to private irrigation districts owned and administered by trusts comprising owners of irrigation properties serviced by the schemes. The Act also specified rules and responsibilities for trusts with respect to operation of the irrigation schemes. In New South Wales, the Irrigation Corporations Act 1994 provided for transfer of ownership or control of government irrigation schemes to either state-owned (Class 1) irrigation corporations or private (Class 2) irrigation corporations. The rules and responsibilities with respect to operations of the corporations are specified within the Irrigation Corporations Act, within the State Owned Corporations Act 1989, and in commonwealth Corporations Law.

The transition costs associated with the transfers of property rights from state governments to irrigators appear to have been small and the process of institutional change relatively quickly achieved. In part, the ease of institutional change would have been as a result of the transition costs being met by government rather than by private irrigators, consistent with previous discussion of successes in development of institutions of collective action where the transition costs of institutional change are subsidised by a central government. Also, the political costs associated with the institutional changes were low as a result of many irrigation farmers perceiving prospects of financial gains through the transfers of property rights and protection against prospective losses by the government payments to improve irrigation infrastructure prior to and after transfer of property rights.

The process of transfer of ownership and control of government irrigation schemes to irrigators has not been completed. Relatively small government irrigation schemes still exist in the Lower Murray region of South Australia and in the Murrumbidgee region of New South Wales. Also, the state government of New South Wales has retained some executive control of the major irrigation schemes in the Murrumbidgee region. Nevertheless, the process of transferring property rights from the state to common-property collectives is likely to continue. The institutions of water allocation would thus be changed to those indicated in Figure 5.8.

CONCLUSIONS: STATIC AND DYNAMIC TRANSACTION COSTS IN INSTITUTIONAL CHANGE

Although largely speculative and qualitative, the above analysis of historical institutional development for water use in the Murray–Darling Basin has indicated that institutional change can in large part be explained in terms of two concepts of the model of institutional change developed in Chapter 2 and examined in more detail at the beginning of this chapter.

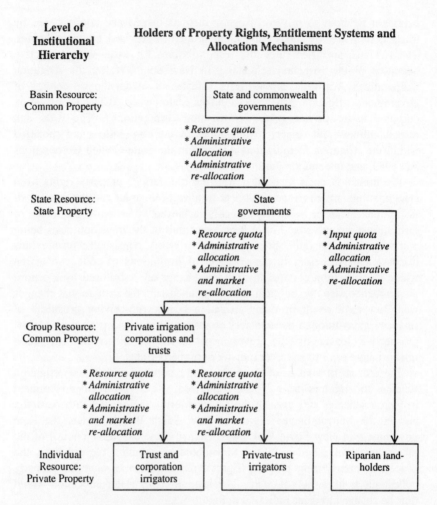

*Figure 5.8: Possible Future Institutional Hierarchy for Surface-Water Use in
New South Wales and South Australia after Privatisation or
Corporatisation of Government Irrigation Schemes*

These two concepts are as follows.

i.   Demand for institutional change is associated with a willingness to pay to
     reduce static transaction costs associated with achieving particular
     economic objectives, in this case objectives relating to the allocation of
     water resources.

ii. Supply of new institutions is constrained by dynamic transaction costs arising in the costs of transition from one institutional structure to another.

Several general features of institutional change can be observed from this historical study.

Firstly, changes in institutions of water allocation have been incremental, making changes at the margin to an existing institutional structure. This is possibly a reflection of high transition costs that may be associated with large institutional reforms that substantially alter existing property-right structures.

Secondly, institutional changes involving transfers of property rights down the institutional hierarchy appear to have been much more easily and quickly achieved than changes involving transfers of property rights up the institutional hierarchy. For example, institutional change was achieved quickly and with relative ease in creating common property rights for group irrigation schemes and introducing market institutions of re-allocation of water entitlements. Both of these changes involved a transfer of property rights down the hierarchy from colonial/state governments. On the other hand, institutional change proved difficult, with attenuation of riparian rights during enactment of water-resources legislation at the turn of the century, and in the creation of institutions for interstate common property rights. Both of these changes involved a transfer of property rights up the institutional hierarchy, in the first case from private individuals to state governments and in the second case from state governments to an interstate common-property organisation. The difficulties in property rights previously assigned to subordinate levels of an institutional hierarchy arise from political opposition that translates into high transition costs for the decision makers for institutional change. These transition costs will be discussed later (Chapter 7). However, suffice to say for the moment that these costs result in irreversibilities in institutional change, defined in the broad sense of costly reversibility rather than strict irreversibility.

If decisions for institutional change at any time are constrained by past institutional development, then the corollary holds that decisions for institutional change may constrain the set of possible institutional changes in the future by affecting future transition costs. This represents a new transaction-cost consideration in the problem of institutional choices: the dynamic transaction cost arising from the constraints on future institutional options imposed by a current institutional change.

The implications of path-dependency in institutional change for institutional choice are examined in more detail in Chapter 6, where path-dependency is discussed in terms of institutional flexibility and dynamic transaction costs. Then, in Chapter 7, the concepts of static transaction costs and dynamic transaction costs are combined within a statement of the policy problem for institutional change.

NOTE

1. It may be argued that water entitlements were implicitly traded with ownership of land and thereby subject to re-allocation by a market mechanism. However, there are two reasons why this was not the case. Firstly, the water could only be used on the land to which the entitlement pertained. Secondly, there was at the time no limit on allocation of further water entitlements. Hence any entitlement would have had a zero market value.

6. Dynamic Transaction Costs and Option Values in Institutional Change

INTRODUCTION

Prior to the 1970s, property rights to irrigation water in the Murray–Darling Basin resided largely with state governments. The governments maintained control over access of individual irrigators to water, the land areas to which water could be applied, the quantities of water that could be used, and the types and areas of crops that could be irrigated. Since the 1970s there has been a transfer of property rights from state governments to either individual irrigators or to collectives of irrigators that have taken over ownership and/or management of the distribution infrastructure of group irrigation schemes. The principal changes to property rights and associated institutions have been as follows.

- Enhanced security of water supplies pertaining to irrigation licences as a result of embargoes on issue of further water entitlements by three of the states in the basin (New South Wales, Victoria and South Australia).
- The introduction of transferability of water entitlements allowing water entitlements to be divided and traded, accompanied by strengthening of *de facto* and *de jure* private property rights of water users.
- Improved 'quality of title' of water entitlements with more explicit descriptions of rights in water licences. For example, specification of security of water supplies through classification of entitlements as high-security or low-security, more detailed specification of rights and duties associated with water use, and description of opportunities and constraints pertaining to water transfers and trading.
- Increased management flexibility in relation to water use with removal of many government controls over crop types, crop areas and times of water application.

These reforms have substantially strengthened the private property rights of irrigation farmers, corresponding to a transfer of property rights down the institutional hierarchy for water use. It was noted in Chapter 5 that transfers of property rights down an institutional hierarchy can be difficult to reverse in so far as the transition costs of 'clawing back' the property rights at a later date are likely to be high. Consequently, devolution of property rights down the hierarchy may reduce the flexibility of the institutional structure with respect to future reforms.

It was proposed in Chapter 5 that a reduction in future flexibility of an institutional structure may constitute a cost to society. Institutional change is mostly directed at reducing static transaction costs associated with decisions for resource allocation, while being constrained by the dynamic transaction costs arising from the transition from one institutional structure to another. A reduction in future flexibility of the institutional structure arises where an institutional change at a given time increases the transition costs associated with institutional changes that may be required or desirable in the future. The main example of this described in Chapter 5 was the institutional reforms associated with enactment of state water-resources legislation and creation of state property rights near the turn of the century. The resulting strong state property rights caused very high transition costs to be incurred in the later development of the institutions of interstate common property. These transition costs have greatly impeded the management of water resources across the entire Murray–Darling Basin.

It is arguable that the costs associated with a loss of institutional flexibility should be recognised as a transition cost of institutional change and should be taken into account in decisions for institutional change. In this chapter, the nature of the cost associated with a loss of institutional flexibility is explored. It is proposed that institutional flexibility has an option value in instances where uncertainty exists over the future state of the resource system and future requirements for institutional change.

IMPERFECT KNOWLEDGE AND UNCERTAINTY IN THE MURRAY–DARLING BASIN

From an economic perspective it would probably not be desirable to have perfect or complete knowledge of the Murray–Darling Basin for the purposes of determining an appropriate institutional structure for regulating use of water resources. The optimal 'quantity' of information for decision making would balance the marginal costs of procuring additional information with the marginal benefits to resource management. As the knowledge of the Basin increases, the marginal costs of procuring further information would increase and the marginal benefits to decision making would decrease. After some point, the marginal cost of additional information would exceed the marginal benefit. An optimal level of information would in all likelihood be less than complete information.

For the Murray–Darling Basin, calls for further increases in knowledge have come from many sources: research hydrologists, ecologists, biologists and other scientists; resource managers in the Murray–Darling Basin Commission and other regulatory agencies; and politicians. Such calls do not necessarily indicate a sub-optimal level of knowledge, at least from the economic perspective of resource management. There are other motivations for seeking information, such as vested interests in research programmes, procrastination on making difficult resource-management and political decisions, and reducing opposition to management initiatives.

Nevertheless, there are indications that knowledge of the Basin is far from complete, with a consequence of substantial uncertainty as to the environmental/ecological consequences of current levels and patterns of water and land use. Much of this uncertainty arises from an inherent dynamic variability in the river system. This variability is so high that, despite the current concern about the health of the system, it is not possible to demonstrate a statistically significant reduction in river flows, and there is similar statistical imprecision in regard to water quality and fish populations (Mackay and Eastburn, 1990).

This variability of the river system and consequent difficulty in discerning and evaluating changes in the system have led to a lot of calls for further information centring on improving long-term data bases. For example, high-priority 'knowledge gaps' identified by the commonwealth Department of Industry, Science and Tourism (1996 p. 67) were as follows.

- 'The significance of flows relative to other environmental variables – especially water quality and structural habitat issues such as in-stream barriers, snag removal and siltation – affecting aquatic ecosystems.'
- 'Long-term data sets that allow comprehensive assessment of the role of flow regimes in the recruitment processes of native and introduced fish species.'
- Measures of river flows that take into account both instantaneous flows and variability across periods of time, and correlation of these measures with other measures of environmental health.

A lack of knowledge on the hydrological and ecological dynamics of the river system has also been cited as constraining management decisions in recent submissions to the Murray–Darling Ministerial Council by member governments in relation to setting a 'cap' on water withdrawals from the rivers (Department of Land and Water Conservation New South Wales, 1997; Department of Natural Resources and Environment Victoria, 1997).

In addition to imperfect knowledge relating to the complexity and variability of the river systems as they exist at the moment, uncertainty as to long-term effects of resource management arises as a result of unknown impacts of the greenhouse effect. Predictions have been made of changes in rainfall across the basin in the order of ±10 per cent, accompanied by changes in seasonal rainfall incidence, temperatures and cloud cover (CSIRO Climate Impact Group, 1991; Pigram *et al.*, 1992; Pigram, 1995).

In the following section, the implications of imperfect information for decisions on institutional change are investigated using a conceptual model.

A MODEL OF INSTITUTIONAL CHANGE, BENEFITS OF LEARNING, AND QUASI-OPTION VALUE

Conceptual Model

In this section, a conceptual model is developed of decision making for institutional change in a situation that may resemble that of the Murray–Darling Basin. The model is formalised in mathematical notation and a numerical extension of the model is used to examine how environmental uncertainty could be addressed in decisions on institutional change. Features of the conceptual model are described below.

- An irrigation industry utilises water from a river basin, maximising profit within the constraints of an institutional structure that defines property rights to water. The profits of the irrigation industry are proportional to the 'strength' of private property rights in the institutional structure for utilising the water resource, that is, the power of individual irrigation farmers to make allocation decisions for water.
- A government regulatory agency has two functions: (i) determining the institutional (property-right) structure for use of the water resource by the irrigation industry; and (ii) maintaining the ecological and environmental 'quality' of the river basin at a predetermined standard.
- There is imperfect knowledge of hydrological and ecological processes in the river basin. The regulatory agency is unsure of the state of nature that will exist in the river basin in the future: a favourable state of nature in the form of environmental resilience to irrigation; or an adverse state of nature in the form of environmental susceptibility to irrigation. With current

knowledge, the government agency can only assign subjective probabilities to possible future states of nature. These probabilities can, however, be revised over time as knowledge of the river basin increases.

- The costs to the government agency of managing the river basin are determined by the realised state of nature and the institutional structure. Under a favourable state of nature, costs are low and largely independent of the institutional structure. Under an adverse state of nature, costs are high and increase with the strength of private property rights. With strong private property rights, the regulatory agency has less flexibility in altering patterns of water use to maintain the standard of environmental quality. Consequently, costs of environmental management are higher. For example, with strong private property rights the regulatory agency may have limited powers to unilaterally reduce water entitlements under unfavourable states of nature characterised by water shortages. A need to participate in water markets to purchase water for environmental purposes would increase the costs to government of achieving environmental objectives.

- Institutional change is path-dependent in so far as any devolution of property rights from the state to private water users is costly to reverse. At the commencement of 'modelled time' property rights are held predominantly by the state government. Institutional change would initially involve a transfer of property rights from the state to private irrigators. Reversal of this change would involve a transfer of property rights back from irrigators to the state. In the first case, the private irrigators do not pay for the gains in property rights and effectively experience windfall gains (consistent with the implementation of institutional reform in the Murray–Darling Basin). However, with a reversal of institutional changes, irrigators demand and receive compensation for attenuation of private property rights. The capacity to demand compensation results in high transition costs being associated with reversal of institutional changes that involve a transfer of property rights back to the state. This is generally consistent with observations of institutional change, for example by Dixit (1996 p. 26): 'Policy acts shape the future environment by creating constituencies that gain from the policy, who will then fiercely resist any changes that take away these gains.' Compensation is a transition cost arising from the need of political decision makers to overcome resistance to institutional change.

Formal Specification

A formal specification of this conceptual model is described below. This model follows a similar form to that of Conrad (1980). The objective is to determine if there may be value in delaying or making conservative institutional changes in situations where the changes are costly to reverse, the benefits of change are uncertain, and future learning will reduce this uncertainty.

Time is considered as comprising three periods: the past (Period 0), the present (Period 1) and the future (Period 2). Policy decisions on institutional change are being made at the beginning of Period 1 and relate to water use over Periods 1 and 2.

The institutional structure for any time period is characterised by a level of private property rights held by irrigators. The level in any period can be quantified as a scalar parameter, I_τ, for $\tau = 0, 1, 2$.

An initial institutional structure, I_0, is inherited from the past and may be altered in either of Periods 1 or 2. Transition equations for institutional structures are:

$$I_1 = I_0 + d_1; \text{ and} \tag{6.1}$$
$$I_2 = I_1 + d_2 = I_0 + d_1 + d_2, \tag{6.2}$$

where d_1 and d_2 are scalar quantities indicating the level of change in I in Periods 1 and 2, respectively. The quantities d_1 and d_2 may be positive (enhancing private property rights) or negative (attenuating private property rights).

The states of nature in Periods 1 and 2 are represented by random variables S_1 and S_2, with higher values of either S_1 or S_2 signifying an increasingly adverse state of nature for the relevant time period. For Period 1 ($\tau = 1$), S_1 has a subjective probability distribution:

$$p_j\{S_1 = S_{1j}, j = 1 \dots m\}. \tag{6.3}$$

Learning through Period 1 allows revision of subjective probabilities for Period 2. Thus for Period 2 ($\tau = 2$), S_2 has a subjective joint probability distribution conditional on the value of S_1:

$$q_j\{S_2 = S_{2j} \mid S_1, j = 1 \dots m\}. \tag{6.4}$$

The learning process is not particularly important to the model, but the revision of probabilities is consistent with a Bayesian process.

The net benefits from irrigation in each of Periods 1 and 2 are positively related to the strength of private property rights and to the state of nature:

$$B_\tau = B\{I_\tau, S_\tau\} \text{ for } \tau = 1,2; \text{ and} \tag{6.5}$$

$$\frac{\partial B_\tau}{\partial I_\tau} > 0 \; ; \; \frac{\partial^2 B_\tau}{\partial I_\tau^2} \le 0 \; ; \; \frac{\partial B_\tau}{\partial S_\tau} < 0 \; ; \; \frac{\partial^2 B_\tau}{\partial S_\tau^2} \le 0.$$

The costs of environmental management by the government agency are negatively related to the strength of private property rights and positively related to the state of nature:

$$C_\tau = C\{I_\tau, S_\tau\} \text{ for } \tau = 1,2. \tag{6.6}$$

Costly reversibility of institutional change arises from requirements that 'negative' institutional changes ($d_1 < 0$ or $d_2 < 0$, implying attenuation of private property rights) be accompanied by compensation payments. The compensation payments are proportional to the absolute magnitude of any negative institutional change:

$$M_\tau = \begin{cases} |\alpha d_\tau| & \text{if } d_\tau < 0 \quad \text{(i.e. if property rights are attenuated)} \\ 0 & \text{if } d_\tau \ge 0 \quad \text{(i.e. if property rights are strengthened).} \end{cases} \tag{6.7}$$

Decisions on institutional change are made with the objective of maximising welfare according to a welfare function that is defined as the benefits from water use minus the costs of environmental management and any compensation costs associated with institutional change. The welfare functions for each period are:

$$W_\tau = B_\tau - C_\tau - M_\tau \text{ for } \tau = 1,2. \tag{6.8}$$

The total welfare is the sum of the welfare in each period is:

$$W = W_1 + \delta W_2 \tag{6.9}$$

where δ is a discount factor.

The decision problem being addressed is that of what level of institutional change should be selected in Period 1 to allow maximisation of the present value of welfare over both periods. Due to the state of nature being a random variable, the decisions on institutional change are made with imperfect knowledge and on the basis of expected welfare. Assuming a policy objective of maximising net present value and faced with uncertainty about states of nature, a risk-neutral decision maker for institutional change in Period 1 would have an objective of maximising the expected present value of welfare over Periods 1 and 2. In calculating expected welfare, this decision maker would assume that the decision maker in Period 2 would likewise make decisions on institutional change to maximise welfare.

Decisions for institutional change in Period 1 could be made under two scenarios.

i.   No learning takes place. The decision maker for Period 1 selects d_1 to maximise expected welfare over the two periods on the basis of subjective probabilities of the state of nature in Period 1 and subjective conditional probabilities of the state of nature in Period 2.

ii. Learning of the state of nature in Period 1 takes place before Period 2 so the decision maker in Period 2 will be able to observe S_1 prior to determining d_2.

For the no-learning scenario, d_1 and d_2 are chosen without knowledge of S_1 or S_2. This is functionally equivalent to choosing both d_1 and d_2 in Period 1. The problem of the decision maker in Period 1 is to select values of d_1 and d_2 that maximise the expected present value of welfare over both periods:

$$\underset{d_1,d_2}{\text{Max}}\Big[E[W] = E\big[W_1 + \delta W_2\big]\Big] \qquad (6.10)$$

Expanding this equation gives:

$$\underset{d_1,d_2}{\text{Max}}\left[\begin{array}{l} E[W] = \sum_j p_j\{S_1 = S_{1j}\}. \\[4pt] \left[\begin{array}{l} W_1\big\{B_1\{I_1,S_1\},C_1\{I_1,S_1\},M_1\{d_1\}\big\} \\[4pt] + \sum_j \left[\begin{array}{l} q_j\{S_2 = S_{2j}|S_1\}. \\[4pt] \delta W_2\big\{B_2\{I_2,S_2\},C_2\{I_2,S_2\},M_2\{d_2\}\big\} \end{array} \right] \end{array} \right] \end{array} \right] \qquad (6.11)$$

For the learning scenario, it is assumed that the decision maker in Period 2 will choose d_2 so as to maximise the expected value of W_2 given a realised value of S_1. The problem of the decision maker in Period 1 is:

$$\underset{d_1}{\text{Max}}\left[E[W] = E\left[W_1 + \underset{d_2}{\text{Max}}\ E[\delta W_2]\,\Big|\,S_1 \right] \right] \qquad (6.12)$$

where $E[\delta W_2]|S_1$ denotes the expected discounted value of W_2 given the realised value of S_1.

Expanding this equation gives:

$$\underset{d_1}{\text{Max}} \begin{bmatrix} E[W] = \sum_j p_j \{S_1 = S_{1j}\}. \\ \begin{bmatrix} W_1 \{B_1\{I_1, S_1\}, C_1\{I_1, S_1\}, M_1\{d_1\}\} \\ + \underset{d_2}{\text{Max}} \sum_j \begin{bmatrix} q_j \{S_2 = S_{2j} | S_1\}. \\ \delta W_2 \{B_2\{I_2, S_2\}, C_2\{I_2, S_2\}, M_2\{d_2\}\} \end{bmatrix} \end{bmatrix} \end{bmatrix} \qquad (6.13)$$

The value associated with the opportunity for learning of the state of nature in Period 1 prior to decision making in Period 2 can be defined in two ways. Firstly, the value of learning can be defined as the increase in the maximum expected welfare arising from the prospect of additional information becoming available, that is, the difference between the maximum expected welfare with learning and the maximum expected welfare without learning. This is the concept used by Conrad (1980) to refer to the expected value of information and labelled by Fisher and Hanemann (1985) as the *unconditional value of information* (unconditional on any constraints on the first-period decision). This concept will hereafter be referred to as the 'unconditional expected value of learning'. Secondly, a narrower definition of the value of learning is the increase in the maximum expected welfare arising from the prospect of additional information becoming available, subject to a constraint on the first-period institutional decision. This is the concept labelled by Fisher and Hanemann (1985) as the *conditional value of information* (conditional on a certain first-period decision) and equates to a *quasi-option value* of a particular first-period decision (Arrow and Fisher, 1974; Fisher and Hanemann, 1985; Boardman *et al.*, 1996 p. 228). This value will hereafter be referred to as the 'quasi-option value' of *a specified first-period decision.*

In the above model, the unconditional expected value of learning can be calculated as:

Unconditional expected value of learning
= [Maximum expected welfare with learning (Eq. 6.12)]
− [Maximum expected welfare without learning (Eq. 6.10)].   (6.14)

The quasi-option values of learning are calculated in a similar manner, but with the first-period decision, d_1, constrained to particular values:

Quasi-option value of learning for d_1 equals θ
= [Maximum expected welfare with learning and $d_1 = \theta$ (Eq. 6.12)]
  − [Maximum expected welfare without learning and $d_1 = \theta$ (Eq. 6.10)]
for θ = all possible values of d_1.   (6.15)

Numerical Extension

A simple numerical extension of the above model is described below.

The level of private property rights in an institutional structure is quantified as a scalar parameter for each time period, I_τ, with values of 0 to 1 ($0 \leq I_\tau \leq 1$). An increasing value of I_τ signifies less attenuated or 'stronger' private property rights.   An institutional level of $I_\tau = 1$ signifies completely unattenuated private property rights.

The initial institutional structure inherited from the past is assumed to comprise fully state property rights ($I_0 = 0$). Positive institutional change can occur in Period 1 such that $0 < d_1 < 1$. Institutional change in Period 2 may be negative or positive within the limits of either reversing the institutional change made in Period 1, or making further institutional change in Period 2 up to the maximum possible level. For simplicity in this example, assume that I_1 and I_2 can take values of 0, 0.5 or 1. Thus for $I_0 = 0$, d_1 can take values of 0, 0.5 or 1 and d_2 can take values of:

0, 0.5 or 1 if $d_1 = 0$;
−0.5, 0 or 0.5 if $d_1 = 0.5$; or
−1, −0.5 or 0 if $d_1 = 1$.

The states of nature in Periods 1 and 2 (S_1 and S_2) can take values of 0, signifying a 'favourable' state of nature, or 1, representing an 'adverse' state of nature. The decision maker's subjective probabilities of S_1 are:

$$p\{S_1 = 0\} = p\{S_1 = 1\} = 0.5.$$ (6.16)

Learning through Period 1 allows revision of subjective probabilities for Period 2. With learning, the conditional probabilities of S_2 are:

$$q\{S_2 = 0 \mid S_1 = 0\} = q\{S_2 = 1 \mid S_1 = 1\} = 0.9; \text{ and}$$ (6.17)

$$q\{S_2 = 0 \mid S_1 = 1\} = f\{S_2 = 1 \mid S_1 = 0\} = 0.1.$$ (6.18)

The net benefits from irrigation in each of Periods 1 and 2 are described by the functions:

$$B_\tau = (-0.45)I_\tau^{\,2} + 2I_\tau + 0.6 - (0.2)S_\tau \text{ for } \tau=1,2. \tag{6.19}$$

The benefit functions described by this equation are shown in Figure 6.1. The functional form and values of parameters were arbitrarily selected to derive a concave benefit function with a maximum benefit of approximately 1 under a favourable state of nature ($S_\tau = 0$). The benefits from irrigation are uniformly lower for any institutional structure with an adverse state of nature ($S_\tau = 1$).

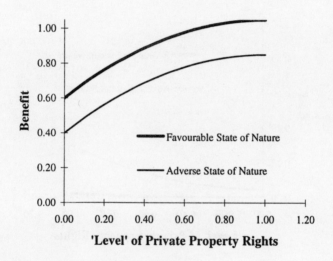

Figure 6.1: Benefits from Irrigation with Different Levels of Private Property Rights and Two States of Nature

The costs of environmental management by the government agency are described by the quadratic and convex functions:

$$C_\tau = (2.5\times10^{S_\tau-2})I_\tau^2 + 0.05 \text{ for } \tau=1,2 . \tag{6.20}$$

The cost functions described by this equation are shown in Figure 6.2. The values of parameters were selected to derive a cost function with a maximum cost of approximately 0.3 under an adverse state of nature. Note that with an adverse state of nature ($S_\tau = 1$) the costs of environmental management are higher and increase at a greater rate with an increasing strength of private property rights.

The compensation function for attenuation of private property rights is:

$$M_\tau = \begin{cases} |\alpha d_\tau| & \text{if } d_\tau < 0 \\ 0 & \text{if } d_\tau \geq 0 \end{cases} \qquad (6.21)$$

where α is a constant that will be referred to as the compensation rate. For this example, a range of values of α from 0 to 0.2 was used to investigate the effects of different costs of compensation for attenuating private property rights on the optimal decision for institutional change.

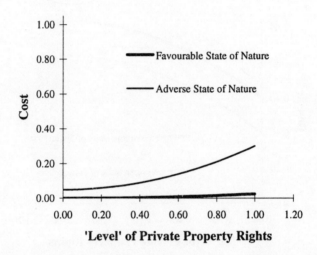

Figure 6.2: Costs of Environmental Management with Different Levels of Private Property Rights and Two States of Nature

The welfare in each period is a function of the benefits from irrigation, the costs of environmental management, and the costs of any institutional change. In this example, the welfare in each time period is described by the functions:

$$W_\tau = B_\tau - C_\tau - M_\tau \text{ for } \tau = 1,2. \qquad (6.22)$$

The total welfare is the sum of the welfare in each period with the discount factor assumed equal to one for simplicity:

$$W = W_1 + W_2. \qquad (6.23)$$

A political decision maker needs to decide on a level of institutional change in Period 1 to maximise the expected total welfare over both periods.

Figure 6.3 shows a decision-tree diagram and the expected values of welfare with the compensation rate $\alpha = 0.1$. The decision maker in Period 1 has a choice of three levels of institutional change indicated in the column headed d_1. For each possible decision for d_1 there are two possible states of nature indicated in column S_1. According to the decision for d_1 there is a resultant institutional structure (I_1). For each institutional structure in Period 1 and each possible realised state of nature, there are resultant levels of welfare, W_1.

The decision maker in Period 2 will also have a choice of three levels of institutional change (d_2), although the choices are dependent upon the decision on institutional change made in Period 1. For this example, d_1 can take values of 0, 0.5 or 1 and thus the range of choices for d_2 is 0, 0.5 or 1 if $d_1 = 0$; −0.5, 0 or 0.5 if $d_1 = 0.5$; or −1, −0.5 or 1 if $d_1 = 1$. According to the decision for d_2, there will be a resultant institutional structure (I_2) and level of welfare, W_2.

In the absence of learning, both d_1 and d_2 are chosen without any knowledge of states of nature. The decision maker in Period 1 will calculate the expected value of total welfare for all possible sets of d_1 and d_2, and select the value of d_1 corresponding to the maximum of these expected values. To illustrate the calculation of these expected values, the expected value of welfare for $\alpha = 0.1$ and for institutional decisions of $d_1 = 5$ and $d_2 = 0$ is determined as follows.

$E(W \mid d_1 = 0.5, d_2 = 0)$
$= E(W_1 \mid d_1 = 0.5) + E(W_2 \mid d_1 = 0.5, d_2 = 0)$
$= p(S1 = 0).(0.93) + p(S1 = 1).(0.63)$
$+ p(S1 = 0).q(S2 = 0 \mid S1 = 0).(0.93)$
$+ p(S1 = 0).q(S2 = 1 \mid S1 = 0).(0.63)$
$+ p(S1 = 1).q(S2 = 0 \mid S1 = 1).(0.93)$
$+ p(S1 = 1).q(S2 = 1 \mid S1 = 1).(0.63)$
$= (0.5)(0.93) + (0.5)(0.63)$
$+ (0.5)(0.9)(0.93)$
$+ (0.5)(0.1)(0.63)$
$+ (0.5)(0.1)(0.93)$
$+ (0.5)(0.9)(0.63)$
$= 1.56.$

Expected values of welfare for $\alpha = 0.1$ and possible values of d_1 and d_2 are shown in Table 6.1. The maximum expected value of welfare without learning and with $\alpha = 0.1$ occurs with institutional decisions of $d_1 = 1$ and $d_2 = 0$, $E(W) = 1.58$. The optimal decision for Period 1 in the absence of learning is therefore $d_1 = 1$.

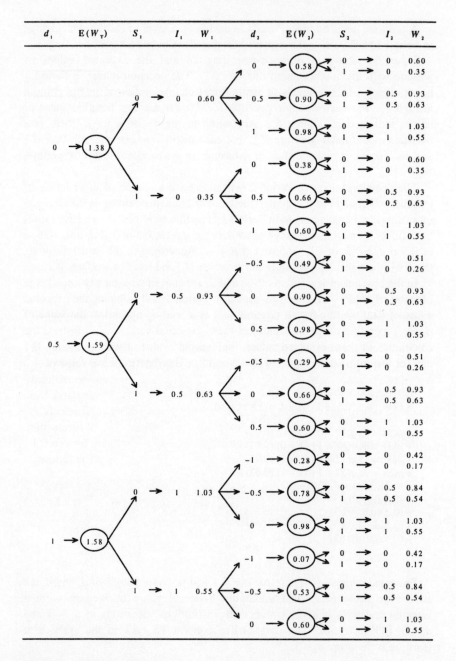

Figure 6.1: Decision Tree showing Calculation of Expected Values of Welfare (α = 0.1)

*Table 6.1: Expected Values of Welfare over Two Periods
              without Learning ($\alpha = 0.1$)*

d_1	d_2	E[W]
0	0	0.95
0	0.5	1.25
0	1	1.26
0.5	−0.5	1.16
0.5	0	1.56
0.5	0.5	1.57
1	−1	1.08
1	−0.5	1.48
1	0	1.58

With learning of the state of nature in Period 1 prior to decision making in
Period 2, the decision maker in Period 2 will be able to select the value of d_2
that maximises the expected value of welfare for Period 2 given the realised
state of nature in Period 1. The decision maker in Period 1 calculates the
expected value of total welfare for all possible sets of d_1 and d_2, and selects d_1
corresponding to the maximum of these expected values. To illustrate the
calculation of these expected values, the expected value of welfare for $\alpha = 0.1$
and for a first-period institutional decision of $d_1 = 0.5$ is determined as follows.

$E[W \,|\, d_1 = 0.5]$
$= E[(W_1 \,|\, d_1 = 0.5) + \text{Max}\,(W_2 \,|\, d_1 = 0.5, S_1 = S_{1j})]$
$= p\{S_1 = 0\}.(0.93)$
$+ \; p\{S_1 = 0\}.\text{Max}\,[q\{S_2 = 0 \,|\, S_1 = 0\}.(0.51) + q\{S_2 = 1 \,|\, S_1 = 0\}.(0.26);$
$\qquad q\{S_2 = 0 \,|\, S_1 = 0\}.(0.93) + q\{S_2 = 1 \,|\, S_1 = 0\}.(0.63);$
$\qquad q\{S_2 = 0 \,|\, S_1 = 0\}.(1.03) + q\{S_2 = 1 \,|\, S_1 = 0\}.(0.55)\,]$
$+ \; p\{S_1 = 1\}.(0.63)$
$+ \; p\{S_1 = 1\}.\text{Max}\,[q\{S_2 = 0 \,|\, S_1 = 1\}.(0.51) + q\{S_2 = 1 \,|\, S_1 = 1\}.(0.26);$
$\qquad q\{S_2 = 0 \,|\, S_1 = 1\}.(0.93) + q\{S_2 = 1 \,|\, S_1 = 1\}.(0.63);$
$\qquad q\{S_2 = 0 \,|\, S_1 = 1\}.(1.03) + q\{S_2 = 1 \,|\, S_1 = 1\}.(0.55)\,]$
$= (0.5)(0.93)$
$+ \; (0.5).\text{Max}\,[0.49;\, 0.90;\, 0.98]$
$+ \; (0.5)(0.63)$
$+ \; (0.5).\text{Max}\,[0.29;\, 0.66;\, 0.60]$
$= 1.59.$

Expected values of welfare for $\alpha = 0.1$ and different values of d_1 are shown in Table 6.2. The maximum expected value of welfare with learning and with $\alpha = 0.1$ occurs with a first-period institutional decision of $d_1 = 0.5$, $E(W) = 1.59$. The optimal decision for Period 1 in the presence of learning is therefore $d_1 = 0.5$.

Table 6.2: Expected Values of Welfare over Two Periods with Learning ($\alpha = 0.1$)

d_1	E[W]
0	1.29
0.5	1.59
1	1.58

From a comparison of Tables 6.1 and 6.2, it is evident that the optimal first-period institutional changes differ between the scenarios of no-learning (optimal $d_1 = 1$) and learning (optimal $d_1 = 0.5$). This is not the case for all values of the compensation rate, α. The ranking of expected welfare for different first-period decisions of institutional change varies with different values of α. Figure 6.4 shows a plot of expected welfare, with learning, for first-period institutional changes of 0, 0.5 and 1 over the range of values for α of 0 to 0.2. For first-period institutional changes of $d_1 = 0$ and $d_1 = 1$, welfare is constant over the range of values of α. For a first-period institutional change of $d_1 = 1$, welfare decreases as the value of α increases up to $\alpha = 0.12$ and thereafter remains constant. For low values of α (< 0.04), expected welfare is maximised with a first-period institutional change $d_1 = 1$. For higher values of α (≥ 0.04), welfare is maximised with a conservative first-period institutional change $d_1 = 0.5$. The differences in expected welfare for $d_1 = 1$ and $d_1 = 0.5$ are small, reflecting the concave shapes of benefit functions and the consequently small marginal gains from incremental institutional change from 0.5 to 1.

For $\alpha < 0.04$, the increase in expected welfare with a conservative first-period institutional change resulted from prospects for learning of the state of nature in Period 1 prior to making a decision on institutional change in Period 2 and thus being able to revise the probabilities for the state of nature in Period 2.

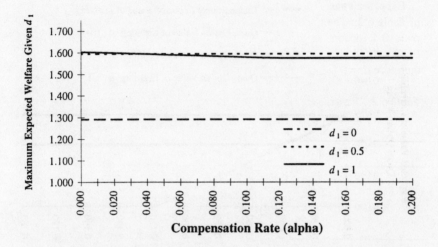

Figure 6.4: Maximum Expected Welfare with Learning for Different First-Period Institutional Changes and a Range of Compensation Rates

Recall that the *unconditional expected value of learning* and *quasi-option values of learning* can be calculated as follows.

Unconditional expected value of learning
= [Maximum expected welfare with learning]
   – [Maximum expected welfare without learning].

Quasi-option value of learning for d_1 equals θ
= [Maximum expected welfare with learning and with $d_1 = \theta$]
   – [Maximum expected welfare without learning and with $d_1 = \theta$]
for $\theta = 0, 0.5$ and 1.

Figure 6.5 shows plots of the unconditional expected values of learning and the quasi-option values of learning over a range of values for the costs of reversing institutional change (a range in values of α from 0 to 0.2).

There are two principal features of the range of values calculated for the unconditional expected value of learning and the quasi-option values. Firstly, the unconditional expected value of learning and quasi-option values are equal where reversal of institutional change is costless ($\alpha = 0$). Secondly, with increasing costs of reversing institutional change ($\alpha > 0$) the unconditional expected value of learning decreases and quasi-option values either remain constant ($d_1 = 0$ and $d_1 = 0.5$) or decrease to zero ($d_1 = 1$).

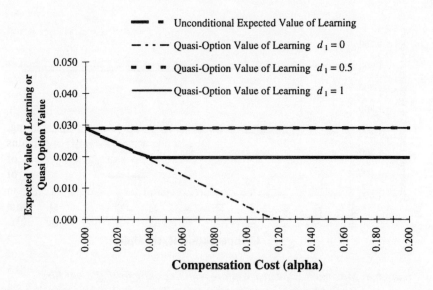

Figure 6.5: Expected Values of Learning for Different First-Period
Institutional Changes and a Range of Compensation Costs

These features of the results arise from the effects on decision making in
Period 2 of both the opportunity for learning and the costs of reversing
institutional change. To understand this further, consider the following two
results from the numerical extension to the model.

i. Without learning, optimal decisions for institutional change result in an
    institutional level in Period 2 of $I_2 = 1$ regardless of whether institutional
    change in Period 1 is unconstrained or constrained to 0, 0.5 or 1.
ii. With learning, optimal decisions for institutional change result in an
    institutional level in Period 2 of $I_2 = 1$ if the realised state of nature in
    Period 1 is $S_1 = 0$, but only $I_2 = 0.5$ if the realised state of nature in Period 1
    is $S_1 = 1$.

With learning and with zero costs of reversing institutional decisions, the
decision maker in Period 2 has the option of ensuring that $I_2 = 0.5$ if an
adverse state of nature is realised in Period 1 and the subjective probability of
an adverse state of nature in Period 2 is consequently revised upwards. This
allows the decision maker in Period 2 to avoid a lower expected benefit than
would occur if $I_2 = 1$. The loss that is avoided by learning and by ensuring that
$I_2 = 0.5$ rather than $I_2 = 1$ is equal to 0.029 regardless of whether the first-

period institutional change was $d_1 = 0$, $d_1 = 0.5$ or $d_1 = 1$. Hence the unconditional expected value of learning and the quasi-option values equal 0.029 and are independent of the first-period decision.

As the cost of reversing institutional change increases, the decision maker in Period 2 will still wish to ensure that $I_2 = 0.5$ upon learning of an adverse state of nature in Period 1. However, achieving $I_2 = 0.5$ requires reversal of institutional change if $I_1 = 1$ and bears a cost of compensation if $\alpha > 0$. Consequently, increasing costs of compensation reduce the value of learning, in terms of expected welfare, if $I_1 = 1$ (and hence also $d_1 = 1$). This explains some results of the numerical example. Firstly, the quasi-option values of learning for $d_1 = 0$ and $d_1 = 0.5$ are constant with respect to the cost of reversing institutional change for the simple reason that if learning reveals an adverse state of nature in Period 1, then no reversal of previous institutional change is necessary to ensure that $I_2 = 0.5$ in Period 2. Secondly, with a first-period institutional change of $d_1 = 1$, the unconditional expected value of learning and the quasi-option value of learning decrease as the cost of reversing institutional change increases, since the benefits of achieving $I_2 = 0.5$ upon learning of an adverse state of nature in Period 1 are reduced by an amount equal to the cost of compensation. Indeed, as the cost of compensation increases beyond $\alpha = 0.11$, this cost exceeds the expected benefits of achieving $I_2 = 0.5$ upon learning of an adverse state of nature in Period 1, and hence the quasi-option value for $d_1 = 1$ reaches a constant value of zero. This is a case of the transition cost of institutional change outweighing the benefits of change.

Finally, what is the explanation for the reduction and then stabilisation in the unconditional expected value of learning as the compensation cost increases? Remember that, with learning, the optimal first-period institutional decision would be $d_1 = 1$ for levels of compensation cost $\alpha \leq 0.04$ (Figure 6.4). Thus, as the compensation cost increases from 0 to 0.04, the expected value of learning decreases, following the same curve as the quasi-option value with $d_1 = 1$. For $\alpha > 0.04$, the optimal first-period institutional decision switches to $d_1 = 0.5$. As already indicated above, with $d_1 = 0.5$ the second-period decision maker will not reverse institutional change upon learning of an adverse state of nature in Period 1, but instead will select $d_2 = 0$ and avoid expected losses that would be associated with an institutional level in Period 2 of $I_2 = 1$. Thus the unconditional value of learning is constant with respect to α for $\alpha > 0.04$.

CONCLUSIONS: DYNAMIC TRANSACTION COSTS AND OPTION VALUES IN INSTITUTIONAL CHANGE

The hypothetical system of natural-resource use and institutional change modelled in this study had the following general characteristics.

- The benefits from resource use, in this case from irrigation, are dependent upon the strength of private property rights in an institutional structure and a state of nature. At the present time the institutional structure is characterised by 'weak' private property rights and 'strong' state property rights. Future benefits from irrigation would be maximised with unattenuated private property rights, regardless of the state of nature, but are lower under an adverse state of nature.
- The net benefits of resource use to society depend on both the benefits from irrigation and the cost of resource management incurred by the government in maintaining environmental quality. This cost is also dependent upon the institutional structure and the state of nature. Management costs are low under a favourable state of nature. With an adverse state of nature, management costs are higher and increase with the strength of private property rights. In combination with an adverse state of nature, strong private property rights cause high costs of environmental management due to reduced flexibility of government in making changes to patterns of water use that are necessary to maintain a predetermined standard of environmental quality. When both the benefits of resource use and the costs of environmental management are taken into account, the net benefits of resource use would be maximised under unattenuated private property rights with a favourable state of nature, but a more moderate strengthening of private property rights would maximise the benefits of resource use under an adverse state of nature.
- The future states of nature are uncertain due to imperfect knowledge of the hydrological and ecological characteristics of the water resource. Knowledge of future states of nature is limited to subjective probabilities. These probabilities are refined over time as learning occurs of the characteristics of the water resource.
- The level of institutional change is determined by a benevolent government. In determining the level of institutional change, the government will seek to maximise a welfare function that has components of the benefits of water use in irrigation, the costs of environmental management, and the potential costs of reversing institutional change. In this model, any reversal of institutional change constitutes an attenuation of private property rights and has an associated transition cost that arises

from a requirement to compensate any irrigation farmers from an attenuation of private property rights. Should learning increase the subjective probability of an adverse state of nature and make reversal of institutional change desirable, the compensation costs impede such reversal.

A formalisation and numerical example of this model indicated that there is a positive value associated with opportunities for learning if the compensation costs of reversing institutional change are sufficiently low to allow reversal of institutional changes or if relatively conservative institutional changes are made in the present period pending future learning. The value that the decision maker in the present period will attach to the opportunity of future learning is conceptually similar to the quasi-option value that has been studied in the context of irreversible decisions of environmental development versus preservation. As with decisions of development versus preservation, explicit recognition of quasi-option values in cost–benefit analyses of institutional change may alter optimal decisions in the present time period towards more conservative changes.

Note that the numerical example involved discrete-choice options and as a result the optimality of a conservative choice was very much dependent upon the specification of the cost and benefit functions, particularly whether the benefits of delayed decision making exceeded the costs of forgone expected benefits in the first period. Nevertheless, other studies of quasi-option values with continuous-choice sets have indicated the general result that when learning is possible, maximisation of expected benefits without recognition of the potential for learning and of quasi-option values will in general lead to a sub-optimal decision (Schmutzler, 1991 pp. 127–8; Hirshleifer and Riley, 1992 pp. 204–7). The only exceptions are the extreme cases where first-period decisions are perfectly flexible (transition costs or compensation costs are zero) or all first-period decisions are strictly irreversible (transition costs are essentially infinite). In the first case, prospects for learning are unimportant because possible decisions in future periods are not restricted by the first-period decisions. In the second case, prospects for learning are unimportant since reaction to this learning is impossible regardless of the first-period decision (Schmutzler, 1991 p. 128).

The Murray–Darling Basin has several general features in common with the model developed in this chapter, as indicated below.

- The future state of nature is uncertain.
- Learning will occur through both research and experience and will result in revision of subjective probabilities of the capacity of the river system to accommodate particular patterns of irrigation activity.

- Environmental management is potentially more costly with stronger private property rights over water. Strong private property rights for irrigators reduce options for a regulatory agency to alter patterns of water use in years of low water supplies. For instance, strong private property rights may reduce the capacity of a regulatory agency to make unilateral decisions for altering water entitlements in years of low water supplies, forcing the government either to buy back entitlements to provide for environmental flows, or to bear a cost through compromised environmental objectives. Strengthening private rights of irrigators effectively transfers risks and costs of water shortages from irrigators to the government and public. An example of this has occurred in the 1997/98 irrigation year. Low water supplies for irrigators in the Murray region of New South Wales plus strong *de facto* property rights over water entitlements has resulted in the government bearing costs of water shortages through release of water from the Snowy Mountains Scheme at the expense of forgone Snowy River flows and generation of hydro-electricity. Nevertheless, the retention by state governments of substantial property rights over water use has had advantages through cost savings to the government in altering water use for the purposes of environmental management. In April 1998, the New South Wales government reduced water allocations for all irrigators in that state by 4 to 6 per cent and in some cases by as much as 12 per cent to provide for environmental water allocations. Compensation amounted to a $25 million package to assist farmers in the adoption of better irrigation practices. This compares with a direct cost of at least $85 million[1] for the Murray–Darling Basin alone if the government had to buy back water entitlements from irrigation farmers.
- It is actually or potentially costly to reverse institutional change that has enhanced private property rights. At present in the Murray–Darling Basin, state governments have retained rights to alter water entitlements held by irrigators without compensation. With stronger private property rights, it is possible that reductions to entitlements would be subject to payments of compensation in a manner similar to the 'regulatory takings' provisions of state and federal legislation in the USA that in certain circumstances require compensation to be paid to individuals who have had the value of private property reduced by changes in government legislation (Innes, unpublished).

The institutional reforms for water use in the Murray–Darling Basin since the 1970s (described in Chapter 5) can be considered as fairly cautious in so far as state governments have retained substantial property rights over water. The above characteristics of the resource system of the Murray–Darling Basin and the modelling results of this chapter suggest that this may be quite reasonable despite some concerns from irrigation farmers about insecurity and uncertainty in water entitlements. The results thus add weight to such a possibility raised by Pigram *et al.* (1992, p. 77):

> Already, irrigators in the Murray–Darling Basin are pressing for the status of their rights to water to be specified more precisely. Security and reliability of supply are important for management decisions to ensure the continued viability of the irrigation enterprise. Security of entitlement is also important for investment decisions and to underpin a workable system for transferability. Understandably, water authorities tend to react with caution to these moves because of implied legal obligations. Moreover, such binding arrangements might inhibit necessary adjustments to water allocations, for example, to make provision for future environmental needs.

This chapter has thus demonstrated that decisions for institutional change may not only be associated with transition costs at the time of making the decision but may also affect transition costs associated with decisions for future institutional change. Dynamic transaction costs, which are the costs associated with changing an institutional structure, thus include both the transition costs for the actual institutional change as well as potential costs imposed on society in the future through reduction in institutional flexibility and associated reductions in quasi-option value. In the next chapter, these two types of dynamic transaction cost will be incorporated into a formulation of the policy problem for institutional change in combination with considerations of static transaction costs.

NOTE

1. The estimate of $85 million based on a total water allocation to irrigation farmers in the Murray–Darling Basin of New South Wales of 6 838 000 megalitres (Murray–Darling Basin Ministerial Council, 1995) and a conservatively low estimate of the price for permanent sale of water entitlement of $250 per megalitre.

7. Policy Analysis for Institutional Change

INTRODUCTION

Previous chapters have examined institutions of water allocation from largely conceptual and *ex post* perspectives. Chapter 2 drew on the existing literature on institutional economics and transaction-cost economics to develop a general model of regulatory institutions for the use of natural resources. This model developed the concept of institutional hierarchies that had previously been touched on in the literature and provided explanations for the nature of particular hierarchical structures in terms of transaction costs. Three core premises were developed in this chapter: (i) transaction costs are associated with any institutional structures for regulation of resource use; (ii) particular institutional structures develop in response to efforts by economic and political agents to reduce the transaction costs associated with achieving particular objectives in resource use; and (iii) processes of institutional change are themselves influenced by transaction costs, resulting in institutional development being characterised by irreversibilities and path-dependencies.

Chapters 3 to 5 sought to determine the extent to which these premises hold true for the regulation of water use for irrigation in the Murray–Darling Basin. Chapter 3 provided background information on the irrigation industries in two states of the Murray–Darling Basin: New South Wales and South Australia. Institutions of water use in these states were described in accordance with the model of institutional hierarchies developed in Chapter 2. Chapter 4 focused on the first two premises and examined transaction costs associated with one part of an institutional hierarchy, that of market allocation of water entitlements in South Australia. The empirical analysis of trading of water entitlements indicated that transaction costs have a substantial impact on the allocation outcomes arising from the institutional arrangements of the 'water market' and that participants in the markets engaged in many initiatives to reduce transaction costs. These results were used as a basis for more general comments on transaction costs arising in other parts of the institutional hierarchy governing water use, and how transaction costs have created, and continue to create, incentives for institutional change.

In Chapter 5, the focus shifted to examining the third premise: that processes of institutional change are themselves influenced by transaction costs resulting in institutional development being characterised by irreversibilities and path-dependencies. The history of institutional development for water use in New South Wales and South Australia was examined and the observation made that the process of institutional change was overwhelmingly incremental, each development building on pre-existing property rights and allocation mechanisms. This historical overview supported the premise of path-dependency in institutional change and indicated that initiatives in institutional development have been greatly constrained by the path of prior development. Chapter 6 examined the implications of this path-dependency and suggested that the current decisions for institutional change will impose constraints on future institutional innovations. Given the irreversibilities of institutional change, uncertainty about the need to alter institutions of water use in the future, and a likelihood of improved knowledge about the river system in the future, there may in some circumstances be quasi-option values associated with relatively conservative decisions for current institutional change that maintain options to respond to improved knowledge.

The material presented so far has thus established the relevance of the central premises to policy decisions relating to changes in institutions for water use. The terms 'static transaction costs' and 'dynamic transaction costs' were used to refer to the two different types of transaction costs relevant to the examination of these issues. Static transaction costs refer to the costs of decision making and resource allocation within a given institutional structure. This is the usual conception of transaction costs in the economic literature. Dynamic transaction costs refer to the costs of institutional change and are the costs that give rise to the irreversibilities and path-dependencies in institutional development.

This chapter explores in more detail the implications of these transaction-cost issues for policy analysis relating to institutional change. A systems representation is used to examine the relationships between the static and dynamic transaction costs and institutional change. The major implications for institutional policy are identified and a statement is made of the general policy problem for institutional change. Attention then shifts to policy analysis and how the different types of transaction costs can be estimated to allow comparative analysis of alternative institutional structures. Finally, conclusions are drawn on the contribution of this formulation of the policy problem to policy analysis and on the implications for future research in institutional choice.

STATIC AND DYNAMIC TRANSACTION COSTS AND INSTITUTIONAL CHANGE

Recall the initial model of institutional change developed from the work of North (1990) in Chapter 2 and considered again in Chapter 5 in relation to the historical development of institutions for water use in the Murray–Darling Basin. Previous chapters examined the implications from this model that both the motivation for institutional change and the constraints on institutional change arise through transaction costs. A given set of institutions and other parameters make up an initial state of the world and determine the set of potential costs and benefits facing economic agents, including both relative prices faced by the agents and the (static) transaction costs of economic exchange. These costs and benefits motivate the economic agents either to engage in economic activity (production, trade, consumption, etc.) or to invest resources in changing the state of the world. This may be achieved by changes in technology or by changing institutions that affect the static transaction costs. In accordance with the theme of this book, attention will focus on institutional change that is achieved through investment in the political process within which the dynamic transaction costs of institutional change are incurred. Since any such investment is made by agents affected by patterns of vested interests in a pre-existing institutional setting, some institutional changes are easier (less expensive) to achieve than others; hence the path-dependency of institutional change.

A simplified model which ignores the identities of the agents for change and focuses instead on motivations and constraints for change is shown in Figure 7.1. An initial set of state variables comprising institutions and other state-of-the-world parameters can be considered as presenting a set of prices. These prices include prices of goods and services, transaction costs for economic exchange and transaction costs of institutional change. On the basis of these, decisions are made in regard to economic exchange and institutional change. These decisions comprise the control variables of the model which, together with exogenous inputs to the system, affect the state of the world at the beginning of the next time period with flow-on effects to prices and transaction costs faced in a subsequent period.

The distinction between static and dynamic transaction costs relates to a focus on different aspects of the model shown in Figure 7.1. Consideration of static transaction costs focuses attention on how a given set of institutions and other parameters create prices and transaction costs that motivate particular decisions in regard to resource allocation and institutional change. This 'subset' of the problem is highlighted in Figure 7.2. This focus is static in so far as assessment of institutional change ignores the link between a particular institutional structure and the costs of institutional change, and thereby ignores the effect of a current decision for change on future options of change. In other words, the transaction costs of institutional change (the dynamic transaction costs) are exogenous to the model and constitute a state-of-the-world parameter.

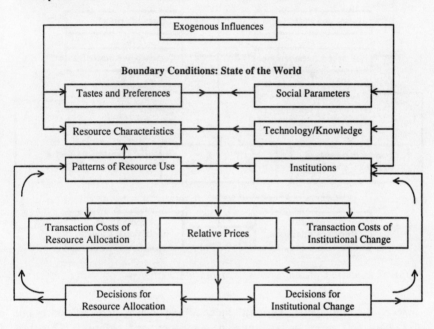

Figure 7.1: Systems Representation of Resource Allocation and Institutional Change

The static transaction costs are the main focus of the body of transaction-cost theory derived from the work of Ronald Coase and Oliver Williamson. Two very general results can be drawn from this body of work that are relevant in considering the static transaction costs of institutional change.

Firstly, the consideration of static transaction costs makes the contract or transaction the unit of analysis. For a given transaction, the objective of analysis is to determine the governance structure or institutional framework by which the transaction costs can be minimised (Williamson, 1979). The implication for institutions of natural-resource use is that for a given set of objectives in relation to resource allocation, such as short-term efficiency, sustainability, equity objectives, etc., the focus of policy analysis is to reduce the transaction costs associated with making the decisions for resource allocation necessary to pursue these objectives.

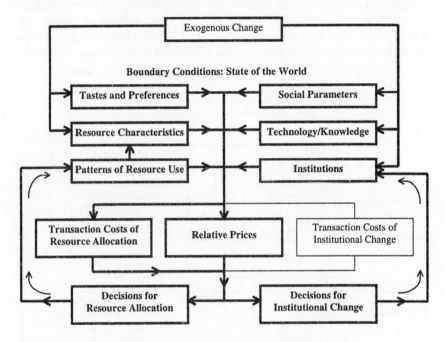

Figure 7.2: Static Considerations in Institutional Change

Secondly, high transaction costs incurred in pursuing particular economic objectives will motivate institutional innovation and reform. This was demonstrated in Chapter 5 in relation to institutional change to allow trading of water entitlements between irrigation farmers. Initially, water entitlements were attached to specific units of land and irrigators wishing to purchase or sell water entitlements would have to undertake a complicated transaction involving trade of both land and water and then subsequently trade the land back to the original owner without the attached water entitlement. The high transaction costs in undertaking such transactions motivated investment in the political process to develop institutions for the trading of water entitlement separately from land.

For the institutions of water allocation in the Murray–Darling Basin, transaction costs associated with alternative institutional structures have rarely, if ever, been explicitly considered in policy analysis. Many historical institutional changes can be explained by reference to a motivation of minimising transactions costs, as described in Chapter 5, but policy analysts have at best given only implicit and subjective recognition to transaction costs of alternative institutional structures in achieving particular allocation objectives.

Consideration of dynamic transaction costs focuses attention on transaction costs of institutional change as endogenous parameters of the model that are determined by the various state variables, with particular attention to the effect of existing institutions (Figure 7.3).

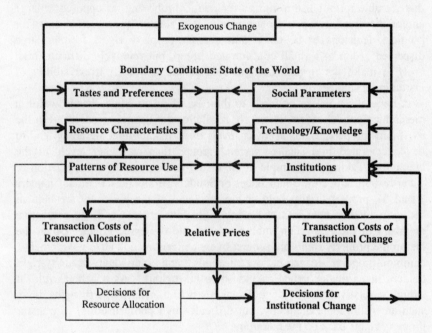

Figure 7.3: Dynamic Considerations in Institutional Change

Dynamic transaction costs associated with institutional change have received some attention in the literature, principally in respect of political repercussions of decisions for institutional change where proposed changes attenuate existing property rights (Dixit, 1996; Horn, 1995). Horn (1995 pp. 30–31) refers to these transaction costs as 'political transaction costs' and argues that these are correlated with the degree of conflict associated with a proposed change. The existence of conflict makes it harder for legislators or other decision makers to agree on institutional change and increases the likelihood that either the decision makers will have to bear political repercussions for the decision or that compensation will need to be paid to the groups in society disaffected by the change.

Arguments presented by Horn (1995) provide reasons why there may be net political costs associated with some transfers of property rights but not others, and also why a particular transfer of property rights may be very politically costly to reverse. This reasoning has to do with the concentration of costs and benefits associated with a proposed institutional change. Generally speaking, the political ramifications of institutional change are greater if the costs and/or benefits of change are incurred by small and/or concentrated groups in society that are able to mobilise resources for political lobbying, as opposed to large and/or dispersed groups. Consequently, it is relatively easy (low cost) for political decisions to be made that transfer property rights from a large dispersed group to a small concentrated group, but relatively difficult (high cost) to make the reverse change. Hence the notion of irreversibility of institutional change.

A generalisation can be made to the case of institutional change within a hierarchical model of institutions for regulations of natural resources. For the most part, property rights at lower levels of an institutional hierarchy tend to be concentrated into smaller societal groups than at higher levels in the hierarchy. Taking the example of the institutional hierarchy for regulation of water resources in New South Wales or South Australia (described in Chapters 3 and 5), property rights held at the top level of the hierarchy are held in common by the state and commonwealth governments and the respective members of the Australian public: a large and dispersed group. Down the hierarchy, property rights are progressively concentrated in state governments, common-property irrigation organisations, and individual property-right holders in particular irrigation industries or regions. As a general rule, it would be relatively easy (low political costs) to transfer property rights down such an institutional hierarchy, but difficult (high political costs) to transfer property rights back up the hierarchy.

As already indicated in previous chapters, the dynamic transaction costs may be divided into two categories: (i) the transition costs of decision making and implementation for institutional change in the current period, where these costs arise as a function of the institutional *status quo*; and (ii) the intertemporal costs arising where institutional change in the current period increases the transition costs of possible future institutional changes, i.e current institutional change reduces the flexibility of the institutional structure to respond to changing circumstances in the future. Both types of dynamic transaction cost arise as a result of path-dependencies and irreversibilities in institutional change.

Consideration of the intertemporal costs is important to policy analysis where certain conditions hold or are recognised in the analysis.

Firstly, transition costs will only be important when it is recognised that static transaction costs are incurred in any decision making for resource allocation and that the position in an institutional hierarchy for which the transaction costs of an allocation decision are minimised will vary according to the nature of the decision. For example, efficient decisions for the allocation of water between irrigation activities at the farm level or between farms in an irrigation district may be made at lowest transaction cost when the decisions rest with individual farmers who can respond readily to signals of market prices, seasonal conditions, etc. For other decisions, such as allocation of water to the environment, transaction costs may be minimised by having the decisions rest with state governments or at the level of common property between state governments, where the decision-making body is the Murray–Darling Basin Commission. Because the static transaction costs are positive for any institutional structure, a policy objective exists to develop new institutional structures in response to changing circumstances. Transition costs will be incurred when changing institutions.

Secondly, consideration of the intertemporal component of dynamic transaction costs will be important where (i) uncertainty or ignorance exists in relation to future institutional arrangements that will need to be in place for resource allocation, and (ii) institutional change is characterised by irreversibility, which can be defined in the broadest sense as meaning that today's choice influences tomorrow's choice possibilities. In the presence of uncertainty and irreversibilities, the value of learning about the resource system and other parameters that affect resource use will be dependent upon the costs of making appropriate changes in the institutional structure. The value associated with flexibility for institutional change in response to learning is a quasi-option value, as described in Chapter 6.

If these general conditions apply to a policy problem for institutional change, then the problem is necessarily an intertemporal one, and needs to consider dynamic transaction costs. In Chapter 6, a conceptual problem of this sort was addressed by specifically including a cost function for reversing institutional change in net present value calculations for institutional change over two periods. This simple conceptual model was useful for the purposes of illustrating how quasi-option values may arise in considerations of institutional change, but a more general statement of the policy problem is necessary to gain insight into the implications for institutional change in more complex situations. This is addressed in the next section of this chapter.

THE INTERTEMPORAL POLICY PROBLEM FOR INSTITUTIONAL CHANGE

Conventional transaction-cost theory deals with static transaction costs and generally considers the benefits of institutional reform to be a reduction in these transaction costs (Eggertsson, 1990 *passim*). The rationale for this approach to problems of institutional change is that in the absence of transaction costs, all institutional structures for allocation of a resource produce the same 'efficient' outcome, a result that has become embodied in the 'Coase theorem'. Williamson (1979) argues that 'if transaction costs are negligible, the organisation of economic activity is irrelevant, since any advantages that one mode of organisation appears to hold over another will simply be eliminated by costless transacting'. Where transaction costs are positive, however, the allocation from any institutional structure will fall short of an efficient 'zero-transaction-cost' allocation. A measure of transaction costs is the discrepancy between these two outcomes, and the institutional structure that most closely approaches the most efficient allocation is that with the lowest transaction costs. The policy goal in considering institutional change is to minimise this discrepancy and therefore in this sense to maximise welfare by selecting an institutional structure to minimise the static transaction costs of decision making for resource allocation.

An objective of selecting an institutional structure to maximise welfare can be expressed as:

$$\underset{I_i}{\text{Max}}\ W = a_i\{I_i\} \tag{7.1}$$

where W = welfare derived from resource use; I_i = alternative institutional structures, possibly comprising a vector of institutional characteristics such as distributions of property rights, entitlement systems, and allocation mechanisms ($i = 1 \ldots m$); and $a_i\{I_i\}$ = net benefits of resource use under institutional structure I_i.

By the argument presented above, the net benefits of resource use under an institutional structure is a function of the level of static transaction costs incurred in decisions for resource allocation. Thus the objective of maximising welfare is equivalent to an objective of minimising static transaction costs:

$$\underset{I_i}{\text{Min}}\ C = c_i\{I_i\} \tag{7.2}$$

where C = transaction costs of decision making for resource allocation; and

$c_i\{I_i\}$ = static transaction costs incurred in decision making for resource allocation under institutional structure I_i.

This statement of the policy problem for examining institutional change is a simplification. At least one study (Griffin, 1991) has shown that, as well as the level of transaction costs, the distribution of these costs is also important in determining welfare benefits of an institutional structure. However, in this initial attempt to incorporate transaction costs into policy decisions of institutional choice, attention was confined to the problem of minimising transaction costs. The objective of selecting an institutional structure to maximise economic welfare is taken to be equivalent to an objective of selecting an institutional structure to minimise static transaction costs.

Consider, in this case, allocation of water resources. An efficient allocation of water exists where the marginal benefit of water use is the same across all water uses. A social planner pursuing such an objective of efficiency could allocate water across all potential uses and users, but the ability to achieve an efficient allocation would be constrained by the static transaction costs associated with requirements for very detailed information on benefit functions across alternative uses. Alternatively, a market system could be relied upon to allocate water, although the capacity of trading to achieve an efficient water allocation would be constrained by the static transaction costs of market search and contracting, as was shown to be the case in Chapter 4. On a conceptual level, the allocation mechanism that would best be able to achieve an efficient allocation, and thus maximise social welfare, would be that with the lowest static transaction costs.

The statement of the policy problem for institutional change in Equation 7.2 is incomplete in that it does not consider dynamic transaction costs: the transition costs and intertemporal costs. The magnitude of transition costs is largely affected by the institutional *status quo*, associated distributions of vested interest, and by other institutional arrangements that determine the process and costs of decision making and implementing a new institutional structure. The magnitude of intertemporal costs depends upon the range of possible future states that would be revealed by learning, and the future transition costs that would need to be incurred in making appropriate institutional responses to learning. In the absence of any potential transition costs in the future, an institutional structure is perfectly flexible and the value of learning about an uncertain future (the quasi-option value) is at a maximum. As potential transition costs in the future increase, institutional structures become increasingly inflexible and unable to be changed in response to learning: quasi-option values decrease. The quasi-option value of an institutional structure thus provides an inverse measure of the intertemporal costs associated with that institutional structure.

Taking into account both the static and dynamic transaction costs, the overall policy problem is to select an institutional structure that minimises a sum of the static transaction costs, the transition costs of moving from the institutional *status quo* to the new institutional structure, and the negative of the quasi-option value of the new institutional structure (an inverse measure of intertemporal cost):

$$\underset{I_i}{\text{Min}}\, C = c_i\{I_i\} + d_i\{I_0, I_i\} - q_i\{I_i\} \qquad (7.3)$$

where I_0 = the existing institutional structure, possibly comprising a vector of institutional characteristics such as distributions of property rights, entitlement systems, and allocation mechanisms; I_i = alternative institutional structures $(i = 1 \dots m)$; $c_i\{I_i\}$ = static transaction costs associated with institutional structure I_i, measured as the difference in economic benefits from the resource system with zero static transaction costs and the economic benefits with the static transaction costs incurred under I_i; $d_i\{I_0, I_i\}$ = transition costs of institutional change from I_0 to I_i ; and $q_i\{I_i\}$ = quasi-option value of institutional structure I_i, measured as the expected net present value of learning under institutional structure I_i, taking into account the potential future transition costs in changing I_i in response to learning.

To illustrate this formulation of the policy problem, consider the situation in the Murray–Darling Basin where state governments determine the extent to which private property rights will be granted in water entitlements. Property rights reside initially with the state governments, and the governments need to decide whether to: (i) devolve property rights down the institutional hierarchy to create and strengthen private rights to the point where security of private water entitlements is guaranteed and any changes in water allocation would need to be accomplished through market transactions with private water users; or (ii) to retain some state property rights, allowing state governments unilaterally to make allocation decisions that affect private water entitlements.

Using notation similar to that adopted by Horn (1995) in formulating a similar problem, let the level of delegation of property rights equal Z with a range [0,1], where $Z = 0$ corresponds to property rights being retained fully by the state government (the institutional *status quo*) and $Z = 1$ corresponds to property rights being fully delegated to private water users.

Let the static transaction costs for private allocation be a function of the level of delegation $\alpha\{Z\}$. The static transaction costs are the costs of making allocation decisions measured by the extent to which the resultant allocation falls short of the efficient allocation that would occur in a world of zero transaction costs. For allocation decisions by a state government, these transaction costs may arise through lack of information and inflexible or time-consuming decision-making processes. For allocation decisions by private water users, transaction costs may arise through market imperfections, including information problems that were examined in Chapter 4 in relation to trading of water entitlements in South Australia.

Let the transition cost in the current period be denoted by the function $\beta\{Z\}$, which reflects path-dependency constraints imposed by the pre-existing institutional structure $(Z = 0)$. The impact of a current decision on the flexibility of the institutional structure and the future costs of institutional change made in response to learning is captured by the quasi-option value associated with any selected level of delegation. Let the quasi-option value associated with any given level of delegation be denoted by the function $\gamma\{Z\}$. The quasi-option value is determined by considering several parameters: the range of possible future states that may be revealed by learning; the subjective probabilities of these states; the possible changes to the institutional structure Z that would be desirable under alternative states; and the effect of the current institutional structure Z on the costs of achieving different institutional structures in the future.

The policy problem faced by a social planner is, for a given objective in resource allocation:

$$\underset{Z}{\text{Min}}\ V = \alpha\{Z\} + \beta\{Z\} - \gamma\{Z\} \quad \text{for } 0 \leq Z \leq 1 \qquad (7.4)$$

where V is the sum of static and dynamic transaction costs associated with a new institutional structure.

Some comment can be made on the signs of the different cost components within the context of the problem being addressed. The static transaction costs $\alpha\{Z\}$ and the variation in these costs would be situation-specific. For example, if the problem is one of allocation of water between farms and irrigation activities within an irrigation region with a very large number of farms and no major constraints on spatial patterns of water use, then the static transaction costs associated with strong private rights and market allocation would probably be low, and indeed possibly much lower than for allocation by a government agency. In other circumstances the static transaction costs for market allocations may be relatively high. For example, if the allocation problem involves 'public-good' uses of water and there are many constraints on allocations, then the information and bargaining costs associated with private property rights and market allocations may be relatively high and allocation decisions may be made at a lower transaction cost by a central state agency. Such a situation may exist where a water resource must be allocated across diverse uses such as irrigation farmers, recreational water users, environmentalists and hydro-electricity generators, and constraints on water allocation arise from capacities of river channels and spatial externalities in water use.   Static transaction costs of allocation would be minimised by a lower level of delegation and the state retaining some property rights.

The transition costs for institutional change, $\beta\{Z\}$, arise both in the form of the direct costs of deciding and implementing institutional change, as well as the indirect political costs or benefits to decision makers.   It is conceivable that for some institutional changes, political benefits may accrue from the change that override the direct transition costs and $\beta\{Z\}$ may be a net benefit to the decision makers.   For example, with delegation of property rights from a state to private water users, it is likely that there would actually be a benefit, or negative cost, to the decision maker as the rights are being transferred down an institutional hierarchy from a large, diffuse group (the state population) to a small, concentrated group (the private water users).   Whilst costs may be incurred in drafting and establishing the systems of private property rights, the political benefits of such an institutional change may exceed these costs and cause a net 'transition benefit' to the political decision makers.

The quasi-option value, $\gamma\{Z\}$, is always non-negative, as indicated in Chapter 6.   The magnitude would depend on the factors described earlier in this chapter: the level of uncertainty in relation to future states of the world; the future decisions that may need to be made for resource allocation; the optimal distribution of property rights for these decisions in terms of minimising static transaction costs; and the extent to which delegation of property rights is characterised by irreversibility.   For example, consider a situation where the potential environmental impacts of irrigation are largely unknown but could be greatly influenced by the spatial distribution of water use.   If the static transaction costs of allocation under private property rights were too high to provide for an efficient allocation of water to balance productive use and environmental quality, an efficient allocation under an adverse future outcome may require an administrative allocation of water and therefore require the state governments to hold the property rights.   If a delegation of property rights to private users is costly to reverse, such a delegation would reduce flexibility to respond to learning about the environmental impacts of irrigation and the quasi-option value, $\gamma\{Z\}$, would be decreasing in Z.   Situations of proposed institutional change can also be envisaged where the quasi-option value would be increased.   An institutional change involving a state government resuming private rights (a redistribution of property rights up an institutional hierarchy) could reduce the costs to government of making future institutional changes in response to learning, and result in an increase in quasi-option value.

Given ranges of the different transaction-cost parameters as $\alpha\{Z\} \geq 0$, $\beta\{Z\} \geq$ or < 0, and $\gamma\{Z\} \geq 0$, the value of V may be $\geq$ or < 0.   A positive value of V indicates that for the given institutional structure, the sum of static transaction costs and transition costs exceeds the quasi-option value.   This may be the case where there is little uncertainty about the future or minimal flexibility costs associated with the relevant institutions, both contributing to a small quasi-option value. A negative value of V indicates that the quasi-option value exceeds the sum of static transaction costs and transition costs. This may be the case where there is substantial uncertainty about the future and strong irreversibilities in institutional change that contribute to a high quasi-option value. The sign of V does not in itself determine whether institutional change will or will not occur. What matters is whether an institutional change will result in a net reduction in V over the institutional *status quo*. Recalling that the institutional *status quo* is represented by $Z = 0$, the sum of transaction costs for this institutional structure can be represented as:

$$V\{0\} = \alpha\{0\} - \gamma\{0\} .\qquad(7.5)$$

For the institutional *status quo*, the transition costs of $\beta\{Z\}$ are, of course, equal to zero as there is no institutional change.

Thus as a general statement, institutional change to a new structure Z' is desirable where:

$$V\{Z'\} < V\{0\} \text{ for } 0 < Z' \le 1.\qquad(7.6)$$

This formulation of the policy problem for institutional change indicates that the decision maker may have to consider a trade-off between current benefits (reduced static transaction costs), transition costs, and quasi-option values associated with flexibility in future institutional change. The need to make policy decisions involving trade-offs between minimising current allocation costs and maintaining flexibility in the face of uncertainty has been previously recognised (for example Segerson, 1992) but not expressed as part of a cohesive framework for policy analysis.

POLICY ANALYSIS

Given the policy decision problem described above, policy analysis for the purposes of institutional choice requires estimation of transaction costs associated with alternative institutional structures. This represents a major shift from current practices of policy analysis, particularly *ex ante* analysis, which generally ignores transaction costs. This section of the chapter explores issues associated with estimating transaction costs and quasi-option values and assesses the prospects for being able rigorously and quantitatively to apply the policy analysis problem for institutional change as formulated in the previous section.   The three transaction-cost parameters of static transaction costs, transition costs and quasi-option value are considered in turn.

Static Transaction Costs

Static transaction costs are the costs of making decisions for resource allocation within a given institutional structure.   As already indicated, a measure of these costs is the extent to which a resource allocation arising from a particular institutional structure falls short of an efficient allocation that would arise in a situation of zero transaction costs.   The reasoning for this is that, in the absence of transaction costs, all institutional structures for allocation of a resource produce the same efficient outcome. When transaction costs are positive, the allocation from any institutional structure will fall short of the efficient allocation. A measure of the transaction costs is the discrepancy between these two outcomes.

Static transaction costs arise through costs of administering an institutional structure, and the costs of decision making for resource allocation under that structure.   These two sources of transaction costs are described further below.

Costs of administering an institutional structure arise though the use of resources in maintaining and administering institutions, such as management of records of property rights and changes in ownership of the rights, and in policing and enforcement.   These costs may be borne by different parties within an institutional hierarchy and effects on resource allocations will differ accordingly.   For example, costs associated with administering private water licences and entitlements of private water users are typically met by the state agency or common-property group that issues the licences and entitlements. Costs of enforcing riparian rights, however, may be incurred largely by the holders of those rights through civil processes of enforcement.   To the extent that institutions are not policed and enforced due to high costs of doing so, additional transaction costs may be imposed on agents within a property-right hierarchy through having to make allocation decisions under greater uncertainty about the outcomes of those decisions.

Costs of decision making for resource allocation within an institutional structure arise largely through costs of obtaining information.   In a world of perfect information, decision making for allocation would be perfect and costless: government agencies would be perfectly informed about relative benefits of alternative uses of resources and private decision makers in markets would have no search or bargaining costs in transactions.   However, in the real world there is not perfect information.   Decision makers under regimes of market allocation of resource entitlements face costs of identifying potential trading partners, developing contracts and monitoring contract outcomes.   Administrative decision makers under regimes of state property or common property face costs of collecting information on interest groups, assessing benefits of alternative allocations, and of monitoring and enforcing allocations. In both cases, decision makers are faced with both direct costs of obtaining information and indirect costs associated with incomplete or sub-optimal contracts and allocation decisions.

Together, the various types of transaction cost will cause allocation decisions to be 'sub-optimal' relative to those decisions that would be made in the absence of transaction costs. Estimating the extent of sub-optimality for use as a measure of transaction costs may, in principle at least, be achieved through estimating various transaction costs and transaction-cost functions and incorporating these costs into models of allocation decisions. Estimating the transaction-cost functions is likely to be the difficult step in this approach as there has only been very limited empirical work undertaken on transaction costs of allocation decisions and the relationships of these costs with institutional structures and other parameters of system of resource use.

There have been several conceptual studies of transaction costs associated with alternative institutions for regulating air and water pollution. Stavins (1995) developed a model of permit trading with transaction costs specified as an increasing function of a number of permit trades and, not surprisingly, found that positive transaction costs constrain trade, raise the costs of pollution control, and make the initial assignment of permits an important determinant of trading outcomes. The conclusion was reached that the cost-efficiency of alternative policy instruments (i.e. alternative institutions) for pollution control is an empirical question, dependent upon the transaction costs incurred for each instrument in different situations. Montero (1997) introduced uncertainty of costs of pollution control into a model of trading of pollution permits, and derived similar results. Uncertainty is effectively an additional transaction cost, reflecting a cost of information, and the model had similar implications to that developed by Stavins. Both these studies, however, gave little attention to the estimation of transaction costs. Stavins relegated this issue to a footnote: 'We assume that [the transaction cost function] is known with certainty. This is not unreasonable, but it is restrictive. ... further work could lead to representations linked to other aspects of the taxonomy of transaction costs. For example, transaction costs are likely to be a function not only of the size of trades but of other attributes as well ... .'

Empirical studies of transaction costs in market institutions have generally comprised studies examining the impact of transaction costs on trading outcomes without making any estimate of transaction costs *per se*. Chapter 4 described one such study which examined consequences of information costs on markets for water entitlements in South Australia. Other similar studies include those of Crocker (1971) and Leffler and Rucker (1991), who undertook empirical applications of transaction-cost analysis to the resolution of resource-allocation problems in air pollution and timber harvesting, respectively. Stavins (1995) briefly reviews several *ex post* studies of transaction costs in markets for tradable pollution permits and finds a correlation between the 'success' of tradable permit schemes and envisaged levels of transaction costs, although these studies made little attempt to estimate the transaction costs faced by traders in these markets. Actual *ex post* estimation of transaction costs in markets for water rights has been attempted by several researchers (Boggs, 1989; Colby, 1990, 1995; Howitt, 1994; Hearne and Easter, 1995). These studies generally estimated the direct costs to traders in water rights associated with the regulatory approvals process for proposed transfers of rights. Other transaction costs such as those incurred in negotiating trade contracts and the costs associated with uncertainty of trading outcomes were not considered.

There are fewer studies looking at transaction costs in administrative mechanisms for resource allocation. This is perverse, given an almost ubiquitous presumption amongst modern-day resource economists that government decision making for resource allocation is associated with very high transaction costs arising from imperfect information and costly decision-making procedures. On a conceptual level, Horn (1995) applied a transaction-cost analysis to examining institutional choice in the context of allocating regulatory functions amongst different levels of government in the USA, particularly between the legislature and appointed administrators. A transaction-cost model was used to explain the existence of a range of different institutions of administration: the role and employment practices of government bureaux; the choice between use of state-owned enterprises and the private sector for the provision of particular goods or services; and government provision of goods and services by bureaux or state-owned enterprises. Also on a conceptual level, Smith and Tomasi (1995) developed a model of policy choice for control of water pollution that included transaction costs as an exogenous parameter. The model suggested that recognition of transaction costs may affect policy choices between taxation schemes or standards for allocating rights to pollute.

Ostrom (1990) indirectly examined costs of decision making for resource allocation in an assessment of common-property institutions when she investigated the 'success' of common-property arrangements in developing and implementing allocation rules for common-pool resources. Transaction costs were not quantified, but strong correlations were shown to exist between factors presumed to affect the costs of decision making and enforcement, and the difficulties experienced by common-property groups in implementing allocation rules.

Quantitative estimation of transaction costs in government decision making for allocation of natural resources are rare. McCann (1997) undertook an investigation of policy choice for non-point pollution which involved estimation of transaction costs associated with four regulatory proposals for reducing phosphorus runoff from farmlands. Transaction costs that would be incurred by government agencies in administering the hypothetical policy programmes were estimated through interviews with agency staff. Other transaction costs, such as uncertainty about the effectiveness of alternative policies and political repercussions were not considered other than to the extent that they motivated research and information collection. Several problems in the estimation of transaction costs were encountered. These included limited abilities of agency staff to conceptualise hypothetical policies and estimate the associated costs, and biases and imprecision in survey results. Thompson (1997) estimated transaction costs associated with two alternative policy proposals for reducing water pollution from textile mills. As with the study by McCann, estimates of transaction costs were made by specifying hypothetical policy programmes and interviewing staff of regulatory agencies to determine the potential costs associated with the programmes.

On the basis of published studies, it thus appears that there is a general lack of established techniques for empirical estimation of the types of transaction costs associated with decision making for resource allocation, referred to as static transaction costs. Some effort has been made to estimate static transaction costs both *ex post* and *ex ante* for alternative institutional structures. However, this work has focused on estimating the actual costs incurred or likely to be incurred in specific situations rather than estimating 'transaction-cost functions' that relate levels of different types of transaction costs to parameters of the institutional structures and other variables of resource systems. The ability to generalise from this empirical work is thus limited.

Transition Costs

Transition costs have received reasonably substantial attention in the literature. Hutter (1986) described transition costs as 'the transaction costs which are expended to bring the institutions into being and to maintain them'. This differs slightly from the definition used in this book, which includes the costs of maintaining institutions within the scope of static transaction costs. Dorfman (1981) defined transition costs as 'the costs of adapting to a change in circumstances', which may include institutional change. According to Dorfman, the distinguishing feature of transition costs is that the costs would not be incurred in the absence of a change in circumstances, and the costs will not recur after the transition to the new set of circumstances is complete.

The types of costs that may be classed as transition costs are many and varied, and may arise from the following processes of institutional change.

- Research and institutional design.
- Negotiation, bargaining and decision making.
- Political repercussions to decision makers.
- Institutional creation, including the drafting of legislation, policies, regulations, etc.
- Implementation, including establishing regulatory organisations and programmes and conducting education activities.
- Redundancy of organisations and human capital associated with pre-existing institutional structures.
- Social displacement of individuals and firms affected by institutional change.
- Compensation payments to persons or firms disadvantaged by institutional change.
- Costs associated with lobbying and rent-seeking behaviour of interest groups.
- Increased perceptions of sovereign risk and policy uncertainty.

The types and magnitudes of transition costs will be determined by the nature of the proposed institutional change as well as the institutional *status quo*. This is implicitly recognised by Dorfman (1981): 'the kinds of transition cost that will be incurred and their magnitude, of course, depend to a great extent on the kind of regulation that is involved and whether the change is an introduction, a recision, or an alteration'. Also, the magnitude of transition costs will be influenced by the process by which an institutional change is implemented. This is often evident with institutional change by governments where particular strategies of change are often determined in recognition of transition costs associated with political repercussions, compensation payouts and social dislocation.

Transition costs are probably the most generally acknowledged and studied transactions costs associated with institutional change, and in some instances procedures have been established for estimation of particular transition costs as a component in processes of institutional change. For example, 'regulatory takings' provisions of state and federal legislation in the USA require compensation to be estimated and paid to individuals that have the value of private property reduced by changes in government legislation (Innes, unpublished). In Australia, changes in firearms legislation in 1996/97 were accompanied by assessments and payments of compensation to persons affected by new laws, including in some instances owners of retail gun shops that suffered business losses. In relation to institutional change for regulation of use of water resources in the Murray–Darling Basin, reforms of property-right regimes over group irrigation schemes have often been accompanied by government subsidies to reduce the costs of change that would be incurred by irrigation farmers and thus to reduce the transition costs implicit in political opposition to the institutional reforms.   Transition costs are also widely recognised as a barrier to institutional change. Reforms of tax law that would replace income taxes with consumption taxes are generally acknowledged to be constrained by the transition costs that some people would have to bear and the associated political costs to any government implementing the reforms (Dixit, 1996 p. 23). Avoidance of transition costs has impeded development of the General Agreement on Tariffs and Trade where national governments have sought to protect special interests and arrangements (Dixit, 1996 p. 23).

Despite the attention given to transition costs, however, the level of empirical work into estimating transition costs associated with institutions for allocation of natural resources seems to be on par with that for static transaction costs. That is, some attention has been given to estimating costs in particular circumstances but there has been a lack of effort given to determining 'transition-cost functions' that relate the levels of transition costs to parameters of institutions and variables of the resource system. The studies of McCann (1997) and Thompson (1997), already discussed above, gave some attention to estimating transition costs associated with changes in policy for pollution control. Thompson referred to enactment costs: social losses from opportunity costs of the legislature's time and social losses from lobbying expenditures by interest groups. An attempt was made to predict lobbying costs that may occur with two hypothetical policy proposals for reducing water pollution from textile mills. It was found, however, that these costs were not readily observable or measurable and estimation relied upon *ad hoc* assumptions of lobbying expenditure by certain interest groups as a percentage of the losses that would be incurred by these groups under alternative policies. McCann (1997) measured political costs through estimates made by regulatory agencies of the expected costs for different policy proposals of responding to lobbying by interest groups, and also by direct survey of policy decision makers. However, as with the estimation of static transaction costs, the ability to generalise from this empirical work is limited by estimation of costs in specific circumstances rather than giving attention to estimating 'transaction-cost functions' that relate levels of different types of transaction costs to parameters of the decision-making environment.

Quasi-Option Value

The above discussion of measurement of static transaction costs and transition costs indicated that there are substantial problems in measuring or predicting these costs due to their diversity, uncertain functional relationships between the costs and their determinants, many costs being implicit or indirect, and many costs not being easily quantified in dollar terms. Many of these difficulties will occur with estimation of quasi-option values which, to all intents and purposes, entails prediction of future transition costs. However, estimation of quasi-option value has to deal with an additional difficulty: that of uncertainty over future states.

How can quasi-option values be estimated and applied to decision making for institutional change? Previous studies looking at quasi-option values in policy decisions have been relatively simple: two-period models with a very limited number of discrete policy options and possible future states of the world. These models have often considered only two policy options, for example preservation or consumptive use of a natural resource. The numerical model presented in Chapter 6 used three policy options. Also in these simple problems, learning was stochastically predictable in the sense that the possible learning scenarios and their probabilities were known *a priori*. Given the small number of policy options and knowledge of prospective learning, quasi-options values associated with selection of flexible positions in an early period could be estimated by comparison of expected values of learning under different initial policy decisions and for the stochastically predictable future states of the world. These studies indicate that option values are probably important in many policy decisions dealing with uncertainty, irreversibility and potential for learning, but are limited in the extent to which the concept may be practically applied in more complex situations of multi-attribute policy decisions and many possible future states. What is needed is a way of more directly estimating or considering quasi-option values, considering trade-offs between quasi-option values and current benefits (reductions in static transaction costs), and incorporating these trade-offs into policy decisions for institutional change.

Parallels exist with the problems of irreversible or partly irreversible capital investment under uncertainty, and with financial call options. The problem of capital investment under uncertainty is described by Dixit and Pindyck (1994 pp. 3–9). Business firms hold investment opportunities by virtue of control of patents, ownership of land or natural resources, holding of certain managerial resources or technological knowledge, market positions and scale of existing operations. Dixit and Pindyck demonstrated that these opportunities to invest resemble a financial call option:

> A call option gives the holder the right, for some specified amount of time, to pay an exercise price and in return receive an asset (eg. a share of stock). Exercising the option is irreversible: although the asset can be sold to another investor, one cannot retrieve the option or the money that was paid to exercise it. A firm with an investment opportunity likewise has the option to spend money (the exercise price)

now or in the future, in return for an asset (eg. a project) of some value. Again, the asset can be sold to another firm, but the investment is irreversible. As with the financial call option, this option to invest is valuable in part because the future value of the asset obtained by investing is uncertain (Dixit and Pindyck, 1994 p. 9).

Dixit and Pindyck apply the theory of call options in financial economics to estimating the option value associated with investment decisions under uncertainty and irreversibility. Fisher (1997) shows that the Dixit–Pindyck model of the investment decision under uncertainty and irreversibility is formally equivalent to the models of quasi-option value developed in the context of irreversible development of an environmental resource, discussed in Chapter 6.

Decisions for institutional change under uncertainty and irreversibility have already been shown to be similar to the irreversible-development versus preservation decision for environmental resources. Decisions for institutional change are also similar to decisions of investment under uncertainty and irreversibility. A decision maker invests resources (the transition costs of a new institutional structure) to obtain a stream of benefits (reduced static transaction costs in future allocation decisions), but in undertaking the investment may extinguish future options or at least increase the costs of pursuing some options (moving to alternative institutional structures). For illustration, consider an institutional hierarchy for use of a water resource that has two levels: a state government and private users of the resource. Property rights are distributed between the state and the private users in such a way that the private users hold an entitlement for water use, but the government may at any time compulsorily reduce these entitlements or alter the rules under which the water may be used. In this situation, the state effectively holds a call option over the water entitlements and property rights of the private users. The government may exercise the option if there is deemed to be a benefit in constraining the way the resource is used or in re-allocating the resource to an alternative use.

Given the established similarities under conditions of uncertainty and irreversibility of decisions for capital investment, environmental development, and institutional change, it appears worthwhile to pursue the lead of Fisher (1997) in examining the relevance of financial theory of call options to the evaluation of quasi-option values in institutional change. Following is an examination of the relevance of pricing models for financial economics to estimating quasi-option values associated with property rights over natural resources.

Financial economists distinguish between two types of call option: an American-type call option where the holder of the option has the right to purchase stock on or before a given date; and a European-type call option where the holder of the option has the right to purchase stock only on the last date of the contract (Merton, 1990 p. 256). Both types of call option implicitly exist in the powers often held by governments over the use of natural resources that are otherwise considered to be private property. For example, with freehold ownership of land, private landowners have broad powers to determine the use of the land, but various levels of government hold powers either to compulsorily resume the land or to constrain the uses to which the land can be put. These powers of governments resemble American-type call options that can be exercised at any time over an indefinite contract period. An exercise price varies with the nature of the option exercised by government. Resumption of land usually entails compensation of the landowner at a 'fair market price', while options to change rules of land use through zoning provisions or environmental laws may entail a direct exercise price to the government of zero, although there would be an implicit exercise price paid by society equal to the opportunity cost of benefits from forgone land uses. As another example, regulation of fisheries and water resources in Australia typically occurs by issue of licences and quotas providing private individuals with rights of access to resource stocks. The licences are issued for finite periods and although such licences are conventionally renewed automatically upon expiry, the regulating governments retain the option to alter entitlements or to alter the conditions under which the resources are used. These options resemble a European-type call option since the options can be exercised at the end of the 'contract' implicit in the licences.

A financial call option is essentially the opportunity or flexibility to purchase stock in response to learning about the value of the stock. This is analogous to the opportunity or flexibility of a government to alter institutions for use of a resource in response to learning about the state of the resource system. The value of a financial call option is itself a quasi-option value.

Financial economists have derived formulae for the valuing and pricing of call options where the options are defined by the stock or asset to which they pertain, the length of the contract period and the exercise price for the option. The formulae vary in complexity according to the assumptions made, principally in regard to the characteristics of the option contract, the nature of the underlying stock, the nature of price movements for the stock, and the investment strategy of the option buyer or seller. One of the earliest approaches to option pricing was the Black–Scholes formula (Black and Scholes, 1973). Examination of this formula provides some insights into determinants of quasi-option values and the limitations of concepts from financial economics in estimating these values.

Estimation of the value of an option assumes that the option is purchased as part of a risk-free portfolio, that is, a portfolio that has an end-of-period value that is exactly the same, regardless of whether the price of the asset moves up or down. The portfolio comprises a mix of a quantity of the underlying asset 'sold short'[1] and a quantity of call options purchased on this asset in a proportion h that results in a risk-free portfolio. If the initial asset price is P, the exercise price of the call is E, and the period of the option is t, then under certain conditions about the price process of the underlying asset, the fair price[2] on a European-type call option on a stock with no dividends is given by the Black–Scholes formula:

$$V = PN(d_1) - Ee^{-rt}N(d_2) \tag{7.7}$$

where $N(x)$ is the cumulative standard normal distribution function,[3] and

$$d_1 = [\log(P/E) + rt + 0.5\sigma^2 t]/\sigma\sqrt{t} \tag{7.8}$$

$$d_2 = d_1 - \sigma\sqrt{t} \tag{7.9}$$

where r is the risk-free rate of interest and σ^2 is the instantaneous variance of the return on the common stock (Cox and Rubinstein, 1985 pp. 204–5).

Interpretation of the formula can be made as follows (Cox and Rubinstein, 1985 p. 205). If the call finishes 'in the money',[4] then the call will be exercised and the stock will be received in return for payment of the exercise price. The first term in the formula, $PN(d_1)$, is the present value of receiving the stock if and only if $P^* > E$. The second term, $Ee^{-rt}N(d_2)$, is the present value of paying the exercise price if and only if $P^* > E$. If P is very large relative to E, then $C \approx P - Er^{-1}$, that is, the value of the option is approximately equal to the value of the stock minus the present value of the exercise price.

Five fundamental determinants of the value of a financial call option are evident from the Black–Scholes formula (Cox and Rubinstein, 1985 pp. 33–4).

- Current stock price: the higher the value of the underlying stock, the higher the value of a call option.
- Exercise price: the higher the exercise price, the lower the value of a call option.
- Variability in the stock price (also referred to as the stock volatility): the higher the variability in the stock price, the greater the likelihood that the owner of stock would do very well or very poorly. The owner of a call option would gain full benefit from any rise in the stock price, but could avoid most losses from any fall in stock price by not exercising the option. Consequently, the higher the variability of the stock price, the higher the value of a call option relative to the stock price.
- Time to expiration of the option: the greater the time to expiration, the greater the value of a call option. This arises for two reasons. Firstly, the greater the time to expiration, the more uncertain is the future value of the

stock. This raises the value of a call option in a similar way to a higher stock volatility. Secondly, a greater time to expiration reduces the present value of the exercise price and hence increases the value of a call option.

- Interest rates or discount rates: high interest rates or discount rates reduce the present value of the exercise price but have no effect on the expected present value of the stock price. The stock price is, under strict assumptions of risk-neutrality, assumed to increase at the interest rate. Hence, higher interest rates increase the value of a call option.

How relevant is the Black–Scholes option-pricing formula to consideration of quasi-option values in institutional change? Consider an institutional structure over a water resource or other natural resource where a state government issues licences to resource users and these licences are of finite duration and specify conditions of resource use. As already indicated above, the ability of the government to not renew licences or to alter the conditions of resource use for the licensees essentially comprises a call option over the resource. Since the call can be exercised at the expiry of the licence, it resembles a European-type call option. Parameters relevant to ascertaining a value of the option are as follows.

- The stock or asset underlying the option is the resource to which the licensing system relates. This stock will probably have a positive asset value, as evident by positive values of entitlements to water and fish stocks where these have been made tradable, and this value would be characterised by variability arising from changes in supply of and demand for the resource.
- Since the government may be able to exercise the call option over the resource without any compensation payment to the former licensee, there may be no explicit exercise price. There would, however, be an implicit exercise price arising from the opportunity cost to society in transferring resources away from the licence holder or in altering the conditions of resource use which effectively transfers resources away from particular uses.
- The call option has a time to expiration determined by the duration and expiry dates of licences.

Given these similarities between a government's power to alter institutions of resource use and financial call options, it appears that methods of pricing financial options may provide a way of estimating quasi-option values associated with a government's residual property rights over a resource. The government option resembles a European-type option inasmuch as a call option exists over an asset which itself has a market value, the option has an exercise price, and the option is able to be exercised at the end of a defined contract period. However, a closer examination of a government's call option over a resource stock reveals that there are some problems with application of the pricing methodologies developed for financial options. These problems relate both to practical difficulties in measuring the parameters for option-pricing formulae, and to fundamental differences between financial call options and call options relating to property rights and other institutions for use of natural resources.

Firstly, the market price of entitlements to resources is generally not a true indicator of the marginal value of the resource to society. The reason for this is that trading in entitlements is usually restricted to certain resources users, whilst other users are excluded. For example, trading of water entitlements may be restricted to irrigation farmers and as a consequence the market prices for the entitlements do not reflect the marginal value of water for environmental or recreational uses. In considering exercising an option over private property rights in water, a government would most likely be interested in the latter values. Consequently, unlike a financial option, the market value of the asset underlying the option is not a good indicator of the value of exercising the option.

Secondly, with call options associated with property rights over a resource the value of the stock is affected by the existence of the option. This is a significant departure from the model of financial call options for which the value of the stock is an exogenous parameter. For financial stocks, ownership of the stock is, by and large, irrelevant for the firm to which the stock pertains. Within limits, changes in ownership of the stock do not affect the incentives of the firm's managers, the operations of the firm, or the stream of benefits generated by the firm. The value of the stock is therefore independent of the existence of call options. This independence of the value of the stock and the existence of the call option do not hold for a government's call option over property rights to a natural resource. Exercise of a government's option would alter the distribution of property rights and resource allocations between government and private resource users. This would affect the flow of benefits from resource use, and therefore alter the value of the resource. Any assessment of the value of the resource under an institutional *status quo* would have to give consideration to the possibility of the government's option being exercised. For example, the property rights in water held by irrigation farmers in the Murray–Darling Basin are subject to policy changes by state governments that may reduce water entitlements or constrain the ways in which water may be used. The probabilities that such options would be exercised are significant, and indeed have been exercised in the recent past.[5] Uncertainty over future government policy relating to water use may affect investment in irrigation capital and infrastructure and hence the value of water use in irrigation. It is also likely that the policy uncertainty would be reflected in market prices for water entitlements.

Thirdly, in the valuation of financial call options the exercise price is an exogenous parameter with an unrestricted domain: for any given exercise price, there is a corresponding value of the option. This is not the case for a government's call option over a natural resource and the property rights associated with the resource. Instead, the exercise price would be an endogenous variable of an option-pricing model, probably as a function of the asset value. In some instances, such as with altering the conditions of water use associated with an irrigation licence, a government's call option may be able to be exercised without any payment to the holders of the private rights. A direct exercise price does not exist for the option, although an exercise price may implicitly be paid by society through the opportunity cost of the change in institutions and changes in resource use. In other instances, the government may pay an exercise price to the rights holder affected by an institutional change where this price is determined at the time of exercising the option. An example exists with the recent changes in firearms legislation in Australia where the government exercised an option to 'recall' property rights from private individuals relating to ownership of certain types of firearms, but paid compensation to the affected individuals for the loss of property rights. The level of compensation was set as estimated market values of the various types of firearms made illegal by new legislation.

Fourthly, calculation of the value of a financial call option requires knowledge or estimation of the variability or volatility of the stock price. This is usually estimated from historical time-series data on the stock price (Merton, 1990 pp. 282–3). Knowledge of the variability of the stock value effectively represents a probability distribution for learning about the future state of the value of the asset, and in particular the probability of learning that the value of the asset at the termination of the option contract will be sufficiently high to justify exercising the option. Learning is implicitly assumed to be 'risky' in so far as the probability distribution of future possible states is assumed to be known. For a government's option over natural resources, similar knowledge of the variability in the value of stock underlying the option may not exist. Even if some historical time-series data exist for market prices of the resource, these may not be sufficient for making a good estimate of future variability in the value of the asset. It has already been argued that market prices for entitlements to resource use are not necessarily a good indicator of the true value of the resource since not all interests may be represented in markets, including those interests of particular relevance to a government's call option over the resource. A further problem exists where markets and market prices do not exist for a resource and it is not possible to obtain an estimate of the variance of the stock value from historical trading data. Various implicit pricing methods may be able to estimate a value for an asset although high levels of debate in the literature over non-market-pricing methods for valuing natural resources suggest that it is difficult enough to establish a value at any one point in time, let alone estimate the variability in this value. In some circumstances, dynamic stochastic programming models could possibly be used to estimate shadow prices for a resource and a variance in these prices, although it is likely that only relatively simple problems could be addressed by computable models. Overall, estimating quasi-option values for resources may be greatly restricted by knowing the probability distribution of future states. This problem is compounded if it is considered that many policy problems of institutional change deal with situations of future uncertainty rather than risk, where it is recognised that the probability distribution for future states is not known.

In summary, although the quasi-option value associated with flexibility in future institutional change has conceptual similarities to the value of a financial call option, the pricing formulae for financial call options are inappropriate for estimating quasi-option values. There are two significant departures from the financial model of valuing a call option: the value of the stock and the exercise price are endogenous to any consideration of the value of an option or a decision to secure an option. Furthermore, there are measurement difficulties for parameters of the value of the stock and the variability in this value which are critical parameters in estimating the value of an option over the stock. It is possible that the models for valuing financial call options could be developed to handle endogeneity of the stock price and exercise price, and hence provide greater insight into measurability of quasi-option values. This, however, remains a difficult problem that has yet to be solved, if it can be.

CONCLUSIONS: A NEW FRAMEWORK FOR INSTITUTIONAL POLICY ANALYSIS

Despite the success of the new institutionalists in providing new insights into economic history, very little work has been undertaken to apply the insights to *ex ante* policy analysis. This problem of applying the theory of institutions and transaction costs to *ex ante* policy analysis was addressed in this chapter.

The problem of institutional choice was posed as follows: for a particular allocation decision or class of allocation decisions, what is the best institutional arrangement that establishes the processes for the decisions to be made and the mechanisms for the decisions to be implemented? In the absence of transaction costs, this is a meaningless question since costless decision making under perfect information will result in the same allocation outcome regardless of the institutional structure. Where transaction costs are positive (imperfect information, costly processes of decision making, uncertainty, etc.) the choice of institutional structure matters, since the structure determines the transaction costs and thereby determines how closely the ultimate resource allocation will approach the hypothetical 'efficient allocation' that would occur in a system of zero transaction costs. Under an assumption that the distribution of transaction costs is of no importance, the policy problem in choosing an institutional structure to resolve a particular allocation problem becomes one of selecting the institutional structure (including property-right regimes, entitlement systems and mechanisms of allocation and re-allocation) that minimise transaction costs.

In previous chapters transaction costs were classified into two types: static transaction costs and dynamic transaction costs. Dynamic transaction costs were further divided into transition costs and intertemporal costs. Taking into account these different classes of transaction costs, the policy problem becomes one of optimising an objective function with components of static transaction costs, transition costs and quasi-option value, where the last provides an inverse measure of intertemporal costs. Earlier in this chapter, this decision problem was framed in cost-effectiveness terms as a problem of selecting an institutional structure to minimise a sum of static transaction costs, transition costs, and the negative of the quasi-option value.

Problems arise in using this formulation of the problem as a basis for policy analysis due to a lack of procedures and techniques for measuring and quantifying the different types of transaction costs and the quasi-option value. There has been a reasonable amount of both conceptual and empirical study of static transaction costs. This includes examining effects of transaction costs on outcomes from institutional structures, and some incorporation of transaction costs into conceptual models of market institutions to indicate how these costs may affect potential allocative outcomes from these institutional arrangements. What is lacking, however, is methodology and experience in *ex ante* estimation of transaction costs in particular resource systems under alternative institutional structures. The problem is similar to that identified by Oliver Williamson almost twenty years ago in relation to transaction costs and the allocation of resources at the level of the firm: 'Further progress in the study of transaction costs awaits the identification of the critical dimensions with respect to which transaction costs differ and an examination of the economising properties of alternative institutional modes for organising transactions' (Williamson, 1979). Without this, opportunities are very limited for objective prediction of allocative outcomes from alternative institutional structures, and hence for comparison of these structures.

For transition costs, the situation is a little better in so far as political expediency often requires that economic and social impact assessments of policy initiatives recognise transition costs implicit in social and economic dislocation, and these costs are often taken into account in decision making. Some attention has been given to considering costs of political decision making in institutional change (Dixit, 1996) but there has been little, if any, attention given to *ex ante* prediction of such costs for policy proposals relating to institutional change for the allocation of natural resources. Many political constraints and costs to political decision makers may not be readily quantifiable.

Finally, the estimation of quasi-option values for particular institutional structures presents perhaps the greatest difficulty in quantitative policy analysis for institutional choice. Whilst dynamic–stochastic programming models may demonstrate the importance of quasi-option values in simple policy scenarios, these models are unlikely to be able to accommodate the complexities of real problems of institutional choice. It is for similar reasons that alternative methods have been developed in financial economics to estimate option values. The problem of valuing financial options has some conceptual similarity with determining quasi-option values, but there are some significant differences that prevent a direct adoption of financial methodologies to the determination of quasi-option values.

Given these difficulties in measurement of the different parameters of the institutional choice problem, there may perhaps be some criticism of this formulation. In the words of Lancaster (1966) the formulation may be thought to 'run the danger of adding to the economist's extensive collection of non-operational concepts'. Other researchers applying the concepts of transaction costs to problems of institutional choice have been pessimistic about empirical application. Griffin (1991), for example, stated that 'because a proper analysis incorporating transaction costs has never been performed to investigate the global efficiency of a prospective institution, the applicability of ... [the terms externality correction, resolution and internalisation] ... is highly questionable in all but conceptual work. Moreover, the empirical difficulties to be encountered in such a rich analysis imply that the chances of ever satisfying this requirement are quite remote.'

Despite the problems of quantifying and predicting transaction costs, particularly flexibility costs as measured by quasi-option value, there is considered to be value in the formulation of the problem of institutional change as one of minimising a sum of transaction costs. Regardless of the problems of measurement, this formulation of the problem of institutional choice provides a useful conceptual framework for considering alternative institutional structures and the costs and benefits of institutional change. Indeed, the formulation provides a cohesive structure for some existing *ad hoc* procedures of policy analysis that seem to give implicit attention to all three types of transaction costs included in the problem formulation. Examples of instances where implicit attention is given to the three types of transaction costs are as follows.

In regard to static transaction costs, attention to markets as a means of improving allocation efficiency of resources can be interpreted as an often unwitting search for allocative institutions with lower transaction costs than existing institutions of administrative allocation. Most economists have been educated to consider markets as being free of transaction costs while acknowledging the transaction costs of government decision making arising from imperfect information. It is therefore not surprising that so many models of zero-transaction-cost markets have been put forward as a panacea for problems of resource allocation and have formed the basis for many initiatives in institutional change away from government decision making. These policy analysts are on the right track, but perhaps not fully aware of the diversity of institutional options for allocation of natural resources and the different implications for transaction costs and efficiency of allocative decisions.

Transition costs are often given explicit recognition in policy analysis for institutional reform, particularly as the subset of costs arising from the social and economic dislocation of the people affected by proposed institutional changes.

Recognition of quasi-option values is implicit in many policy decisions based on the precautionary principle. An underlying presumption of the precautionary principle is that under conditions of uncertainty and irreversibility, it may be better to take a cautious stance in resource allocation for the time being, with the possibility of revising the stance at some later date as new information becomes available. A preservation of quasi-option value is implicit in preferences for gradual institutional change. As indicated by Dorfman (1981): 'one motivation, surely, for the prevalence of introducing regulations or dismantling them by graduated steps is uncertainty about the consequences of the regulatory change. It is felt to be desirable to be able to watch the adjustments as they evolve and to be able to make mid-course corrections as they are needed.' Quasi-option values have also been implicitly recognised in reform of institutions of water allocation. In Western Australia, for example, the following statement was recently made by the relevant regulatory agency in regard to institutional reform for water licences. 'Long term licences will be issued where it can be shown that there is little risk to the resource or other users. In other areas, where the risk is high, licences will be issued for shorter periods to allow periodic review' (Water and Rivers Commission, 1998). Maintaining options for government decision making over resource allocation is implicit in a reluctance to grant long-term licences where the future state of the resource system is 'risky' and where reducing licence terms at some future time would be politically difficult.

Previous chapters of this book have demonstrated the significance of all three classes of transaction costs in shaping the development of institutions for water use in the Murray–Darling Basin over the past century. The framework for institutional analysis developed in this chapter allows for lessons of history to be applied in current and future reform, at least at the level of conceptually framing the problem of institutional choice. There are shortcomings in this formulation of the general policy problem for institutional change: effects of the distribution of transaction costs have been ignored and opportunities for quantitative application are limited. Nevertheless, the formulation of the problem does provide a framework for many existing *ad hoc* approaches to policy analysis and offers direction to future research aimed at more rigorous comparative studies of institutions within contexts of history and of imperfect information on economic outcomes of institutional change.

NOTES

1. An asset is 'sold short' if a contract exists for sale of the asset at some future time and the vendor does not own sufficient quantities of the asset to meet the contract. To meet the commitment for sale of the asset, the vendor must purchase additional units of the asset before the sale date or pay a penalty specified in the contract. A portfolio comprising a quantity of the asset sold short and a quantity of call options on the asset can be risk-free since changes in the asset value will produce counteracting changes in value of each component of the portfolio. An increase in the asset price results in an increase in the value of the options, but increases the costs of meeting the contract for sale of the asset. Conversely, a reduction in the asset value reduces the value of the options, but also reduces costs of meeting the sales contract.

2. The fair price of an option is the price at which the value of the risk-free portfolio is zero given the expectations of variability in the value of the asset over the option contract.

3. A standardised normally distributed random variable has a mean of zero and a standard deviation of one. The standard normal density function is:

$$N'(x) \equiv (1/\sqrt{2\pi})e^{-x^2/2}.$$

The standard normal distribution function, $N(z)$, gives the area under this density from $-\infty$ to z. That is, it gives the probability that the random variable will take on a value at most equal to z (Cox and Rubinstein, 1985 p. 202).

4. 'In the money' has the meaning that the asset price at the end of the contract exceeds the exercise price, and hence it is worthwhile exercising the option, i.e. $P^* > E$, where P^* is the asset price at the option date and E is the exercise price.

5. In April 1998, for example, the New South Wales government made a unilateral decision to reduce water allocations by up to 12 per cent for irrigation farmers throughout that state for the purposes of providing water for the environment.

8. Conclusions

SUMMARY OF FINDINGS

At the commencement of research for this book in 1994, much attention was being given by resource economists and policy makers to systems of private property and tradability of water entitlements. The Council of Australian Governments was finalising agendas for water reform that included requirements to define water entitlements and property rights, with some implicit suggestion that these be private property rights, and to establish market institutions for the allocation and re-allocation of these entitlements. Simultaneously, the rate of institutional reform was at a peak in the Murray–Darling Basin with newly implemented 'water markets' in New South Wales and processes well under way to privatise government-owned group irrigation schemes in New South Wales and South Australia. There were, however, problems and difficulties in designing and implementing some institutional reforms. For example, in New South Wales, difficulties were encountered in defining the security of supply associated with water entitlements; determining allocations of water between consumptive uses and the environment while accommodating steadily increasing public demands for improved environmental management; and defining distributions of rights between individual water users and collective organisations in group irrigation schemes. In both New South Wales and Victoria, private water entitlements were being reduced by governments to provide for environmental flows and increasing restrictions were being applied by state governments on water use so as to reduce environmental impacts of irrigation. The Murray–Darling Basin Commission was continuing efforts to exert management control over the entire catchment with respect to levels of water but was impeded in doing so by resistance from state governments in the upstream states on issues such as reducing or at least stabilising levels of consumptive water use.

These problems associated with institutional reforms in water use made it apparent that there were many issues associated with allocation of water use that would not easily be resolved by enhancing private property rights in the resources. This is not to deny the economic benefits that have probably resulted from enhancement of private property rights and the introduction of water trading. Rather, it is recognising that the water resource of the Murray–Darling Basin is a large and complex common-pool resource. Many of the issues being grappled with in relation to institutional reform related to collective-action dilemmas and externality problems that complicate and limit the effectiveness of private rights and other existing property-right structures as institutions for resource allocation.

Given these issues and problems, an initial objective of this study was to take a sceptical view of the agenda for creating private property rights in water resources and compare the economic merits of different systems of property rights, in particular regimes of common property and private property. However, it soon became apparent that examination of alternative institutional structures for resource allocation is far more complicated that dichotomous choices between discrete property-right regimes. Institutional structures governing the use of natural resources are typically complex with simultaneous existence of multiple types and numbers of agents with decision-making powers (property rights) for resource allocation, and institutions providing the mechanisms for implementing these decisions (entitlement systems and mechanisms of allocation and re-allocation). Alternative institutional structures vary mainly with respect to distributions of rights between rights holders rather than discrete differences in property-right regimes.

In view of the complexity of institutions for resource allocation, it was necessary first to develop a conceptual model for interpreting and describing institutions. This was achieved by a model described in Chapter 2 that incorporated distributions of property rights between levels in an institutional hierarchy, and the associated institutions of entitlements and allocation. In Chapter 3 this model was applied to an examination of institutions of water use in the Murray–Darling Basin and demonstrated the coexistence of regimes of common property, state property and private property over the water resources of the basin.

As well as developing the model of institutional hierarchies, attention was also given to explaining why institutional hierarchies have particular sets of characteristics with respect to property rights, the allocation of these rights, and the processes underlying institutional change through time. Exploration of these issues drew on the theoretical insights of the new institutionalists that use transaction-cost theory to explain the nature of institutions with two underlying premises: (i) institutions develop to reduce transaction costs occurred in making and implementing decisions for resource allocation; and (ii) institutional change and development is itself only achieved through incurring transaction costs, and these costs create path-dependencies in institutional change. These two classes of transaction costs were labelled as static transaction costs and dynamic transaction costs, respectively. Chapters 4 and 5 demonstrated the importance of these transaction-cost concepts in examining institutions and institutional change. Chapter 4 demonstrated the importance of static transaction costs in influencing outcomes of institutions of private property rights and water markets. In Chapter 5 an examination of the history of institution of water use in the Murray–Darling Basin indicated that consideration of both static and dynamic transaction costs could provide insights into the emergence of institutional structures. Institutional change was partially explained by reference to objectives for reducing static transaction costs and constraints imposed by dynamic transaction costs. Together, Chapters 4 and 5 demonstrated that transaction costs are important considerations in institutional reform both in development of new institutions to promote the interests of societies in utilisation of the water resources, and in the stagnation of institutional structures due to high costs of institutional change.

Chapters 6 and 7 explored implications of static and dynamic transaction costs for *ex ante* policy analysis for institutional change. In Chapter 6, it was shown that the existence of dynamic transaction costs and consequent path-dependencies in institutional change may result in an option value being associated with 'flexible' institutional arrangements. That is, where the future state of the resource system and associated socioeconomic parameters are uncertain, there may be an option value associated with an institutional arrangement with low transition costs for change and consequently with flexibility to be altered in response to learning and new knowledge. This option value was shown to be conceptually similar to the idea of 'quasi-option value' previously developed in relation to problems of irreversible development versus preservation of environmental assets. The option value may be eroded by any institutional change at the present time that increases the transition costs associated with achieving a potentially desirable institutional structure in the future.

In Chapter 7, a general policy problem was defined for assessing the benefits of options for institutional reform. This formulation of the policy problem was based on the conventional neo-institutional view that new institutions develop to reduce static transaction costs, but also incorporated issues of dynamic transaction costs that impose constraints on institutional change. The policy problem was stated as one of choosing an institutional structure for a particular resource-allocation objective that minimises a sum of: (i) the static transaction costs associated with making the necessary allocation decisions; and (ii) the dynamic transaction costs of institutional change from the *status quo*. The dynamic transaction costs comprised two variables: (i) the transition costs that would be incurred in any shift from the institutional *status quo*; and (ii) the negative of the quasi-option value of the new institutional arrangement, where the quasi-option value provides a measure of expected benefits from institutional flexibility.

Also in Chapter 7, an examination was made of prospects for application of this formulation of the policy problem for institutional change. The general conclusion from this examination was that whilst the formulation of the policy problem provides a useful conceptual framework to examine institutional change, rigorous practical application is impeded by a lack of techniques and methodology for *ex ante* estimation of transaction costs. Existing literature indicates that some effort has been given to estimation of static transaction costs, but these are predominantly for *ex post* analyses of institutions. Transition costs have received more attention in *ex ante* studies because of their importance to political decision makers. Quasi-option values probably represent the greatest challenge in estimation, particularly where there are multiple options or a continuum of options for institutional change, and multiple possible future states of the world that affect the relative benefits of alternative institutional arrangements. Some conceptual similarity exists between the options associated with flexibility of an institutional structure and financial call options, but in-principle differences prevent direct adoption of valuation methods from finance theory.

Notwithstanding problems of practical application, the formulation of the problem of institutional choice provides a useful conceptual framework for considering alternative institutional structures and the costs and benefits of institutional change. Indeed, the formulation provides a cohesive structure for some existing *ad hoc* procedures of policy analysis that seem to give implicit attention to all three types of transaction costs included in the problem formulation.

IMPLICATIONS FOR INSTITUTIONAL REFORM IN USE OF WATER RESOURCES

This work has demonstrated the importance of different types of transaction costs as central parameters in the consideration of institutional change for water use in the Murray–Darling Basin and for other natural resources. Prospects for reductions in static transaction costs provide incentives for institutional change and determine the relative merits of alternative institutional structures. An emphasis in current institutional reform centring on private rights and market trading can be interpreted as an effort to reduce transaction costs incurred in achieving an efficient allocation of water amongst end-users of the resources, albeit not generally recognised as such. Other property-right regimes and allocation mechanisms should be included in comparative institutional analysis. Transition costs constrain institutional change, particularly where proposed institutional arrangements threaten to attenuate the existing private property rights of farmers or the state property rights of state governments. In the latter case, transition costs have greatly impeded institutional reform for management of the Murray–Darling Basin as a single resource system. Quasi-option values probably accrue to the maintenance of at least some state property rights over the water resources of the basin, given imperfect knowledge on the biophysical characteristics of the basin, future impacts of irrigation on environmental quality, future economic parameters of the irrigation industry, and future preferences for environmental quality.

By recognising transaction costs as the central economic parameters in institutional change, the framework for addressing problems of institutional change developed in this book may contribute to a more rigorous approach to policy analysis. For instance, the notion of option value in the flexibility of institutional structures may provide a useful conceptual link between policy makers and the many research programmes aimed at improving knowledge of ecological processes in the Murray–Darling Basin and developing new technologies of irrigated agriculture. The process of learning and gaining new knowledge can be considered as a reduction in uncertainty and ignorance about the resource system. This is illustrated conceptually in Figure 8.1.

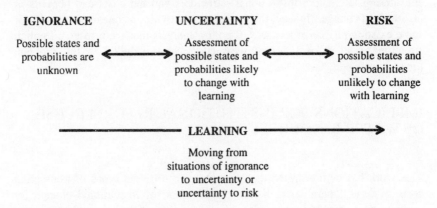

Figure 8.1: States of Knowledge and Learning

Figure 8.1 uses Knight's (1921) classification of risk and uncertainty and Faber and Proops's (1993) notion of ignorance to describe knowledge as a continuum between risk and ignorance. Risk refers to a situation of knowing all possible states and their probability distributions, of which 'certainty' is the special case of a particular state having a probability of one. Ignorance occurs where possible states cannot be specified and, therefore, the probability distributions also cannot be specified. In between these two extremes is a state of uncertainty where there is knowledge of possible states but incomplete knowledge of probability distributions. Learning refers to a process by which new information is accumulated and causes a shift in the state of knowledge from ignorance towards risk.

The possible scope of risk, uncertainty and ignorance in relation to the resource system of the Murray–Darling Basin is shown in Figure 8.2.

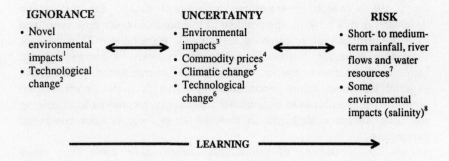

IGNORANCE	UNCERTAINTY	RISK
• Novel environmental impacts[1]	• Environmental impacts[3]	• Short- to medium-term rainfall, river flows and water resources[7]
• Technological change[2]	• Commodity prices[4]	• Some environmental impacts (salinity)[8]
	• Climatic change[5]	
	• Technological change[6]	

◄─────────────────── LEARNING ───────────────────►

Figure 8.2: Risk, Uncertainty and Ignorance in the Murray–Darling Basin

Notes:
1. Novel environmental impacts refer to unanticipated outcomes of economic–environmental interactions. Examples have occurred in the past, including algal blooms, the ecological impact of the European carp on native fish populations, and impacts of river regulation on native fish populations.
2. Technological change may be unanticipated.
3. Some short-term or 'acute' environmental impacts are known in terms of possibility but cannot readily be predicted as a result of the complexity of environmental systems and multitude of causative factors. Algal blooms and fish populations are examples.
Commodity prices, particularly for internationally traded commodities, are subject to uncertainty.
4. Knowledge exists about possible levels of prices but price movements cannot be stochastically predicted.
5. Climatic change refers principally to changes resulting from the greenhouse effect. Such changes are predicted in terms of possibility but not probability.
6. Technological change may be predictable in terms of the possible outcomes of research programmes, but not the probability of successful development of new techniques.
7. Long-term historical records of rainfall and river flows in combination with contemporary modelling of river flows and water storages allow annual water resources to be stochastically predicted.
8. Slowly developing and long-term environmental problems such as river and land salinity are relatively well understood and predictable. Predictions are often presented as definite and deterministic but would in fact be stochastic.

Use of this model of learning to make an assessment of research programs and prospects for new knowledge may allow some idea to be gained of the likely value of new knowledge in terms of improving resource management. To the extent that this value would depend upon flexibility within the current institutional structure, the value of new knowledge could be used to make judgements about the option value associated with maintaining flexibility in management institutions to accommodate the new knowledge.

AGENDAS FOR RESEARCH

As a new approach in examining institutional change, the formulation developed in this book for the problem of institutional choice may contribute to new directions of research in institutional economics. This involves examining economic institutions within the contexts of history, broader institutional structures, alternative institutional arrangements, politics, and expectations about future circumstances. This is quite different from conventional approaches to institutional analysis that are limited to examining particular allocation problems in isolation from these broader contextual parameters.

Calls for broadening of institutional analysis have come from many quarters with attention to areas such as political economy and political constraints on institutional change (Horn, 1995; Dixit, 1996), game-theoretic considerations of strategic behaviour in collective action and institutional development (Gardner and Ostrom, 1991; Ostrom *et al.*, 1993; Sened, 1997), alternative efficiency criteria (Bromley, 1991a), and consideration of institutional alternatives rather than exclusive focus on market mechanisms (Ostrom, 1990). There is obviously a vast range of considerations in such agendas, many of which have not been considered in the research for this book. Nevertheless, it is considered that this does contribute to a broadening of institutional analysis. Furthermore, this is achieved in a manner that is of practical value, at least in conceptualising institutional problems in a manner than should reduce the *ad hoc* nature of associated policy analysis.

The research agenda that this work points towards is further conceptual and empirical studies of transaction costs within a consistent framework such as that offered here. The acknowledged lack of techniques at present for estimating and predicting transaction costs is no reason to suppose that techniques cannot be developed. This area of study is in its infancy, with relatively few empirical studies of transaction costs as yet. However, the few studies that have empirically estimated transaction costs associated with institutions for use of natural resources have lacked two important components: (i) a consistent conceptual approach to identifying, classifying and quantifying transaction costs; and (ii) generalisation of research findings within a conceptual model of institutional choice. Without these two components, empirical studies do not go beyond collecting of data.

The suggested direction for research is similar to that initiated by Elinor Ostrom (1990, 1992), who explored the features of resource systems and institutional structures that give rise to static transaction costs and transition costs associated with regimes of common property for utilisation of natural resources. This has included the capture of the results of many past empirical studies of resource use under common property and use of these results to construct general models that allow prediction of the transaction costs that may be incurred under common property in particular resource situations, and thus the potential economic value of common-property institutions in the different situations.

This book extends the conceptual model of transaction costs and institutional choice to provide a cost-effectiveness framework for comparative analysis of alternative institutional structures. Thus whereas Ostrom's model of common property allows prediction of whether or not common property provides a suitable institutional structure for use of a natural resource, the model developed in this book allows analysis to be extended to address: (i) comparisons of common property with alternative institutional structures; and (ii) the place and functions of particular property-right regimes and allocation mechanisms within an institutional hierarchy. It is suggested that future research should involve empirical work within this framework, particularly developing methodologies and techniques for more readily estimating and predicting transaction costs and applying the framework to comparative institutional analysis.

An immediate application to institutional reform for water use in the Murray–Darling Basin and elsewhere may be in the design and selection of institutional structures to deal with threats to environmental quality. Such institutional reform is affected by, and itself affects, the static transaction costs of decision making for environmental quality, the transition costs of institutional change, and quasi-option values associated with maintaining institutional flexibility. Many environmental impacts of irrigation have characteristics of economic externalities. Consequently an important issue is the static transaction costs that may arise in different allocations of property rights across the multiple levels of the institutional hierarchy and decision making by different parties in regard to water use and environmental protection. Transition costs are important to the extent that strong property rights are currently held by private irrigators, almost in the form of a 'right to farm', and by state governments as the 'owners' of the water. These costs constrain institutional reform that may otherwise be desirable for addressing environmental problems through, for example, transferring property rights to either the level of common property between the states (the Murray–Darling Basin Commission), or common property at the level of sub-catchments or local regions. Quasi-option values may be important given uncertainty about the future extent and costs of environmental degradation, future climatic change and technological change. The framework for institutional analysis provided in this book allows these issues to be addressed using a consistent metric.

References

Alchian, A.A., 1988. Some economics of property rights, in M. Ricketts (ed.) *Neoclassical Microeconomics* Vol. 1, Thought in Economics Series no. 3, Aldershot, Edward Elgar, pp. 289–311.

Armstrong, C.W., 1994. Cooperative solutions in a transboundary fishery: the Russian–Norwegian co-management of the Arcto-Norwegian cod stock, *Marine Resource Economics* 9: 329–51.

Arrow, K., 1969. The organisation of economic activity: issues pertinent to the choice of market versus non-market allocation, in *The Analysis of and Evaluation of Public Expenditure: The PPB System, Volume 1*, US Joint Economic Committee, 1st Session, 59–73.

Arrow, K.J. and Fisher, A.C., 1974. Environmental preservation, uncertainty and irreversibility, *Quarterly Journal of Economics* 88: 312–19.

Attwater, W.R. and Markle, J., 1988. Overview of California water rights and water quality law, *Pacific Law Journal* 19: 957–1030.

Australian Bureau of Agricultural and Resource Economics, 1995. *Australian Commodity Statistics 1995*, Canberra, ABARE.

Bardhan, P., 1989. Alternative approaches to the theory of institutions in economic development, in P. Bardhan (ed.) *The Economic Theory of Agrarian Institutions*, Oxford, Oxford University Press.

Bartlett, R., 1995. The development of water law in Western Australia, in *Water Resources – Law and Management in Western Australia*, Proceedings of a conference held at the University of Western Australia, 23–4 February 1995, Western Australian Water Resources Council, Perth.

Barzel, Y., 1989. *Economic Analysis of Property Rights*, Political Economy of Institutions and Decisions series, Cambridge, Cambridge University Press.

Bates, R.H., 1988. Contra contractarianism: some reflections on the new institutionalism, *Politics and Society* 16: 387–410.

Baumol, W., Panzar, J. and Willig, R., 1982. *Contestable Markets and the Theory of Industrial Structure*, New York, Harcourt Brace Jovanovich.

Becker, L.C., 1977. *Property Rights: Philosophic Foundations*, Boston, Routledge and Kegan Paul.

Bjornlund, H. and McKay, J., 1996a. TWE policy in horticultural South Australia – a major player in the water market, in J. Pigram (ed.) *Security *and Sustainability in a Mature Water Economy: a Global Perspective*, Armidale, Centre for Water Policy Research, University of New England pp. 305–23.

Bjornlund, H. and McKay, J., 1996b. Transferable water entitlements: early lessons from South Australia, *Water* September/October, pp. 39–43.

Black, F. and Scholes, M., 1973. The pricing of options and corporate liabilities, *Journal of Political Economy* 81: 637–54.

Blaug, M., 1992. *The Methodology of Economics: or How Economists Explain*, 2nd edn, Cambridge, Cambridge University Press.

Boardman, A.E., Greenberg, D.H., Vining, A.R. and Weimer, D.L., 1996. *Cost-Benefit Analysis: Concepts and Practice*, Upper Saddle River, NJ, Prentice Hall.

Boggs, C.S., 1989. *Analysis of Transaction Costs Associated with Water Transfers in Colorado*, Masters Thesis, Department of Economics, University of Colorado.

Borenstein, S. and Rose, N.L., 1994. Competition and price dispersion in the U.S. airline industry, *Journal of Political Economy* 102(4): 653-83.

Branson, J. and Eigenraam, M., 1996. Water policy reform in Victoria – a regional perspective, Paper presented at the 40th annual conference of the Australian Agricultural and Resource Economics Society, Melbourne, Victoria, 13–15 February 1996.

Bromley, D.W., 1989. *Economic Interests and Institutions: the Conceptual Foundations of Public Policy*, New York and Oxford, Basil Blackwell.

Bromley, D.W., 1991a. *Environment and Economy: Property Rights and Public Policy*, Oxford, UK and Cambridge, MA, Blackwell.

Bromley, D.W., 1991b. Testing for common versus private property: comment, *Journal of Environmental Economics and Management* 21: 92–6.

Bromley, D.W. and Cernea, M.M., 1989. *The Management of Common Property Natural Resources: Some Conceptual and Operational Fallacies*, World Bank Discussion Papers 57, Washington, DC, The World Bank.

Bromley, D.W. and Segersen, K. (eds), 1992. *The Social Response to Environmental Risk: Policy Formulation in an Age of Uncertainty*, Boston, Kluwer Academic.

Buchanan, J.M. and Tullock, G., 1962. *The Calculus of Consent: Logical Foundations of Constitutional Democracy*, Ann Arbor, University of Michigan Press.

Bureau of Agricultural Economics, 1987. *The Rice Industry: a BAE Submission to the IAC*, BAE Project 41100, Canberra, Australian Government Publishing Service.

Cadell Land and Water Management Plan Working Group, 1995. *Cadell Community's Land and Water Management Plan*, Deniliquin, NSW, Cadell Land and Water Management Plan Working Group.

Campbell, H.F. and Lindner, R.K., 1990. The production of fishing effort and the economic performance of licence limitation programs, *Land Economics* 66(1): 56–66.

Campos, J.E.L., 1989. Legislative institutions, lobbying and the endogenous choice of regulatory instruments: a political economy approach to instrument choice, *Journal of Law, Economics and Organization* 5(2): 333–53.

Ciriacy-Wantrup, S.V. and Bishop, R.C., 1975. Common property as a concept in natural resources policy, *Natural Resources Journal* 15: 713–27.

Clark, S.D., 1971a. The Murray River question: part I – colonial days, *Melbourne University Law Review* 8: 11–40.

Clark, S.D., 1971b. The Murray River question: part II – federation, agreement and future alternatives, *Melbourne University Law Review* 8: 215–53.

Clark, S.D., 1982. The River Murray waters agreement: down the drain or up the creek?, *Transactions of the Institution of Engineers Australia Civil Engineering* 24(3): 201–8.

Clark, S.D., 1983. The River Murray waters agreement: peace in our time?, *Adelaide Law Review* 9: 108–41.

Coase, R.H., 1937. The nature of the firm, *Economica* 4: 386–405.

Coase, R.H., 1960. The problem of social cost, *Journal of Law and Economics*, 3: 1–44.

Colby, B.G., 1990. Transaction costs and efficiency in western water allocation, *American Journal of Agricultural Economics* December 1990: 1184–92.

Colby, B.G., 1995. Regulation, imperfect markets, and transaction costs: the elusive quest for efficiency in water allocation, in D.W. Bromley (ed.) *The Handbook of Environmental Economics*, Cambridge, MA, Blackwell, pp. 475–502.

Colby, B.G., Crandall, K. and Bush, D.B., 1993. Water right transactions: market values and price dispersion, *Water Resources Research* 29(6): 1565–72.

Colby Saliba, B., Bush, D.B., Martin, W.E. and Brown, T.C., 1987. Do water market prices appropriately measure water values?, *Natural Resources Journal* 27: 617–51.

Cole, P.J., 1978. Soils and land use of the River Murray valley in South Australia, *Proceedings of the Royal Society of Victoria* 90: 167–74.

Coleambally Land and Water Management Plan Committee, 1996. *Coleambally Land and Water Management Plan*, Coleambally, NSW.

Commons, J.R., 1968. *Legal Foundations of Capitalism*, Madison, University of Wisconsin Press.

Conrad, J.M., 1980. Quasi-option value and the expected value of information, *Quarterly Journal of Economics* 94: 813–20.

Cox, J.C. and Rubinstein, M., 1985. *Options Markets*, Englewood Cliffs, NJ, Prentice Hall.

Cox, S.R., DeSerpa, A.C. and Canby Jr, W.C., 1982. Consumer information and the pricing of legal services, *Journal of Industrial Economics* 30: 305–18.

Crabb, P., 1988. *The Murray–Darling Basin Agreement*, Australian National University Centre for Resource and Environmental Studies Working Paper 1988/6, Canberra, Australian National University.

Crocker, T.D., 1971. Externalities, property rights, and transactions costs: an empirical study, *Journal of Law and Economics* 14(2): 451–64.

CSIRO Climate Impact Group, 1991. *Climate Change Scenarios*, CSIRO Division of Atmospheric Research, Melbourne.

Dahlby, B. and West, D., 1986. Price dispersion in an automobile insurance market, *Journal of Political Economy* 94: 418–38.

Dahlman, C.J., 1980. *The Open Field System and Beyond*, Cambridge, Cambridge University Press.

Dales, J.H., 1968. *Pollution, Property and Prices*, Toronto, University of Toronto Press.

Deakin, A., 1884. *Irrigation in Western America so far as it has relation to the Circumstances of Victoria* and *Irrigation in Egypt and Italy*, Royal Commission on Water Supply First and Fourth Progress Reports, Melbourne, Victorian Government.

Demsetz, H., 1967. Toward a theory of property rights, *American Economic Review* 57: 347-59. Reprinted in E.G. Furubotn and S. Pejovich, 1974. *The Economics of Property Rights*, Cambridge, MA, Ballinger, pp. 33–42.

Department of Industry, Science and Tourism, 1996. *Managing Australia's inland waters: roles for science and technology*, a paper prepared by an independent working group for consideration by the Prime Minister's Science and Engineering Council at its fourteenth meeting, 13 September 1996, Canberra. Department of Industry, Science and Tourism.

Department of Land and Water Conservation New South Wales, 1997. Water Audit – Implementation of the Diversion Cap in New South Wales, Presentation to the Murray–Darling Basin Ministerial Council on 25 July 1997 by the Hon. K. Yeadon, Minister for Land and Water Conservation.

Department of Natural Resources and Environment Victoria, 1997. Murray–Darling Basin Ministerial Council: Implementing the Cap in Victoria, Progress report July 1997, Melbourne, Department of Natural Resources and Environment.

Department of Water Resources New South Wales, c. 1993. *Water Resources of the Murrumbidgee Valley: Doing More with Water*, Sydney, Department of Water Resources, New South Wales.

Department of Water Resources New South Wales, 1995. *Water Resources of the Border Rivers System in Northern New South Wales: Doing More with Water*, Sydney, Department of Water Resources, New South Wales.

Dixit, A.K., 1996. *The Making of Economic Policy: a Transaction-Cost Politics Perspective*, Munich Lectures in Economics, Cambridge, MA, MIT Press.

Dixit, A.K. and Pindyck, R.S., 1994. *Investment Under Uncertainty*, Princeton, NJ, Princeton University Press.

Dorfman, R., 1981. Transition costs of changing regulations, in A.R. Ferguson (ed.) *Attacking Regulatory Problems: an Agenda for Research in the 1980s*, Cambridge, MA, Ballinger, pp. 39–54.

Dragun, A.K. and Gleeson, V., 1989. From water law to transferability in New South Wales, *Natural Resources Journal* 29: 647–61.

Eggertsson, T., 1990. *Economic Behaviour and Institutions*, Cambridge Surveys of Economic Literature, Cambridge, Cambridge University Press.

Eigenraam, M., Stoneham, G., Branson, J., Sappideen, B. and Jones, R., 1996. Water policy reform in Victoria: a spatial equilibrium model, Paper presented at the 40th annual conference of the Australian Agricultural and Resource Economics Society, Melbourne, Victoria, 13–15 February 1996.

Faber, M. and Proops, J.L.R., 1993. *Evolution, Time, Production and the Environment*, 2nd edn, Berlin, Springer-Verlag.

Fernandez, R., and Rodrik, D., 1991. Resistence to reform: status quo bias in the presence of individual specific uncertainty, *American Economic Review* 81(5): 1146–55.

Fisher, A.C., 1997. Investment under uncertainty and option value in environmental economics, Working Paper no. 813, Department of Agricultural and Resource Economics, University of California at Berkeley.

Fisher, A.C. and Hanemann, W.M., 1985. Endangered species: the economics of irreversible damage, in D.O. Hall, N. Myers and N.S. Margaris (eds) *Economics of Ecosystems Management*, Dordrecht, Dr W. Junk, pp 129–38.

Flinn, J.C. and Guise, J.W.B., 1970. An application of spatial equilibrium analysis to water resource allocation, *Water Resources Research* 6(2): 398–409.

Gangadharan, L., 1997. Transactions costs in tradable emissions markets: an empirical study of the regional clean air incentives market in Los Angeles, Research Paper 591, University of Melbourne, Department of Economics.

Gardner, R. and Ostrom, E., 1991. Rules and games, *Public Choice* 70: 121–49.

Gardner, R.L. and Miller, T.A., 1983. Price behaviour in the water market of northeastern Colorado, *Water Resources Bulletin*, 19(4): 557–62.

Gaynor, M. and Polachek, S.W., 1994. Measuring information in the market: an application to physician services, *Southern Economic Journal* 60(4): 815–31.

Goodin, R.E. (ed.), 1996. *The Theory of Institutional Design*, Cambridge, Cambridge University Press.

Goodin, R.E., 1996. Institutions and their design, in R.E. Goodin (ed.) *The Theory of Institutional Design*, Cambridge, Cambridge University Press, pp. 1–53.

Gordon, H.S., 1954. The economic theory of a common property resource: the fishery, *Journal of Political Economy* 62: 124–42.

Griffin, R.C., 1991. The welfare analytics of transaction costs, externalities and institutional choice, *American Journal of Agricultural Economics* 73(3): 601–14.

Hall, N., Poulter, D. and Curtotti, R., 1994. *ABARE Model of Irrigation Farming in the Southern Murray–Darling Basin*, ABARE Research Report 94.4, Australian Bureau of Agricultural and Resource Economics, Canberra.

Hallowell, A.I., 1943. The nature and function of property as a social institution, *Journal of Legal and Political Sociology* 1: 115–38.

Hardin, G., 1968. The tragedy of the commons, *Science* 162: 1243–8.

Hartwick, J.M. and Olewiler, N.D., 1986. *The Economics of Natural Resource Use*, New York, Harper and Row.

Hay, D.A. and Morris, D.J., 1991. *Industrial Economics and Organization*, 2nd edn, Oxford, Oxford University Press.

Hayami, Y. and Ruttan, V., 1985. *Agricultural Development: An International Perspective*, Baltimore, Johns Hopkins University Press.

Hearne, R.R. and Easter, K.W., 1995. *Water Allocation and Water Markets: an Analysis of Gains-From-Trade in Chile*, World Bank Technical Paper Number 315, Washington, DC, World Bank.

Henry, C., 1974. Investment decisions under uncertainty: the irreversibility effect, *American Economic Review* 64(6): 1006–12.

Hirshleifer, J. and Riley, J.G., 1992. *The Analytics of Uncertainty and Information*, Cambridge Surveys of Economic Literature, Cambridge, Cambridge University Press.

Hofler, R. and Murphy, K.J., 1992. Underpaid and overworked: measuring the effect of imperfect information on wages, *Economic Inquiry* 30(3): 511–29.

Hohfeld, W.N., 1913. Some fundamental legal conceptions as applied in judicial reasoning, *Yale Law Journal*, 23, 16–59.

Hohfeld, W.N., 1917. Fundamental legal conceptions as applied in judicial reasoning, *Yale Law Journal*, 26, 710–70.

Honoré, A.M., 1961. Ownership, in A.G. Guest (ed.) *Oxford Essays in Jurisprudence*, Oxford, Oxford University Press.

Horn, M.J., 1995. *The Political Economy of Public Administration: Institutional Choice in the Public Sector*, Political Economy of Institutions and Decisions, Cambridge, Cambridge University Press.

Howitt, R.E., 1994. Empirical analysis of water market institutions: the 1991 California water market, Nota di Lavoro 13.94, Economics, Energy and Environment, Fondazione Eni Enrico Mattei.

Hubbard, M., 1997. The 'new institutional economics' in agricultural development: insights and challenges, *Journal of Agricultural Economics* 48(2): 239–49.

Hunt, E.K., 1986. *Property and Prophets: the Evolution of Economic Institutions and Ideologies* 5th edn, New York, Harper and Row.

Hutter, M., 1986. Transaction cost and communication: a theory of institutional change, applied to the case of patent law, in van der Schulenburg, J.-M. and Skogh, G. (eds) *Law and Economics and the Economics of Legal Regulation*, International Studies in Economics and Econometrics Vol. 13, Dordrecht, Kluwer Academic, pp. 113–29.

Innes, R., c. 1996 unpublished. The economics of takings and compensation when land and its public use values are in private hands, Department of Agricultural and Resource Economics, University of Arizona.

Jones, R. and Fagan, M., 1996. Estimated demand and supply for irrigation water in southern NSW, Paper presented at the 40th annual conference of the Australian Agricultural and Resource Economics Society, Melbourne, Victoria, 13–15 February 1996.

Kay, N.M., 1997. *Pattern in Corporate Evolution*, Oxford, Oxford University Press.

Knight, F., 1921. *Risk, Uncertainty and Profit*, Boston, Houghton Mifflin.

Knight, J., 1992. *Institutions and Social Conflict*, Cambridge, Cambridge University Press.

Lancaster, K.J., 1966. A new approach to consumer theory, *Journal of Political Economy* 74: 132–57.

Leffler, K.B. and Rucker, R.R., 1991. Transaction costs and the efficient organization of production: a study of timber harvesting contracts, *Journal of Political Economy* 99(5): 1060–87.

Lindblom, C., 1977. *Politics and Markets*, New York, Basic Books.

Lindner, R.K., 1990. Something fishy in the ITQ market, Paper presented at the Australian Agricultural Economics Society 34th Annual Conference, University of Queensland, 13–15 February 1990.

Lippman, S. and McCall, J., 1976. The economics of job search: a survey, *Economic Inquiry* 14: 347–68.

Lo, L.J. and Horbulyk, T.M., 1996. Potential welfare gains from rural–urban water reallocation in southern Alberta, Canada, Paper presented at the 40th annual conference of the Australian Agricultural and Resource Economics Society, Melbourne, Victoria, 13–15 February 1996.

Maass, A. and Anderson, R., 1978. *... and the Desert Shall Rejoice: Conflict, Growth and Justice in Arid Environments*, Cambridge MA, MIT Press.

Mackay, N. and Eastburn, D. (eds), 1990. *The Murray*, Canberra, Murray Darling Basin Commission.

Maddala, G.S., 1992. *Introduction to Econometrics*, 2nd edn, Maxwell Macmillan.

Marvel, H.P., 1976. The economics of information and retail gasoline behaviour: an empirical analysis, *Journal of Political Economy* 84(5): 1033–60.

Mason, C.F., Sandler, T. and Cornes, R., 1988. Expectations, the commons and optimal group size, *Journal of Environmental Economics and Management* 15: 99–110.

Matthews, R.C.O., 1986. The economics of institutions and the sources of growth, *Economic Journal* 96: 903–18.

McCall, J., 1970. Economics of information and job search, *Quarterly Journal of Economics* 84: 113–26.

McCann, L., 1997. *Evaluating Transaction Costs of Alternative Policies to Reduce Agricultural Phosphorus Pollution in the Minnesota River*, PhD Dissertation, University of Minnesota.

Menzies, B. and Gray, P., 1983. *Irrigation and Settlement in the South Australian Riverland*, South Australian Department of Agriculture Technical Paper no. 7, Adelaide, South Australian Department of Agriculture.

Merton, R.C., 1990. *Continuous Time Finance*, Cambridge, MA, Blackwell.

Montero, J.P., 1997. Marketable pollution permits with uncertainty and transaction costs, *Resource and Energy Economics* 20(1): 27–49.

Murray–Darling Basin Act 1993, No. 38 of 1993, Commonwealth of Australia.

Murray–Darling Basin Agreement 1992. Schedule to the Murray–Darling Basin Act 1993, Commonwealth of Australia.

Murray–Darling Basin Ministerial Council, 1995. An Audit of Water Use in the Murray–Darling Basin, Canberra, Murray–Darling Basin Ministerial Council.

National Competition Council, 1997. *Compendium of National Competition Policy Agreements*, Canberra, Commonwealth of Australia.

National Farmers' Federation, 1998. *Wik Bill Already a Compromise*, news release 6 April 1998, Canberra, National Farmers' Federation.

Nicholson, W., 1995. *Microeconomic Theory: Basic Principles and Extensions* 6th edn, Fort Worth, Dryden Press.

North, D.C., 1981. *Structure and Change in Economic History*, New York, Norton.

North, D.C., 1990. *Institutions, Institutional Change and Economic Performance*, Political Economy of Institutions and Decisions series, Cambridge, Cambridge University Press.

North, D.C. and Thomas, R.P., 1973. *The Rise of the Western World: A New Economic History*, Cambridge, Cambridge University Press.

Olson, M., 1971. *The Logic of Collective Action: Public Goods and the Theory of Groups*, Cambridge, MA, Harvard University Press.

Ostrom, E., 1990. *Governing the Commons: the Evolution of Institutions for Collective Action*, Political Economy of Institutions and Decisions series, Cambridge, Cambridge University Press.

Ostrom, E., 1992. The rudiments of a theory of the origins, survival and performance of common-property institutions, in D.W. Bromley (ed.), *Making the Commons Work: Theory, Practice and Policy*, San Francisco, International Center for Self-Governance, pp 293–318.

Ostrom, E., Gardner, R., and Walker, J., 1993. *Rules, Games and Common-Pool Resources*, Ann Arbor, University of Michigan Press.

Pendse, S.G., 1986. *Trilateral Governance – an Extension of the Transaction Cost Approach*, Occasional Paper no. 84, Deakin University School of Management.

Pesaran, M.H. and Pesaran, B., 1995. *Microfit 4.01* (Beta Test Version), Oxford, Oxford University Press.

Pigram, J.J., 1995. Climate change and irrigation: an Australian response, *Canadian Water Resources Journal* 20(4): 227–35.

Pigram, J.J., Shaw, K.L., and Coelli, M.L., 1992. Climate change and irrigated agriculture: implications for the Murray–Darling Basin, Armidale NSW, Centre for Water Policy Research, University of New England.

Posner, R.A., 1972. *Economic Analysis of Law* 2nd edn, Boston, Little Brown.

Quiggin, J., 1988. Private and common property rights in the economics of the environment, *Journal of Economic Issues*, 22(4): 1071–87.

Quiggin, J., 1995. Common property in agricultural production, *Journal of Economic Behaviour and Organization* 26: 179–200.

Randall, A., 1981. Property entitlements and pricing policies for a maturing water economy, *Australian Journal of Agricultural and Resource Economics* 25(3): 195–220.

Randall, A., 1987. *Resource Economics: an Economic Approach to Natural Resource and Environmental Policy*, 2nd edn, New York, John Wiley.

Reinganum, J.F., 1979. A simple model of equilibrium price dispersion, *Journal of Political Economy* 87(4): 851–8.

Rosen, M.D. and Sexton, R.J., 1993. Irrigation districts and water markets: an application of cooperative decision-making theory, *Land Economics*, 69(1): 39–53.

Rothschild, M. 1973. Models of market organisation with imperfect information: a survey, *Journal of Political Economy* 81(6): 1283–308.

Salop, S. 1977. The noisy monopolist: imperfect information, price dispersion and price discrimination, *Review of Economic Studies* 44: 393–406.

Salop, S. and Stiglitz, J., 1977. Bargains and ripoffs, *Review of Economic Studies* 44: 493–510.

Santopietro, G.D. and Shabman, L.A., 1992. Can privatization be inefficient?: the case of the Chesapeake Bay oyster fishery, *Journal of Economic Issues* 26(2): 407–19.

Schlager, E., 1990. Model Specification and Policy Analysis: the Governance of Coastal Fisheries, PhD Dissertation, Workshop in Political Theory and Policy Analysis, Indiana University, Bloomington.

Schmutzler, A., 1991. *Flexibility and adjustment to information in sequential decision problems: a systematic approach*, Lecture Notes in Economics and Mathematical Systems, Berlin, Springer-Verlag.

Scoccimarro, M., Branson, J., Wall, L. and Mallawaarachchi, T., 1996. Modelling the impact of water policy reforms on dairy farm performance in the southern Murray–Darling Basin, Paper presented at the 40th annual conference of the Australian Agricultural and Resource Economics Society, Melbourne, Victoria, 13–15 February 1996.

Scoccimarro, M. and Collins, D., 1995. Implications of the COAG recommendations for rural water use, in Australian Water and Wastewater Association, 1995, *16th Federal Convention Sydney 1995: Delivering the Vision for the Next Century*, Proceedings, Volumes 1 and 2, Sydney, Australian Water and Wastewater Association Incorporated.

Scott, A.D., 1989a. Conceptual origins of rights based fishing, in P.A. Neher, R. Arnason and N. Mollet (eds) *Rights Based Fishing*, NATO ASI Applied Sciences Series, Vol. 169, Dordrecht, Kluwer Academic.

Scott, A.D., 1989b. Evolution of individual transferable quotas as a distinct class of property right, in H. Campbell, K. Menz and G. Waugh (eds) *Economics of Fishery Management in the Pacific Islands Region*, Proceedings of an international conference held at Hobart, Tasmania, Australia, 20–22 March 1989.

Scott, A.D., 1993. Obstacles to fishery self-government, *Marine Resource Economics* 8: 187–99.

Seabroke, W. and Pickering, H., 1994. The extension of property rights to the coastal zone, *Journal of Environmental Management* 42: 161–79.

Segerson, K., 1992. The policy response to risk and risk perceptions, in D.W. Bromley and K. Segerson (eds) *The Social Response to Environmental*

Risk: Policy Formulation in an Age of Uncertainty, Boston, Kluwer Academic, pp 101–30.

Sened, I., 1997. *The Political Institution of Private Property*, Cambridge, Cambridge University Press.

Simmons, P., Poulter, D. and Hall, N.H., 1991. Management of irrigation water in the Murray–Darling Basin, Australian Bureau of Agricultural and Resource Economics Discussion Paper 91.6, Canberra, Australian Government Publishing Service for ABARE.

Simon, H.A., 1955. A behavioural model of rational choice, *Quarterly Journal of Economics* 69: 99–118.

Simon, H.A., 1979. Rational decision making in business organizations, *American Economic Review* 69: 493–513.

Smith, R.B.W. and Tomasi, T.D., 1995. Transaction costs and agricultural nonpoint-source water pollution control policies, *Journal of Agricultural and Resource Economics* 20(2): 277–90.

Staatz, J.M., 1983. The cooperative as a coalition: a game-theoretic approach, *American Journal of Agricultural Economics*, 65(December): 1084–9.

Standing Committee on Agriculture and Resource Management, 1995. *Water Allocations and Entitlements: a National Framework for the Implementation of Property Rights in Water*, Task Force on COAG Water Reform Occasional Paper no. 1.

Stavins, R.N., 1995. Transaction costs and tradeable permits, *Journal of Environmental Economics and Management* 29: 133–48.

Stevenson, G.G., 1991. *Common Property Economics: a General Theory and Land Use Applications*, Cambridge, Cambridge University Press.

Stigler, G.J., 1961. The economics of information, *Journal of Political Economy* 69(3): 213–25.

Sturgess, G.L. and Wright, M., 1993. *Water Rights in Rural New South Wales: the Evolution of a Property Rights System*, Sydney, Centre for Independent Studies.

Takayama, T. and Judge, G.G., 1971. *Spatial and Temporal Price and Allocation Models*, Contributions to Economic Analysis 73, Amsterdam, North-Holland Publishing Company.

Thompson, D.B., 1997. *Comparing Water Quality Policies Through an Institutional- Transaction-Cost Framework*, Olin Working Paper Series OLIN-97-24, John M. Olin School of Business, Washington University, Saint Louis.

Vaux, H.J. Jr and Howitt, R.E., 1984. Managing water scarcity: an evaluation of interregional transfers, *Water Resources Research* 20(7): 785–92.

Water and Rivers Commission, 1998. *Water Reform in Western Australia: Allocation and Trading in Water Rights: Phase 1 Consultations Analysis and Response to Submissions*, Water Reform Series, Water and Rivers

Commission Report WR 7, Perth, Western Australia, Water and Rivers Commission.

Wilkinson, C.F., 1985. Western water law in transition, *University of Colorado Law Review* 56(3): 317–45.

Williams, M., 1974., *The Making of the South Australian Landscape: a Study in the Historical Geography of Australia*, London, Academic Press.

Williamson, O.E., 1971. The vertical integration of production: market failure considerations, *American Economic Review* (Papers and Proceedings) 61: 112–23.

Williamson, O.E., 1979. Transaction-cost economics: the governance of contractual relations, *Journal of Law and Economics* 22: 233–61.

Williamson, O.E., 1985. *The Economic Institutions of Capitalism*, New York, Free Press.

Williamson, O.E., 1993. The logic of economic organisation, in O.E. Williamson and S.G. Winter (eds) *The Nature of the Firm: Origins, Evolution and Development*, New York, Oxford University Press.

Wong, B.D.C. and Eheart, J.W., 1983. Market simulations for irrigation water rights: a hypothetical case study, *Water Resources Research* 19(5): 1127–38.

Working Group on Water Resource Policy, 1995. *The Second Report of the Working Group on Water Resource Policy to the Council of Australian Governments*, February.

Index